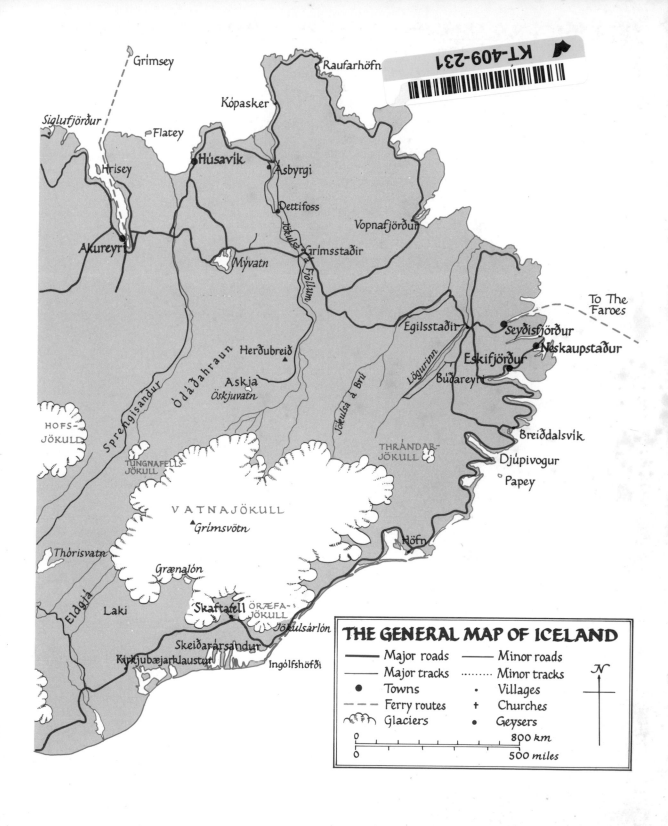

Grimsey

Siglufjörður

Flatey

Kópasker

Raufarhöfn

KT-409-231

Hrísey

Húsavik

Ásbyrgi

Dettifoss

Vopnafjörður

Akureyri

Mývatn

Grimsstaðir

Jökulsá á Fjöllum

To The
Faroes

Egilsstaðir

Seydisfjörður

Neskaupstaður

Herðubreið

Lögurinn

Eskifjörður

Ódáðahraun

Askja

Öskjuvatn

Jökulsá á Brú

Búðareyri

HOFS-
JÖKULL

Sprengisandur

THRÁNDAR-
JÖKULL

Breiðdalsvík

TUNGNAFELLS-
JÖKULL

Djúpivogur

Papey

VATNAJÖKULL

Grímsvötn

Thórisvatn

Höfn

Graenalón

Eldgjá

Laki

Skaftafell

ÖRÆFA-
JÖKULL

Jökulsárlón

Skeiðarársandur

Kirkjubæjarklaustur

Ingólfshöfði

THE GENERAL MAP OF ICELAND

— Major roads   — Minor roads
— Major tracks   ······ Minor tracks
● Towns   · Villages
– – Ferry routes   + Churches
Glaciers   ● Geysers

N

0   800 km
0   500 miles

ICELAND
THE VISITOR'S GUIDE

DAVID WILLIAMS

Introduced by DAVID BELLAMY

Editorial
John Blackett-Ord

Design
Keith Savage
David Cringle

Maps and Diagrams
Reginald Piggot

Drawings
Keith Savage

Iceland: The Visitor's Guide published by Stacey International, 128 Kensington Church Street, London W8 4BH
Telex 298768 Stacey G

ISBN 0 905743 38 5

Set in Linotronic Baskerville by
SX Composing Limited, Essex, England

Colour origination by
Hong Kong Graphic Arts Limited, Hong Kong

Printed and Bound by
Dai Nippon Printing Co. Limited, Hong Kong

Publishers' Acknowledgements
The publishers wish to thank the Iceland Tourist Board for kindly checking the text for accuracy.

All photographs are by David Williams, except p.104 (illuminated manuscript) which is by kind permission of Sólarfilma, Reykjavík.

THE AUTHOR
David Williams is a 36-year-old teacher living in Glasgow, Scotland. After travelling extensively in Central Europe and along the Asian Highway to India, he turned westwards, drawn to Iceland by the grandeur of its stark and contrasting scenery. Like many other visitors he has returned on numerous occasions to explore and photograph the varied landscape.

Author's Acknowledgements
This book owes a great deal to the many individuals and organisations who have helped me so much over the last few years and to all of them, both in Iceland and Britain, go my thanks. In particular, I should like to mention the following:
in Iceland
Icelandair, Gunnar Sveinsson of BSI, Úlfar Jacobsen Travel Bureau, Auður Jacobsen.
in Britain
Sonicworld UK, Clive Stacey.

Finally, I must pay special tribute to my parents and my sister for all their encouragement and help throughout the planning of my visits to Iceland and the preparation of the book.

CONTENTS

INTRODUCED BY DAVID BELLAMY

WHEN I WAS ten years of age I read a book entitled *The Wonders of Creation*. It was one of those fabulous Victorian volumes which recorded the experiences of the great travellers who took up the challenge of the Grand Tour of the World when it could only be accomplished by sailing boat, horseback and on foot.

The book told of the vastness and fascination of Amazonia, of North America, Africa, Eurasia and more. But the chapters which held my attention and to which I returned again and again concerned Iceland.

So it was that as a student I decided to enter an essay competition for a travel bursary. The subject was simple: "If you had £30 where would you travel and why?"

I wrote about Iceland saying that I wanted to follow in the footsteps of Lord Dufferin and Sir William Hooker to see "the wonders nature had afforded there."

To my surprise I won and my father, who was then fifty and had never done anything very adventurous in his life, decided to come too. So later that year we boarded the M/S 'Gullfoss' at Leith, en route to Reykjavík and my first real adventure abroad.

Since that fantastic trip I have travelled the world and seen all the things described in that little book and yet I still like to return to Iceland, for it *is* one of the great Wonders of the World, offering so much both in spectacle and welcome.

Great glaciers which ebb and flow with the pulse of world climate – awesome majesties of living ice – gouge, bulldoze and water new landscapes which burst with spring flowers and autumn seed and fruit, providing refuge for tourists and wildfowl alike which fly across the world.

Volcanic activity, though dire in certain of its consequences (no wonder Mount Hekla was thought to be the Mouth of Hell), holds a special fascination for all of us. An eruption viewed from a safe distance is the ultimate experience of creative and destructive power. I defy anyone not to wonder at the diversity of Iceland's volcanoes, the power of Strokkur, little brother of the great Geysir itself, and the hiss and gurgle of fumeroles and boiling mud pools. All are still there as the early travellers described.

Everywhere you care to look, from the Westman Islands in the south-west to Grímsey across the Arctic Circle in the north, there are new landscapes in the making. The uneasy alliance between fire and ice, be it volcanic heat or the gentle warmth of summer sun, pours water over the falls, the power of which catches the breath of every visitor and refracts rainbows into their pictures and their thinking.

Iceland is one of the youngest slabs of real estate in the world and yet it supports a nation which through its Sagas boasts the oldest democracy on this earth. A nation in which literacy and learning still hold pride of place and where streets are as free of litter as streets can be.

Don't take my word for it but go and see it all for yourself.

This magnificent book will, I am sure, help to make your visit as rewarding as it can be. It will also be a perfect souvenir of the experience of a lifetime and make you want to return again and again.

See you there.

David J Bellamy
Bedburn, 1984

PART ONE
AN INTRODUCTION TO ICELAND

HISTORY

'There came into view a large and misty mountain in the ocean . . . with misty clouds above it, and a great smoke issuing from its summit . . . Then they saw the peak of the mountain unclouded and shooting up flames into the sky which it drew back again to itself so that the mountain was a burning pyre . . . Soon after, one of the inhabitants came forth . . . he was all hairy and hideous, begrimed with fire and smoke.'

(*Navigatio Sancti Brendani*, c.575)

ST BRENDAN'S fanciful description records what was probably one of Hekla's eruptions more than fourteen hundred years ago. This strange, fiery land 'rugged and rocky, covered over with slag, without trees or herbiage, but full of smiths' forges', struck terror into the hearts of the earliest visitors. Alarming tales such as these and Iceland's isolation in the northern reaches of the Atlantic helped ensure that it was another three centuries before any major colonisation took place.

It is not clear who the earliest inhabitants of the island were. Some Roman coins of the third century have been found, but we do not know who brought them or when. The island was probably first explored by Irish monks during the sixth to ninth centuries AD; these brave men sailed north in frail curraghs, landing on the island's southern coast and establishing a settlement at Kirkjubær. St Brendan's description quoted above probably refers to one of these early inhabitants. Although there were as many as 1,000 of these exiles by 874, little is left to show how they lived or worked, and the reasons for their disappearance after the settlers' arrival remain shrouded in mystery.

The first Scandinavian known to have arrived was the Norwegian pirate Naddod, who left his native Norway in 860 and, blown off his course to the Faroes, landed in Reyðarfjörður in the eastern fjords. Four years later the Swede Gardar Svafarsson sailed round the island, staying a winter at Húsavík, and, encouraged by Svafars-son's description of this new land, the Norwegian Flóki Vilgerðarson spent two years exploring the island. He and his party stayed at Vatnsfjörður in the north-western peninsula.

However they spent too much time fishing to the detriment of the cattle, which had no winter fodder, and therefore did not survive the winter, forcing Flóki to move on. The following spring was very cold too, and, on climbing a hill near their winter home, Flóki saw Fossfjörður full of icefloes that had drifted in from Greenland and named the land 'Iceland'.

Undeterred by the country's new name, the first permanent settlers arrived in 874. They were Vikings from Norway and their arrival must have horrified the Irish monks who had fled to this lonely island to escape the depredations of just such men as these.

Generally considered to have started in 793 with an attack on the unprotected monastery at Lindisfarne off the coast of Northumbria in England, the 'Viking Age' lasted for some two hundred years, during which time the sight of Viking ships was to strike terror from Labrador in the west to Istanbul in the east as these farmers turned sailors conquered and colonised wherever they went.

Just what caused the waves of conquest and colonization that typified the 'Viking Age' remains open to debate; the primary cause of Iceland's colonization, however, is fairly well established. While the tribes in Sweden and Denmark had been welded into something approaching nationhood by the dominant tribes in each region (the Swedes and Danes respectively), Norway at this time was still fragmented into a large number of minor kingdoms ruled by tribal chiefs. In the late ninth century, Harald Finehair (862-930), a minor chiefling from the south, unified the country by force of arms during a bloody ten-year campaign that saw the major opposition to his rule subdued.

The defeated chieftains were faced with a choice: to subjugate themselves to his rule, to resist further, or to leave the country. Many left, a good number ending up in Iceland, although often only after a generation or so settled in the more familiar and prosperous British Isles.

Unusually, therefore, in world history, this emigration and colonization of new territory was carried out by some of the noblest, richest and ablest inhabitants of the 'mother' country. They were accompanied by many ordinary farmers simply seeking a new life and a chance to farm in peace, as well as, less voluntarily, by Irish slaves who were probably carried off to provide labour by settlers en route from Norway to Iceland. These latter were freed in the fullness of time, becoming independent settlers in their turn (the Westman Isles are so named as they were the 'Isles of the West Men', ie the Irish).

Iceland is the only country in Europe that possesses a record that dates, to all intents and purposes, from the beginning of its inhabited history. This is the *Landnámabók* ('Book of Settlements') compiled in the twelfth and thirteenth centuries, which gives an account of the first four hundred or so settlers, their origins, their land and the subsequent histories of their families.

The first settler to arrive was Ingólfur Árnarson. On sighting land he is said to have thrown his wooden 'high seat' pillars into the sea, vowing that he would settle wherever they reached land. Decorated with elaborate mythological carvings, the pillars were sacred and their removal to the new home was an act of great symbolic significance to the early settlers. A long search for the pillars ensued before they were found at the site of the present capital of the country. Behind the broad sheltered bay into which the pillars had drifted, plumes of vapour rose from warm water springs. Impressed by this sight, Ingólfur named the place Reykjavík ('Smoky Bay').

The Age of the Settlement

THESE Nordic Iron Age farmers were soon joined by others from Viking settlements in the British Isles and Ireland, who began to establish themselves in the south-west – the major fertile region – of the island, and in the other coastal areas, the interior being uninhabitable. This period which lasted from 874-c.930 is known as the 'Age of the Settlement'. By 930 nearly all the farming land had been divided up; as it became scarce a rule was made that no man could have more land than he could carry fire round in a day. (For women the rule was different: they could have as much land as a two-year-old heifer could run round in a day.)

The first settlers were of course pagans, and took with them to their new home the tales of the Norse gods and their place in the ancient mystic beliefs. These gods lived in Ásgard, said to be situated far to the east of the river Don in Asia. Chief amongst them was Óðin (god of poetry and magic) who lived in Valholl (Valhalla), the home of all who perished in battle. Perhaps the most popular of the gods was Thór, one of Óðin's sons. He was the god of thunder and protector of the peasants; he also protected the gods from their enemies, especially the giants, with whom they were in frequent conflict. In this he was helped by his magic hammer 'Mjöllnir' which was all-powerful and had the ability to always return to Thór's hand after it had been hurled. Its sacredness was so respected by the ancients that the sign of the hammer was often made to ward off evil spirits.

Estimates of the total population of Iceland by 930 range between 20,000 and 45,000. At first, the situation resembled that which had existed in Norway before Harald disrupted the old order; the principal settlers became *goðar* (chieftain-priests), whose followers paid allegiance to them in return for their protection. The *goði* (sing.) was normally of noble birth, and held both religious and secular authority. Iceland was divided loosely into a number of 'mini states' which were independent of one another, each under the authority of its *goði*. This was by no means a feudal system however, for the authority of the chieftain was not clearly defined, and the allegiance of his followers was heavily dependent on the justice and effectiveness of his rule.

Nevertheless there was a need for a system of law common to all the island's inhabitants and c.920 one of the settlers, Úlfljót, chosen for his wisdom and experience, was sent abroad to study the laws of south-western Norway and recommend a code of law for his country.

In 930 his recommendations were put into effect with the founding of the *Althing* (General Assembly), which marked the beginning of the Icelandic Commonwealth that was to last for the

A statue of Ingólfur Arnarson, Iceland's first settler, by Einar Jónsson.

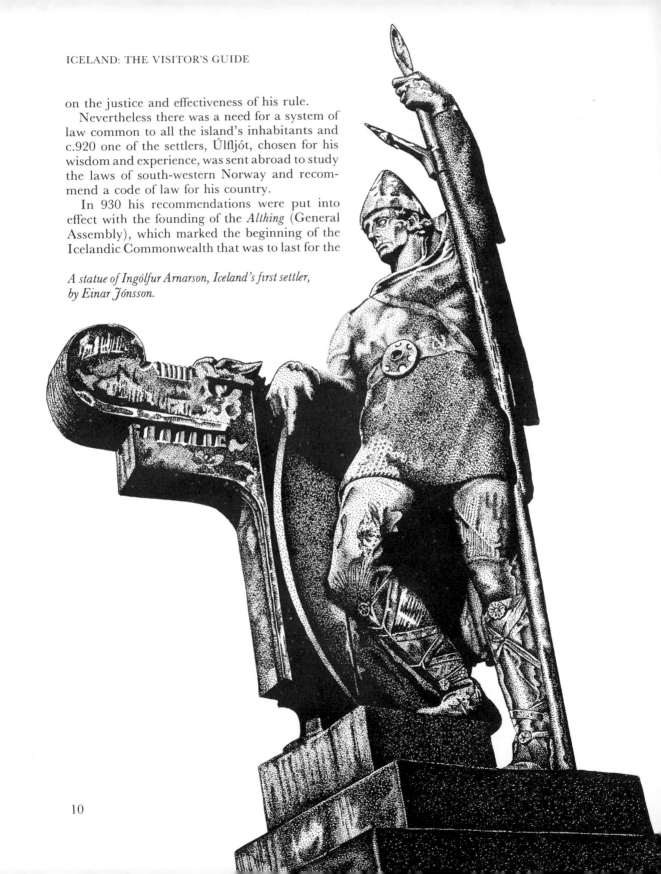

next 330 years. The number of principal *goðar* was fixed at 36 (later 39), and government of the country was vested entirely with them. The Althing was divided into two distinct bodies, one law-making, the other judicial. Local *Things* (Assemblies) were held in the spring in each of the Commonwealth's twelve (later thirteen) districts, under the aegis of the Althing. Once a year the Althing itself met, for two weeks in summer, at the site chosen for it at Thingvellir (Plain of the Assembly). It was attended by a large part of the population, providing an excuse for a fortnight-long festival and celebration, as well as making laws and settling those disputes left unsettled by the local *Things*.

Since the code of law was not written down, the elected 'Lawspeaker' had to memorise the laws and recite one-third of them at the Althing each year of his three-year period of office.

The Althing has been called the first parliament in history; certainly it was far in advance of other European political institutions in the Middle Ages, and represented a remarkable achievement for so young a nation.

Conversion to Christianity

TOWARDS the end of the tenth century, the effect of Christianity's widespread adoption in Northern Europe began to make itself felt in Iceland. The numbers of Icelandic travellers to mainland Europe who returned converted increased steadily, particularly after Ólaf Tryggvason became King of Norway.

While Iceland paid no allegiance to the Norwegian king, links between the two countries naturally remained close, with many prominent Icelanders paying annual visits to Norway, and seeking wealth, advancement and distinction at the Court. King Ólaf was an enthusiastic Christian: he had been converted by Aelfea, Bishop of Winchester, during a military campaign against the British Isles and had pledged to bring Christianity to the Northlands.

He now did all he could to convert Icelandic visitors to his court, rewarding them well for conversion, and sending his chaplain, Thang-

brand to preach in Iceland. Thangbrand's robust style of conversion – he was not averse to fighting duels to prove the superiority of his religion – met great success and between 997-999 many leading *goðar* were baptised.

Matters were now clearly coming to a head, with religious tensions rising as there had been some bloodshed. In 1000, the Althing met, and the Christian *goðar* and their followers, unwilling to accept the ruling of the official pagan Althing, proposed that they should secede and set up their own Christian commonwealth.

Faced with the prospect of the religious civil war this secession would almost inevitably produce, and aware that the powerful and aggressive King of Norway stood behind the Christians, the Althing, with impressive pragmatism, took the political, rather than religious, decision to convert to Christianity.

The Discovery of Greenland and America

GREENLAND may first have been sighted by an Icelander called Gunnbjörn Úlfsson, c.900. At any rate rumours of its existence led to its discovery some eighty years later by the celebrated Viking Eirík the Red, c.982, who had settled in Iceland after being outlawed from Norway as the result of a blood feud. However he was banished from Iceland, too, for 3 years as the result of further feuding, and spent the period exploring Greenland's southern coast.

Returning to Iceland at the end of his three year banishment, he named the country he had discovered 'Greenland', in the hope, so the Sagas say, that such a name would attract settlers. It seems to have worked for he set out next year with twenty-five ships full of colonists. Eleven were forced to turn back by bad weather, but the remainder, including that of Eirík the Red, reached Greenland and founded two settlements, one on the south coast near Cape Farewell, the other near where Godthaab now lies on the west coast.

Recent research indicates that Greenland's climate was much milder from the eleventh to the thirteenth centuries than it is now and the colonies prospered for some time, having at their peak a combined population of some 2,000 people. Climatic conditions greatly deteriorated during the fourteenth century, however, and the settlements died out, most probably at some point during the fifteenth century.

Eirík the Red had three sons, all well-known as sailors and travellers, but one of them, Leif Eiríksson, was considered the greatest navigator of his day, in 999 making the first direct trans-oceanic Atlantic voyage from Greenland to Norway.

Another Icelander, Bjarni Herjólfsson, is credited with having first sighted America after losing his course in fog on his way from Iceland to Greenland. Leif Eiríksson is said to have bought Bjarni's ship and set off to find and explore the land he had sighted. This he succeeded in doing, arriving first at a barren rocky shoreline with glaciers in the mountains beyond, which he named 'Helluland' ('Stoneland'). This is thought to have been Baffin Island or Northern Labrador. Next he reached wooded country which he named 'Markland' ('Woodland'), now thought to have been Southern Labrador.

Finally, after two days further sailing, he came to a fertile country with so mild a climate that there were grapes growing wild, causing Leif to name the country 'Vinland' ('Wineland'). He erected dwellings and explored the country more thoroughly before returning to Greenland.

Not surprisingly, great interest was aroused by Leif's discovery and one of his brothers, Thorvald, returned to the spot where Leif had landed, and explored the country for two years, before he was killed in a fight with natives. It seems probable that colonization of America by the Norsemen was prevented by the hostility of the natives: the well-known later expedition led by Thorfinn Karlsefni, which was at least 100 strong, also suffered casualties at their hands and was forced to withdraw.

The exact site of Leif's landing in 'Vinland' has remained a source of controversy, with locations from New York state to Newfoundland being put forward. The presence of grapes would appear to suggest an area south of Newfoundland, at least.

Such knowledge as we have of these epic voyages is drawn from the (sometimes conflicting) *Vinland Sagas*.

The Collapse of the Commonwealth

DURING the twelfth century the relative equality of power and wealth amongst the *goðar*, which had formed the cornerstone of the Commonwealth's stability, gradually disappeared and by the beginning of the thirteenth century most of the power and wealth in Iceland was shared between six ruling families. A period of unprecedented feuding, murder and bloodshed followed as they struggled for ascendancy: each enlisting in turn the support of the King of Norway, whose plans to arrogate the country were well suited by the increasing anarchy. The traditional independence of the *goðar*'s followers was crushed beneath their burgeoning power and freeholders were now harshly used, often being treated as personal vassals by their increasingly arrogant masters.

The Althing was powerless to prevent these developments, for it had been constituted in such a way that it possessed no centralized basis of power capable of subduing its increasingly lawless members. By 1262, the situation had reached such a pitch that the majority of the population welcomed the intervention of the Norwegian king, who concluded an 'Agreement of Union' with the (incomplete) Althing, by which the king undertook to maintain peace in the country, adhere to the existing Icelandic laws, and ensure that supply ships sailed regularly from Norway to Iceland. In return he was to receive the Icelanders' allegiance and the right to levy taxes on them. The 'Agreement of Union' – and the bloodshed which preceded it – may be said to mark the beginning of the Dark Ages of Icelandic history, for if Iceland had enjoyed a period of relative enlightenment and democracy during Europe's Dark Ages, it was now to suffer five centuries of almost unrelieved misery due to natural disaster and foreign oppression.

Less than 20 years after the 'Agreement of Union', a new code of law was introduced by the king and accepted, reluctantly, by the Althing. This led to the official abolition of the powers of the *goðar*, handing full control of the government of the country to the king. The Althing continued to meet, more or less regularly, until 1800, but its importance and power were much reduced and decreased further through time.

The vacuum left by the *goðar*'s loss of power and the emasculation of the Althing was filled by the Church (by now controlled by Norwegian bishops) which amassed considerable wealth at the expense of the Icelandic landowners. In this the Church was largely abetted by the Norwegian monarchy, whose treatment of its new dominion became increasingly arbitrary. Up until the Reformation in the sixteenth century these bishops, usually foreign, wielded enormous power in Iceland, in many cases taking over as old-style chieftains in all but name. In 1354, the King of Norway began the practice of leasing the country to the highest bidder, who was then appointed 'Governor' for three years. Providing he paid his annual 'rent' he was free to gather taxes by whatever means he wished. This led to a trade monopoly that was to have disastrous consequences for the Icelanders, who suffered considerable depredation, and outbreaks of violence by the starving population against their foreign oppressors were not uncommon.

The Dark Ages

THE STORY of the next four hundred years is one of almost unending catastrophe for the Icelanders. The fourteenth century was marked by three eruptions of Hekla (1300, 1341, 1389) which destroyed farming land and were followed by violent earthquakes. The population was ravaged by recurrent smallpox epidemics, and famine was widespread, brought on by cattle diseases and bad weather.

The one source of external support during this period was trade with Norway, but after the Black Death struck that country in 1349, killing one-third of the population, this trade was drastically reduced and the Icelanders, lacking raw materials for building ships of their own, were left in a desperate position.

The end of the fourteenth century saw Iceland passing under Danish control with the Kalmar 'Act of Union' of 1387 marking the formal union of Sweden, Norway and Denmark under the Danish crown. This development did nothing to improve conditions for the Icelanders, however, as the new Danish officials proved no less mercenary and callous than their Norwegian predecessors had been.

The fifteenth century was to prove even more devastating to the population of Iceland than the previous 100 years. The Black Death struck the island from 1402-4, killing, by conservative estimates, at least one-third of the population and depopulating whole districts. The economic life of the country came almost to a standstill, only to be revived by the first arrivals of English traders seeking to traffic in dried codfish. They were soon followed by the German merchants of the Hanseatic League and the lively (and occasionally violent) commercial competition that ensued over the next century virtually revolutionised Iceland's economy, bringing about a fundamental change in commerce, with fish rather than homespun cloth becoming the principal export.

The evident profitability of this trade led to a number of largely unsuccessful attempts by the Danes to curb the English and German merchants' activities. The latter had originally enjoyed the support of the Danish Crown in their efforts to build up trade. However they were too successful and became, from a Danish point of view, ominously influential in Iceland; around 1530 German merchants even took an active part in the proceedings of the Althing.

In 1547, the King of Denmark acted to prevent this trade, by leasing Iceland to the City of Copenhagen. This was a significant step towards the full trade monopoly, which, when it was eventually put into force in 1602, was to provide 185 years of further economic misery for the Icelandic people.

Church politics played an important part in the history of Iceland in the sixteenth century.

The Reformation, which had swept through the rest of Europe, began to affect the lives of the Icelanders. The fervently Lutheran King of Denmark, Christian III, attempted to establish a Lutheran church in Iceland. When the two Roman Catholic bishops, Ögmundur Pálsson and the legendary Jón Arason, resisted his demands, the king seized his chance to crush the power of the Icelandic Church and to confiscate its enormous wealth for his own use. The eighty-year-old Ögmundur was abducted by the king's representatives and carried back to Denmark where he died. Bishop Arason, however, proved a more formidable adversary and came close to gaining control of the country by force before he was captured and illegally beheaded with two of his sons at Skálholt in 1550.

The Danish Crown now appropriated the Church's vast properties, ultimately gaining control of around one-fifth of the country's landed property. In addition, vigorous steps were taken to suppress Catholic customs, and the severity of the law was increased, with capital punishment introduced for heresy and adultery.

The seventeenth and eighteenth centuries were to prove a period of even greater unrelieved misery for the Icelandic people. Economically, the country was reduced to penury by the Danish trade monopoly. The Danish trade merchants imported putrid food and shoddy goods at exorbitant prices, flouting all regulations, and dictating the terms of trade. In 1662, the King of Denmark declared himself the absolute hereditary monarch of Iceland, and the leading Icelanders were summoned to Bessastaðir (then home of the Danish Governor-General) and forced to take an oath of allegiance to him under threat of arms.

A series of exceptionally severe winters at the beginning of the seventeenth century decimated the livestock; some 9,000 people starved to death in consequence. The century was to end as it had begun: in 1695 and 1696 the weather was so severe that the sea surrounding the island froze.

The seventeenth century was also characterised by repeated attacks on the country by English and Spanish pirates. In 1627 the island of Heimaey was overrun, almost unbelievably, by a band of Algerian pirates who carried away some 240 of the ablest-bodied of the inhabitants and slaughtered the rest.

The eighteenth century saw continuing oppression and exploitation on the political and economic fronts. A series of epidemics swept the country, the worst of which, smallpox in 1707-1709, killed some 18,000 people (one-third of the population), reducing the population to little more than one-half that recorded in 1100.

Intermittent extremely destructive volcanic activity during the seventeenth century (ash from an Icelandic eruption in 1625 fell on Bergen in Norway) proved merely a foretaste to that experienced in the eighteenth century which saw a number of major eruptions (Öræfajökull in 1727 and Katla in 1755), culminating in that of Laki in 1783 (see p.174), the poisonous fumes from which killed half the country's cattle and three-quarters of its sheep and horses, virtually obliterating farming activity in much of the island.

But these centuries of almost unbelievable physical hardship, oppression and calamity for the islanders were witness – as if in compensation – to an intellectual flowering and literary renaissance. The Reformation led to the establishment in 1522 of Latin schools at both Skálholt and Hólar, many of whose pupils went abroad to gain further education at foreign universities. At the same time the introduction of the printing press greatly reduced the cost of books and helped widen ownership of them (primarily Bibles and hymn books), contributing greatly to increased education. The advent of the Reformation in Iceland also saw the abandonment of the practice of appointing foreigners (often corrupt) as bishops of the country; subsequently many Icelandic bishops played prominent roles in promulgating the spread of learning, distinguishing themselves as intellectual, as well as religious, leaders.

Although deep in economic misery and shaken by natural catastrophe, Iceland once more gave birth to literary and intellectual achievements that caught the attention of the outside world.

The work of scholars such as Arngrímur Jónsson (1568-1648), Thormóð Torfaeus (1636-1719) and Árni Magnússon (1663-1730) helped stimulate European interest in the history and literature of the Northlands, and through the collection and preservation of old manuscripts helped preserve Icelandic literature from imminent destruction. No less importantly, Icelanders themselves began to take an increased interest and pride in their history and identity.

One of the greatest Icelanders of the eighteenth century was Skúli Magnússon (1711-94), a man of energy and perseverance, who succeeded in breaking the power of the Hørdkraemmer company (the Danish company which exercised the trade monopoly over Iceland).

Recognising the need to break the trade monopoly and lay a new basis for Iceland's decrepit economy, he established a number of small manufacturing enterprises, with the support of King Frederick V of Denmark, who was well disposed towards the islanders. He was fiercely opposed in his plans by the Hørdkraemmer Company, who were fearful of the competition. Skúli brought a legal suit against the company for the wrong it had done to Iceland and, after a lengthy legal battle, the company was dissolved and all trade with Iceland was carried on by the Danish government. In 1763, the monopoly was once more awarded to a private company which continued most of the Hørdkraemmer's bad practices, until in 1774 its charter was dissolved, with the government once more taking over the trading obligations.

It was not until 1787 that commerce with Iceland was opened up to all subjects of the Danish crown, ending 185 years of starvation and misery caused by the iniquitous trade monopoly.

The Nineteenth Century

THE NINETEENTH CENTURY started with the dissolution of the Althing by royal order in 1800. And yet this century, which began with the extinction of the institution which symbolised Iceland's national entity, was to experience a new upsurge in Icelandic nationalism, a new awareness of national identity and a determination to gain independence from foreign control.

The beginning of the nineteenth century found Iceland still in great difficulty, exacerbated by the effect that the Napoleonic Wars had on European sea-borne trade. As a result of the 'Peace of Kiel' of 1814, Denmark (which had sided with Napoleon) ceded Norway to Sweden but retained control over Iceland, Greenland and the Faroes. In the years following the war, trading was less restricted, allowing some economic recovery and the arts, sciences and education began to prosper again. At the same time the first real stirrings of Icelandic nationalism began to manifest themselves and a determination grew to remove Danish control from the country.

This development followed the events that were taking place throughout much of Europe and well-travelled Icelanders were able to report on what was happening in other countries. The most famous nationalist leader, Jón Sigurðsson, spent much of his time in Copenhagen, arguing for the rights of his country and writing political articles to sustain the fight. The first fruit of the Icelanders' struggle was the reconstitution of the Althing in 1843, but only as a consultative body; however, most of its members were to be elected, with Jón Sigurðsson later representing a district in the north-west.

1848 brought a further revolution in France and also a change in the Danish monarchy, two events that intensified the demands for autonomy. A number of reforms took place in the next decade, including the ending of trade restrictions in 1854 and the establishment of a free press; these advances increased the Icelanders' confidence still further.

In 1874, on the thousandth anniversary of the Settlement, King Christian IX announced a new constitution which gave the Althing control over the nation's finances. Thirty members of the Althing were to be elected (ten more than before) and six would be chosen by the king (as before). However, executive powers were to be held by a governor who was responsible to Copenhagen; thus the king still had a veto over legislation, which the Icelanders opposed.

Towards the end of the century there were important developments in economic life, with the founding of the National Bank (1885) and the first cooperative (1882); by 1902 the cooperative societies were united into a Federation *(Samband)*, which today is one of the country's most important economic organisations.

With the future looking brighter, the Althing continued to press for more power and after the election of a new Danish government (which was more amenable to the Icelanders' demands) a Home Rule agreement was drawn up in 1904. In this, the 'Icelandic Minister' was responsible to the Althing, some of whose members were still appointed by the king. Debate and negotiations still continued on the issue and in 1918 Iceland and Denmark became sovereign states, having the same king and with Denmark being responsible for the defence and foreign interests of the two countries. This agreement was to run until the end of 1940 and if no agreement could be reached within three years (i.e. at the end of 1943) then either country could unilaterally declare the Union to be finished.

This is exactly what happened. On 9 April 1940, Denmark was occupied by Germany and therefore unable to abide by the 1918 Act of Union. On 10 April, the Althing took upon itself the powers over defence (though it had no forces) and foreign affairs. However, one month later a British force occupied the country in order to forestall Germany from doing the same thing, and in 1941, as the British troops were needed elsewhere, the Icelanders agreed (on 8 July 1941) to them being replaced by American troops, who stayed there throughout the war.

Without wasting much time after the expiry of the three-year limit, the Althing declared (on 25 February 1944) the Act of Union to be terminated and put the issue to a plebiscite, with 97 per cent of the votes being cast in favour of the Althing's decision. On 17 June 1944 over 20,000 people went to the historic site of Thingvellir to hear the Althing's President declare the establishment of the Republic; the date was chosen as it was the birthday of Jón Sigurðsson. This great event marked the start of the modern phase of the country's history, but as a celebration of the nation's past, an even larger crowd (some 50,000 or about one quarter of the country's entire population), returned some thirty years later (on 27 July 1974) to celebrate the 1100th anniversary of the Settlement.

CULTURE

A SOCIETY'S cultural achievements are always shaped by the geographical, economic and social circumstances under which they are created and Iceland is far from being an exception to this rule. The country's isolation, its Norse traditions, the long winter nights and the lack of building materials have, among other factors, all contributed towards the development of an unusual cultural heritage.

A discussion of this heritage is perhaps best prefaced by a brief description of what it is *not*, for Iceland's special circumstances have until recently precluded its people from pursuing excellence in many artistic fields that the populations of other countries are fortunate enough to have been able to enjoy for centuries.

As he or she travels round the country, the visitor to Iceland will soon notice that there are no castles, keeps, walls or other fine buildings or architectural monuments. Most of the buildings are new and Reykjavík does not boast a single building that is more than 200 years old. Lack of suitable building materials (due to a great extent to the geological youth of the country) has prevented the development of architectural skills until the most recent times. There are few public buildings made of stone: the Parliament House in Reykjavík is one notable exception. The turf, wood and corrugated buildings seen at the beginning of the century (see pp.142-143) have been replaced by concrete, but there are (happily, perhaps) few buildings more than several storeys high.

The absence of substantial buildings designed to stand for generations inhibited the development of painting, for there were no walls permanent enough to decorate with frescos or murals or splendid enough to serve as settings for fine works of art; nor, thanks to the poverty of much of the island's history, were there rich patrons to encourage artists and provide commissions.

All the same, it is perhaps surprising that the spectacular Icelandic scenery did not inspire a greater response from Iceland's artists. However, the Icelandic attitude to Nature was a very practical one (born no doubt of the vicissitudes that she so frequently showered upon them) and she was regarded more as an adversary than an artistic inspiration. It was only those artists who went abroad for an education that painted landscapes of their homeland: and these were usually romanticised. On returning home, these painters found little public interest in their work.

Such art as did exist was instead largely religious in inspiration, and centred around the painstaking work of illuminating manuscripts.

Old Icelandic Literature

IT IS NO coincidence that the visual arts were largely devoted in Iceland to the beautification of the written word, for Iceland's language and literature are its glory and its crowning achievement, reaching, in the Eddic poetry and the greatest of the Sagas, the pinnacle of literary achievement, an achievement all the more astonishing for being attained in the midst of economic misery and in a country with only two schools for most of its history and no university until 1911. Remarkably, despite these disadvantages, there has been universal literacy in Iceland since the eighteenth century, and her language and literature have long been the valued possessions not just of a minority intellectual caste, but of the whole nation.

Such has been the isolation of the Icelanders (both geographical and artistic) throughout their history that the language has remained virtually unchanged since the time of the Settlement. A twelve-year-old Icelander can read the Sagas without any of the strain his American or British counterpart would feel at reading Langland or Chaucer. This almost miraculous preservation makes Old Norse the oldest extant literary language in Europe, perhaps the world. The Icelanders are fiercely proud of it, and the deleterious effects the all-pervading Western culture may have upon the purity of their language provides a deep-seated source of public controversy for the Icelanders today.

However, the value of Old Icelandic literature lies not only in its literary excellence, but also in its preservation – however imperfectly, and with whatever literary distortion – of much of the pre-Christian history of the Germanic peoples (that is to say the Scandinavians, the Anglo-Saxon, and the other German-speaking peoples). Most of what we know about these pagan peoples – customs, mythology, and way of life – has been learnt from the Sagas and the Eddic poetry (see below). That these were preserved is due to a series of historical 'accidents', beginning with the original Settlement, when a colony of settlers with a rich oral tradition became geographically isolated from the rest of Europe, preserving and passing down from generation to generation the myths and traditions of the society they had left. Next, the curiously pragmatic conversion of Iceland to Christianity (see p.11) seems to have created an air of tolerance, so that in practice the two religions co-existed for a time rather than the one expunging the other – with the rather surprising result that the pagan oral tradition was extensively preserved in written form by Christian scribes in the eleventh and twelfth

17

centuries. Finally the collection by Árni Magnússon (1663-1730) of manuscripts from all over Iceland preserved Icelandic literature from an imminent disappearance during the 'dark ages' of the country's history. Many of the works had been copied down onto cowhide, and it was not uncommon for these to have been put to more practical use, such as clothing or footwear, under the desperate conditions of the time.

The historical value of Icelandic literature is not limited to the ancient pre-Christian legends or mythology it preserves: some of the Sagas and most of the skaldic poetry (see below) deal with events that were recent or contemporary to the time of their creation, and as such provide a semi-reliable record – often the only one we have – of important events in Iceland's history. One example of this is the series of Sagas *(The Vinland Sagas)* dealing with the discovery of Greenland and America.

Eddic and Skaldic Poetry

OLD ICELANDIC LITERATURE can be divided into two main categories, poetry and prose, and the poetry can be further divided into two distinct traditions, 'skaldic' and 'Eddic' poetry. 'Skaldic' poetry was written by *skalds*, young Icelandic poets who often travelled abroad, staying at the courts of foreign kings, in whose honour they would compose poetry in return for favours from the king. So great was their wanderlust, and so popular their works, that Iceland's young poets travelled widely, and were found in many European courts, as well as in Russia and Byzantium. Many of them became influential figures in the courts which they attended, and on their return to Iceland became figures of note in their own country, where the news they brought of events in the outside world was eagerly awaited. Such skalds played an important role, not just for their contemporaries but also for later historians, in recording accurately the events of which they heard tell on their travels.

The skalds drew their material not from legend or myth but from contemporary events and individuals, commemorating battles, or praising the exploits of an influential king or leader. They took pride in elaborate and artificial poetic styles, with frequent use of obscure metaphors and clever phrasing. They are generally known by name (indeed many of the heroes of the Sagas are skalds), unlike the Eddic poets who are anonymous. Skaldic poets were, therefore, essentially skilled versifiers, masters of style who won great reputations for recording the events of their times. The most famous skald was Egill Skallagrímsson (c.910-990), the first of the Icelandic court poets and the hero of one of the *Sagas of Icelanders*.

The phrase 'Eddic poetry' refers to the poetry contained in the manuscript known as the *Poetic Edda*, a collection of thirty-five heroic and mythical poems. Relics of an oral poetic tradition which was written down c.1200, these poems represent a much older, pagan world view; as mentioned earlier, they provide practically the only examples of pre-Christian Germanic literature in existence. Some of the poems recount myths of the pagan gods. From these we learn the world-famous stories of Óðin and Thór, of Balder, Freya and Loki. Others tell semi-legendary tales of historical figures from early German history (for example, Attila the Hun features in one of the oldest poems); others still are devoted to legendary heroes such as Sigurd (Siegfried).

The poetry is far more direct, simple and objective than skaldic poetry, with little elaboration or imagery. It makes great use of dialogue, and strong connections with early forms of drama have been postulated by some commentators. There is frequently an elegiac or melancholy cast to the poems, perhaps foreshadowing the coming of the *Ragnarök* (the great battle in which most of the old gods would perish).

During the fourteenth century, a verse form called the *rímur* was developed by the Icelanders, a mixture of skaldic poetry and European verse forms that employed strict stanza form coupled with elaborate imagery, rhyming patterns and alliterative effects. Over a thousand *rímur* cycles from 330 poets have been recorded. For inspiration they draw largely on the *Sagas of Ancient*

Times: inevitably, with considerable repetition.

This secular poetic tradition developed side by side with sacred poetry which started to replace the pagan Eddic following the formal establishment of Christianity in the island in 1000. Most of this poetry had little literary significance, with the notable exception of *Lilja* (The Lily), written c.1343-4 by Eysteinn Ásgrímsson.

The Sagas

OLD ICELANDIC PROSE is dominated by the Sagas. These have been described as the first prose novels of Europe. They are unparalleled in mediaeval literature, being written in the vernacular at a time when the rest of European literature was given over to religious themes.

The sources for the Sagas remain uncertain: most probably these are a mixture of written 'authorities' and tales passed down via oral tradition, or recorded in the form of skaldic poetry. In the isolated communities that together comprised the Icelandic nation, stories of historical events or the deeds of the leading figures of the day were always in great demand, much as news bulletins are today – with the difference that the Sagas' creators used considerable authorial licence to shape their factual material into a satisfying artistic whole. The annual two-week summer festival of the Althing offered an especially good opportunity for news to be passed, old stories told and new stories learned.

The Sagas take as their subject-matter the lives of the great Icelandic figures of the tenth and eleventh centuries. Underlying the surface narrative, but influencing it at every crucial turning, lies the Viking (and Icelandic) conception of how the individual should conduct himself within the society in which he lives: in other words, their moral code. Honour was of paramount concern, both personal honour, and, equally importantly, the honour of the family. An insult or injury to oneself or to one's family must be avenged without fail: this was the code of behaviour that lay behind the frequently bloody feuding that took place from the time of the Settlement, reaching its peak with the violent infighting of the 'Sturling Age' just before the 'Agreement of Union' of 1262. The Sturling Age was itself the subject of the *Sturlunga Saga*, written by a nephew of one of the main protagonists, the remarkable Snorri Sturluson, who was himself probably the author of *Egil's Saga*.

Most of the important Sagas are gathered into one of several collections, compiled at different times. The earliest of these, *Sagas of Icelanders*, was written mainly in the thirteenth century, and dealt with events of the tenth and eleventh centuries. It includes two of the greatest of all the Sagas: *Njál's Saga* and *Egil's Saga* (see above).

The Kings' Sagas are a group of tales that deal with the lives and exploits of kings and earls from the Norselands, while *The Family Sagas* were written in the thirteenth century and detail the history of leading families, particularly from the north and north-west of the country.

Romantic and chivalrous tales from the rest of Europe form the basis of many later Sagas.

The peculiar brilliance of the best of the Sagas lies in their portrayal of character, their psychological insight and their narrative ability – their fundamental grasp of the art of storytelling. Their style is direct, factual, objective. Many are characterised by restraint, almost understatement, despite frequent detailed descriptions of battles and dramatic confrontations. Fate plays a prominent part in many of the Sagas: a man's heroic conduct can be judged by how he carries himself when Fate turns its hand against him.

Later Literature

AFTER the achievements of the twelfth, thirteenth and fourteenth centuries, Icelandic literature declined during the troubled and difficult fifteenth and sixteenth centuries. But the seventeenth century, although no less harsh to the Icelanders than its predecessors, saw a surge of intellectual and literary creativity. One of the major figures of the century was Hallgrímur Pétursson (1614-74), Iceland's greatest hymn writer. His principle work, *Fifty Passion Hymns*, was ten years in the making, but ranks today amongst the finest examples of its genre found anywhere in the world, and has won a special place in the nation's life. It is recited annually during Lent, and one of the hymns is sung at funeral services.

As mentioned in the history section, during the seventeenth century scholars such as Árni Magnússon and Thormóð Torfaeus greatly advanced the histiography of the Norselands, as well as preserving the country's heritage by collecting and preserving old manuscripts.

The eighteenth century was notable in particular for the appearance for the first time of scientific descriptions of the island, such as the celebrated account by Eggert Ólafsson and Bjarni Pálsson. Many practical (as opposed to literary) books were published during this period, as were translations of important European works.

Thanks to the invigorating influence of Romanticism, the nineteenth century proved to be the most outstanding century since the thirteenth in the history of Icelandic literature.

The great pioneer of Romanticism in Iceland was Bjarni Thorarensen (1786-1841), but his younger contemporary, Jónas Hallgrímsson (1807-1845) is perhaps the best-loved poet that Iceland has produced. During this period much was written that favourably contrasted an idyllic view of Iceland peasant life with the degeneracy enjoyed in Copenhagen, Iceland's foreign capital, with many authors developing a more political stance in their writing.

In prose, Jón Thoroddsen (1818-1868) is widely regarded as the father of the modern Icelandic novel. His best works are considered to be *Lad and Lass* (1850) and *Man and Wife* (1876). During this century too, the first steps were taken to preserve the purity of the language with the formation of the Icelandic Literary Society in Copenhagen in 1816. The Society (now based in Reykjavík) remains active to this day.

Modern Literature

POETRY remains a most popular form of self-expression for the Icelanders. Traditional poetry is still represented by the *rímur* mentioned earlier, whose elaborateness has been increased and refined over the years. More than 2,000 different rhyming schemes have now been recorded and the most complicated of *rímur* (called *sléttubönd* and *hringhenda*), contain stanzas which can be read backwards as well as forwards (and, very occasionally, upwards and downwards!). Like skaldic verse, from which they are descended, these verses are demonstrations of linguistic virtuosity rather than vehicles for poetic truth.

The greatest modern traditional poet, writing in a more serious vein, is the lyricist Tómas Guðmundsson, but serious traditional poetry is now the exception more than the rule. It has been increasingly replaced by modernist poetry, which tends to be less immediately accessible than its traditional counterpart, since each poet seeks to establish his own personal, innovative vocabulary of images, language and symbol, rather than drawing on a well-established convention. Sigfús Daðason, Hannes Pétursson and Thorsteinn frá Hamri stand out as the leading figures (among many contemporaries) in the modernist generation of Icelandic poets. Most modern Icelandic poets share a concern, often expressed in their work, that Iceland's traditional way of life is being eroded by imported Western values.

In prose the epic, narrative traditions of the Sagas dominated new fiction until the 1960s, in part perhaps because the supreme novelist of the age, Halldór Laxness (the 1955 Nobel Prize-winner for Literature) remained firmly in that tradition. Written in the 1930s and 40s, his novels *Independent People* and *The Bell of Iceland* are arguably the finest evocations of Iceland to have been written since the Sagas, and his satirical novel *The Atom Station* (1948) was the most controversial Icelandic publication of its time.

In the mid-1960s women writers began for the first time to contribute to Iceland's literary output, and the prevailing conservatism in fiction was finally shattered by Guðberger Bergsson's novel *Tómas Jónsson Bestseller* (1966), whose use of monologue, breaking away from the conventional narrative form, has opened up a whole new range of possibilities for Icelandic fiction.

Nineteenth-century carved wooden cupboard.

The Icelanders retain their extraordinary passion for books of all kinds, and this enthusiasm supports a flourishing publishing industry. Around 600 different books are published every year in Iceland, an impressive statistic for a country with a population of only 235,000.

Over the last hundred years or so, with the growth of Reykjavík as a cosmopolitan city with a sizeable concentration of population and increasing exposure to the outside world, several branches of the arts which had languished in Iceland for centuries have gained a new lease of life.

Painting, for so long a poor relation of Iceland's culture, is today perhaps the most vigorous and exciting of the arts. The country's newfound wealth and independence produced a wave of new artists around the turn of the century, who established painting for the first time as a significant force in the country's cultural life. Asgrímur Jónsson, Jón Stefánsson and Jóhannes Kjarval are generally considered to have made the largest contribution to this transformation. As prosperity and material comfort increased, the Icelanders' attitude to nature appears to have subtly altered; at any rate there has been an increasing interest in landscape painting, once shunned as a genre. The post-war generation have exhibited an enormous diversity of styles, with the various schools of modernism – expressionism, constructivism, surrealism, abstract painting and so on – all well represented.

Sculpture has never had a strong tradition in Iceland, most probably because the traditional raw materials such as stone and wood were for centuries in exceedingly short supply (the craft of carving small wooden domestic objects was, however, well-established, although it is little practised nowadays). With the development of new sculptural media such as wire and concrete, this obstruction has been removed, and an increasing interest in the sculptural arts is developing. The most important sculptor of the modern age is Ásmundur Sveinsson whose work ranges from representational to abstract forms in a wide variety of media.

21

Examples of the work of many of the artists mentioned here can be found in the National Art Gallery (see p.163).

Music, too, had unpromising origins in Icelandic history. The skalds may have sung some of their poems, and the advent of Christianity introduced chanting and hymn singing. Secular songs were sung, the most common form being the *rímur*-song: sung versions of the *rímur* cycles mentioned earlier.

Only two musical instruments are known to be native to Iceland; these are rather similar to one another, both being stringed instruments which were placed on a table and played with a bow. Not surprisingly, Iceland folk music has a distinctive sound of its own quite unlike that of any other European country.

The growth of Reykjavík and other settlements provided the catalyst for increased musical activity: many musical disciplines such as choir singing, brass bands and orchestras, require group activity (and an audience) that had not really been practicable in the old isolated form of Icelandic existence, with small rural communities scattered throughout the island, and little communication between them.

Since 1970 there has been a biennial International Arts Festival, with music as its principal ingredient, which has attracted many musicians of world renown to Iceland, and the Icelandic Symphony Orchestra and the Icelandic Opera Company nowadays both attract large and enthusiastic followings.

Other communal art forms, such as drama and the other performance arts, have also flourished in recent years.

THE ICELANDERS

ANY ATTEMPT to describe the modern-day Icelanders must take as its starting point the astonishing transformation their everyday life and society has undergone this century. It is no more than two generations since they emerged from six centuries of oppression by foreign powers and resultant destitution. During those two generations Icelandic society has developed from a near-mediaeval existence to its present-day, outward-looking prosperity.

The dawning of the twentieth century saw the Icelanders living in conditions that had changed little since 1100. Icelandic society was overwhelmingly rural, as Reykjavík and Akureyri had not yet started to grow and begin their domination of economic life. On the farms the lack of natural building materials such as workable stone, wood or slate, meant that the houses had to be made of roughly hewn lava blocks and turf. The farmhouses were single-storey affairs with low roofs made from planks (often driftwood), birch bark and turf. Sometimes a number of these hovels were placed side by side, joined by an interconnecting passageway, with earth piled up around the walls to keep out the bitterly cold winds. The family's living quarters consisted of a single room which served as kitchen, workplace and bedroom; there would be a fire in this single small room, the smoke filling its damp corners before rising through a hole in the roof. Some of these old buildings still survive, usually as farm outhouses, while others have been preserved as museums (see pp.142-143).

Life was governed by the seasons: once the welcome spring sun had begun to melt the winter snow and the days grew a little longer, the year's farming could begin in earnest. Few homesteads could provide sufficient income by farming alone so the menfolk would begin fishing in March, once the icy grip of winter had eased a little. The

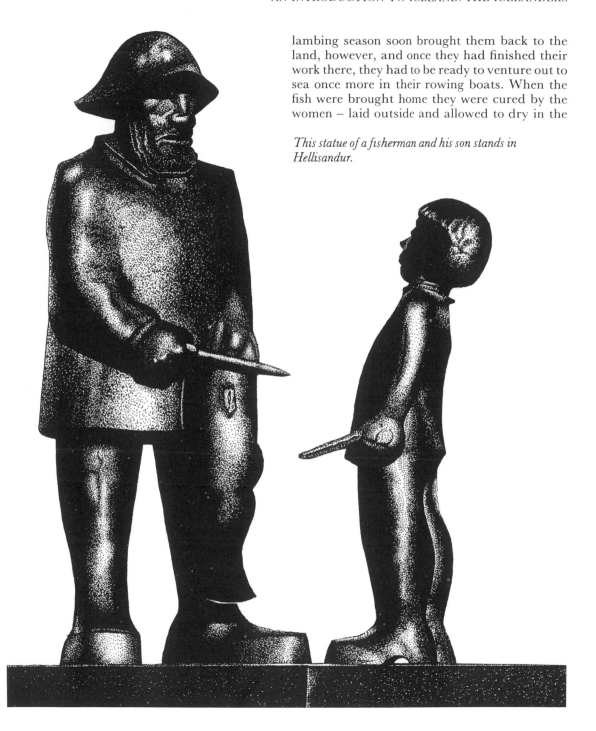

lambing season soon brought them back to the land, however, and once they had finished their work there, they had to be ready to venture out to sea once more in their rowing boats. When the fish were brought home they were cured by the women – laid outside and allowed to dry in the

This statue of a fisherman and his son stands in Hellisandur.

sun – before they were taken to one of the larger settlements to be sold.

Summer was often hectic, especially if its arrival was delayed by drift ice from the north, but the busiest period was harvest time as it often coincided with favourable fishing weather, and on such occasions almost the entire population was involved in winning food by one means or another. Even today, in some places, schoolchildren may leave their schoolbooks behind to go down to help at the harbour when an important catch has to be landed. Food in the summer months could be plentiful; milk and fish, together with mutton and the few vegetables that could be raised, formed the basic diet. Flour had to be imported and was very expensive, so bread and cakes were not as common as in other European countries. The need to stockpile food for winter, together with the difficulty of providing fodder for the animals, meant that many of the sheep had to be slaughtered each autumn and the meat preserved. The national delicacy of *hangikjöt* (smoked mutton) was made in a specially constructed sod hut where the brine-soaked mutton could be smoked over a fire of birchwood or dried sheep-dung. It still remains a popular dish, but the farms no longer smoke their own meat; they now leave this to the urban curing factories. Fish too were often smoked or dried, after which they could be kept a long time until needed; they were usually eaten with butter. When shark was caught the peculiarly Icelandic dish of *hákarl* could be made from the cured flesh.

While the long summer days may be an attraction to today's visitors, in the past for the Icelanders they meant long working hours – and sometimes they still do: jobs like hay gathering which are best done when the weather is fine may be carried out for hours on end with hardly a break. The pace of life used to slow down as winter approached; there was little that could be done on the land and fewer calm days on which a boat could go out to fish. This was the time for preparing for the next year – the men would mend nets, make tools or perhaps learn a new skill while the women made clothes for the family. After brushing and spinning, the raw wool was woven and shared out to give the women about seven metres of homespun each to make up into clothes, while the men received the same length, already made up. The grey undyed wool was by far the most important clothing material, and was used for jerseys, hats, gloves and socks, but in very wet and cold weather the fishermen would also wear a one-piece leather garment – the forerunner in design for today's skiwear. Footwear, tough enough to protect the feet on the rough lava tracks, was made from a single piece of hide from a cow, sheep or seal. The hide would be cured and cut to the right size; after being soaked it would be worn until it had dried out, shrinking to take up the most comfortable shape around the foot.

The long winter nights were family affairs, the women working with the wool while the men practised the ancient craft of wood carving. As the adults worked one of the children read aloud, perhaps from one of the Sagas: reading prose or poetry or singing folksongs were popular ways of whiling away the dark hours in the smoky atmosphere of the farmhouse.

This was the way of life shared by the majority of Icelanders until the beginning of this century. Since then industrialization, the explosive growth of the capital city, Reykjavík, and increased contact and trading with the outside world have revolutionised the Icelanders' lives. At the same time they have retained an exceptionally strong sense of their history and heritage. This is not an easy combination – how could it be? – and tensions arise from the conflict between traditional values and the Western attitudes and materialism that prosperity and exposure to US and European markets have brought.

This is perhaps best exemplified in the deep anxiety with which many Icelanders view the debasement of the language (as they perceive it) by contact with the West. This is a genuine concern – their language is arguably the Icelanders' greatest heritage, and unlike painting or sculpture it is a living thing: it cannot be put behind glass or preserved in museums. Care is therefore taken to ensure that new words with an Icelandic linguistic basis are coined for new technology, to prevent the adoption of foreign expressions in their stead. Thus the computer is *tölva* (number prophetess), the telephone is *sími* (long thread), television is *sjónvarp* (view casting). A law has also been passed forbidding parents to give their children non-Icelandic names.

The Icelanders have a history of hard work – they have had to – and today it is still not unusual for a man to have two jobs at once, especially during the summer. The material gains of the last thirty years are particularly important to the people, and considerable sums are spent building houses and equipping them with all the latest gadgetry which, thanks to recent levels of inflation, may cost two or three times as much as in other Western countries.

The harshness of life in Iceland for much of its history has resulted, too, in a national fortitude that is difficult to overestimate, which has enabled the Icelanders to endure Nature's excesses and finally to prosper on one of the world's most unpredictable and inhospitable land masses. This sterling quality was exhibited to its best advantage during the massive eruption on the island of Heimaey in January 1974. The community fought for over five months to save their town, part of which was engulfed by pumice, the rest threatened by a lava flow that was pushing a ridge of clinker 40 metres high in front of it, and exuding dense poisonous gases.

High pressure pumps were employed to try to cool the advancing edge of the lava with millions of litres of sea water, and thus divert the lava stream behind it. It was a truly herculean task, but finally, after many days and nights of hard and dangerous labour, it was achieved and when the eruption ceased five months later, man had, for the first time in history, successfully fought the destructive power of a volcano.

Over 300 houses had been engulfed, and nearly a million kilos of ash and pumice had to be removed, but the people returned in July to rebuild their shattered settlement, and today, although it still bears the scars of the catastrophe,

Heimaey has recovered from the eruption that – but for the determination of its inhabitants – would undoubtedly have obliterated it.

Calamities such as that at Heimaey have befallen the Icelanders throughout their history and it is not surprising that their geographical position should have forged a people of marked independence and individuality. Up until a hundred years ago the average Icelander lived in very isolated circumstances with little communication with other settlements: he had to be self-reliant. The long history of poverty on the island, and its essentially agricultural base, prevented the emergence of an aristocracy, and class distinctions are less obvious than in other European countries. The almost obsessional interest which an Icelander expresses in his genealogy is not the result of class competitiveness, but of a keen sense of history, and the traditional importance of family and forebears to an individual.

The country lacks sharp intellectual divisions as well: the artists and intellectuals have not become an elite, remote from the average Icelander, as they have in perhaps every other European nation. Icelanders are voracious readers, and farmers and seamen are often remarkably knowledgeable about current developments in literature and poetry. But in Iceland the poet or dreamer and the man of action have never become divorced.

Almost without exception, the greatest figures in Icelandic history distinguished themselves in the artistic or intellectual sphere as well as the political. Men such as Snorri Sturluson, who was a major poet, historian and Saga-writer as well as a warrior and chieftain in the Viking mould, amassing wealth and influence before dying a violent death; Jón Arason who was an accomplished poet as well as a warlike bishop and Jón Sigurðsson, the greatest Icelandic political figure in the nineteenth century, was a noted philologist and historian.

The present lack of intellectual and artistic isolationism is thus firmly grounded in historical precedent. The Icelanders respect their poets as much as their leaders, probably more so, but they take to their hearts a man who is both.

Superstition played an important part in Icelandic literature: only Ireland in western Europe can claim a folklore of comparable richness and fecundity, occurring at the margin where Christianity meets the old religion. The modern Icelanders remain true to their tradition and taken as a whole they are an extremely superstitious nation. A survey in 1975 indicated that 64% of the population had had a supernatural experience of some sort. Dreams are held to have great significance and there is widespread belief in the 'hidden folk' *(huldufólk)* and in 'enchanted spots', areas of particular significance to the 'hidden folk' which must consequently be left well alone by humans. It is not unknown for a new road to be diverted due to public demand to avoid interference with an 'enchanted spot'.

As might be expected from such a superstitious nation, there is a great prevelance of mediums and seances and spiritualism is widely practised (the Norwegian psychologist, Harald Schjelderup, has said that the three countries in which spiritualism is most widely practised are Brazil, Puerto Rico and Iceland). Great store is set by communication with the dead (often in dreams) and ghost stories are too numerous to mention. It is perhaps unsurprising that the Icelanders, isolated in their small communities, beset by natural disasters and possessed of a strong pagan tradition, should have discerned the activities of supernatural beings all around them.

The Icelanders show the extreme tolerance in moral matters that is generally held to be characteristic of Scandinavian countries. Birth out of wedlock is a common occurrence (although often later legitimised), and there is none of the (frequently hypocritical) stigma attached to illegitimacy found in many other European countries. This liberal attitude is probably reinforced by their equally relaxed approach toward institutionalised religion; the Lutheran Church may fairly be said to play little part in national life.

There is little crime in Iceland (although it has increased in recent years), a phenomenon that can perhaps be attributed to the combined influence of the Icelanders' strong sense of personal honour, their independence and their tolerance (one consequence of which is that prisoners' sentences are almost invariably very lenient: on special occasions many of the prisoners are let out!). Despite their Viking forebears they are a gentle and affectionate people, although their insatiable appetite for discussions and argument can raise passions – particularly if the subject is politics. Icelanders generally consume alcohol in moderation (prohibition existed 1915-1922), but their drinking sprees (at New Year, perhaps) can be prodigious.

The population of Iceland is so small that many of its institutions retain a very parochial air. Iceland's national newspapers have much of the air of provincial publications, with a lot of emphasis on minor local news and features. Icelanders are great newspaper readers: in Reykjavík alone there are no less than five daily papers. It is interesting to note that these are all politically orientated, and more overtly partisan than their Western European counterparts.

Besides reading, chess is probably the next most popular national pastime: both are legacies of the long winter nights when there was little choice other than to sit at home and entertain yourself. Reykjavík was put on the international map as a Mecca for chess by Fischer and Spassky's extraordinary series of matches for the world title in the 1970s.

Television and radio nowadays provide less testing forms of entertainment, and indeed threaten to erode the old way of life entirely. The introduction of television in the mid-sixties rekindled the controversy over the 'foreign invasion' of the national culture. Since 1961 the NATO base at Keflavík has had its own internal TV service (not surprisingly dominated by American programmes) and quite a number of people in the capital bought TV sets to pick up the station. This 'importation of culture' was fiercely debated and led to a wide-ranging argument over the programme content of the planned Icelandic service. Today the Keflavík service is limited to the base.

THE LAND

AS THE American and European continents drift slowly apart over the Earth's surface, the void that opens up between them is filled by a great new volcanic mountain chain – the North Atlantic Ridge. Most of the Ridge lies deep beneath the Atlantic, but on occasions it protrudes from the sea, and one such place is Iceland; it is this that makes Iceland so important today as an accessible place in which to study the evolution of planet Earth. The central portion of Iceland is the newest region and to the east and the west of the country are the older land masses that have moved away from the central ridge.

Iceland is Europe's second largest island (Britain is the largest), measuring about 500 km from west to east and about 350 km from north to south. It sits at the junction of the North Atlantic Ridge and another submarine ridge that runs from Scotland to eastern Greenland via the Faroes. The seas around Iceland have a depth of about 600 m towards Greenland and 400 m-600 m towards the Faroes while on both sides of the submarine ridge there are deep troughs of 2,000 m or more.

Iceland lies 290 km south-east of Greenland (its nearest neighbour) and, with the exception of the island of Grímsey and a few small rocks, lies completely south of the Arctic Circle. With an area of some 103,000 sq km, it has an average altitude of 500 m. Only one-quarter of the country lies below 200 m.

It is, geologically speaking, a young country. The oldest rocks, which are basalt, are only about sixteen million years old – much younger than the oldest basalts of Greenland and the Faroes – but the most striking example of the country's youth is that one-tenth of its area is covered by lava less than ten thousand years old. The youngest area lies along the extension of the North Atlantic Ridge which runs from Reykjanes (in the south-west) north-east to Askja, and then northwards through Mývatn. The rocks here are complex and are often composed of different varieties of basalt and debris from volcanoes. In this region there are many prominent fractures, such as Almannagjá (at Thingvallavatn), that run parallel to the direction of the Ridge.

The plateaux in the centre of the country are uninhabited but they provide summer grazing for sheep. Warmth-loving plants grow remarkably well on some of these plateaux as the winter snow protects them from spring frosts, and the relatively dry summer means that soil temperatures are higher than in the flat lowlands. Plant life is not found everywhere, however – vast areas have been laid bare by the glaciers, and the many violent eruptions of the volcanoes have smothered the land in lava, ash and cinders. Where water is present, dwarf shrubs and bogs are found and many lavafields are extensively covered with a rich, soft carpet of moss.

The east coast and the north-west peninsula are dominated by beautiful fjords that were made by great glaciers plucking rocks from valley sides, widening and deepening them in the process. The fjords only occur in the old basalt regions, the ice having changed small V-shaped valleys into steep-sided ones, leaving behind mountainsides with step-like slopes. These steps are formed out of individual lava flows, which were very fluid and flowed long distances from their sources. There were none of the great explosions usually associated with the other types of eruption, but sandwiched between the layers of basalt are beds of ashes that were produced during separate and more violent eruptions.

The hillsides are usually covered with massive scree slopes (caused by frost shattering the rock), leaving little room at their base for cultivation or settlements. While sheep farming was originally the major economic activity of the fjords, this has given way to fishing as they have numerous

27

natural harbours. There is usually only one settlement in each fjord, often in the lee of the hills or sometimes on a spit of sand that may project out into the water.

There are numerous lakes around the country which have been formed in a variety of ways: the largest two, Thingvallavatn (84 sq km) and Thórisvatn (70 sq km), both of which are in the south-west, were formed by a sudden drop in the level of the ground; others, like Lögurinn in the east, were formed by glacial erosion. Mývatn in the north was created by the damming effect of a lava flow, while the craters produced by eruptions may become the site for a lake once the volcanic activity has ceased: an example is Öskjuvatn in Askja, which is the deepest lake in the country (217 m). Grænalón (to the west of Skeiðarárjökull) is an example of an ice-dammed lake; the numbers of these are changing as the glaciers alter their size. Glaciers often form small meltwater lakes at their snout – the number and shape of these is altering too as the climate changes. The last type of lake is a lagoon lake; Hóp (45 sq km), which is in the north, is an interesting example.

There are many rivers in the country, generally running north or south-west. None of them are navigable as their current is often too rapid and varies too much through the year. The three main types of rivers found in Iceland are the *jökulár* (glacial rivers, whose greatest flow is in July or early August), *dragár* (which drain old basalt areas in summer and autumn), and *lindár* (spring-fed rivers which drain lavafields and have a nearly constant discharge).

The rivers that flow from the glaciers carry a huge quantity of sand and gravel downstream, which is then dropped to form the glacial sands *(sandur)* so common on the south coast. The constantly changing paths taken by these rivers have been a great barrier to road transport and in particular to the completion of the ring road.

The surface of the lavafields is so broken and porous that there are few rivers that cross them, so the rain and melted snow seeps through the upper surface, reappearing at the side of a river perhaps a few kilometres away. Those rivers that pass through the old basalt areas have carved some magnificent canyons, often lined with regularly shaped basalt columns that have been exposed by the water.

In many cases, the rivers have produced waterfalls such as Dettifoss (44 m and Iceland's largest waterfall) on Jökulsá á Fjöllum and Gullfoss (32 m, see pp.108-109) on the Hvitá. Some waterfalls, such as Skógafoss (60 m, see pp.112-113), fall over old sea cliffs.

The Volcanoes

A VAST AMOUNT of lava has poured out of Iceland's volcanoes since the end of the last glacial period – enough to cover about one-tenth of the island – and during historical times there have been more than 125 eruptions from over 30 volcanoes. In Iceland the Earth's crust is only about 10 km thick (compared to about 30 km in many other landmasses) and is rent with long fractures; below is the mantle and it is here that the molten rock ('magma') gathers before being erupted to the surface, sometimes after accumulating in a higher 'magma chamber'.

As the visitor travels round the island he is confronted by volcanoes of different shapes and sizes, with different types of lavafields around them. The reason for this variation often lies in the state of the magma just before it comes up to the surface. In the case of a very fluid magma the gases can escape easily and the hot material can quietly pour out of the vent and cover a large area, even if the slope down which it travels is not very steep. If such a flow takes place, a 'shield volcano' is formed, so-called since its final shape is similar to a shield lying on the ground. A fine example is Skjaldbreiður (north-east of Thingvallavatn) which is 1060 m high and has a slope of only seven degrees. At the summit, these volcanoes may have flat-bottomed craters, with steep sides which often collapse, increasing the size of the crater (300 m in diameter in the case of Skjaldbreiður). If the crater is full of magma and regularly overflows then the volcano can be built up by many (perhaps thousands) of sheets of lava with little ash or other airborne material thrown out.

Another type of conical volcano is represented by Hverfjall (452 m) to the east of Mývatn (see p.131). This was built by an explosive eruption, the viscous magma spraying out pieces of hot ash which welded together on cooling and built a steep cone with a slope of some thirty degrees. Many cones, though, are of a composite nature, with alternate layers of lava and airborne material. This combination welds the material together and the volcano can reach a great height. Such a volcano is called a 'strato-volcano', the best known example being Snæfells-jökull on the Snæfellsnes peninsula (see p.144).

Iceland's most common type of volcano is built from a 'crater row' which is often a number of vents that open up along a fissure. When this erupts it results in a volcano building not a cone, but a ridge; a classic example is the country's most famous volcano, Hekla (1491 m, see p.111). Crater rows such as Laki (south-west of Vatna-jökull) have been amongst the most effusive volcanoes in Iceland's history.

One very different type of crater may be found at Mývatn and Kirkjubæjarklaustur: a 'pseudo-crater'. This is formed when a lava stream flows over wet ground; the water is heated, turns into steam and explosively forces its way upwards through the layer of hot lava. As the cooler crust of the flow collapses back on itself, a crater is formed. Since this type of crater is not fed by magma it is not a real crater – hence the name, 'pseudocrater'.

There are two main types of lava that are produced. In the case of a very fluid magma with little or no gas, the lava will be forced out of the vent easily and at great speed, perhaps throwing fountains of the red-hot liquid many metres into the air. The lava from such an eruption can travel quickly over the ground and may produce chan-nels and tunnels ('lava tubes') through which it runs. When the surface of the lava finally solidi-fies, it does so in folds and is called 'ropey lava' ('*helluhraun*'). Great domes of this can be formed (called 'tumuli') which may eventually crack under the strain of their own weight. Ropey lava

is quite easy to walk across (when cold!).

If the magma is more viscous and has a lot of gas dissolved in it, the lava flow often takes the form of big blocks of clinker-like material. While fluid lava runs easily downhill, these large hot jagged blocks move by tumbling clumsily over one another. The progress downhill may be very slow (only a few metres per minute); the front of the advancing pile might be a few metres high. When it has cooled down and set, it forms a great mass of contorted shapes with big spaces between the blocks. The surface of this block lava ('*apalhraun*') is sharp and the rock is brittle. It is almost impossible to cross such a lavafield until it has been weathered and moss-covered.

The material that is thrown through the air from a volcano may land far from the vent that produced it, so it may be difficult to discover the origin of much loose material that is lying around. Such material varies greatly in size and consistency: the large lumps of lava that are thrown out of a vent are called 'bombs', and if they rotate in the air they may become spherical; 'pumice' is a very light material formed when sticky, frothy lava which is plugging a vent is suddenly blown out; 'ashes' are powdery remains of magma that have been sprayed out and have then solidified during flight. While many of these materials may be produced during the same eruption, it is the lightest ones that will be lifted highest and farthest from the vent. Dust from eruptions may stay in the atmosphere for many years, the biggest eruptions creating a dust cloud large enough to produce beautiful red sunsets not only in Iceland but in many other parts of the world as well.

While volcanic eruptions permit solid, liquid and gaseous material to escape from the Earth's interior relatively quickly, there are various secondary volcanic features that release material (and heat) over a long time and at a much less violent rate. The most common examples are the thousands of hot and warm springs found throughout the central (geologically young) region of the country.

'Fumeroles' are vents that produce vapours –

often at such a powerful rate that they make a roaring sound. Vapour may come from lava cooling underground, or from magma sources that are still losing gases, mixed with water that has been turned into steam. Fumeroles may give out steam, hydrochloric acid, carbon dioxide and numerous other gases. When sulphur gases are given out, the fumeroles are called 'solfataras'; these can usually be recognised by the sweet, sickly smell they give out and from deposits of the yellow powdered sulphur beside the vent. All these vents have to be approached with care as they often emit superheated steam. In areas where they are hot and powerful, they may exist long enough to turn the surrounding rock to a cream or yellow coloured clay. Deposits of silica, chlorides and sulphates of various hues can be found at the mouths of the vents, often producing sizeable crystals.

Less dramatic are the acid and alkaline springs. Acid springs are usually found at relatively high altitudes or other places where there is little ground water. Carbon dioxide dissolved in hot water produces hot acid springs which are relatively small. In lower areas where there is a lot of ground water and where the reactions between the rocks and the gases have produced alkaline chemicals dissolved in large quantities of water, there are high volume, warm water springs. It is these springs that are used to provide warm water for domestic heating (as in Reykjavík and Húsavík) and for glasshouses (for instance at Hveragerði). Sometimes the volume of water is sufficient to produce a warm lake as at Laugarvatn. Since the hot rocks that produce this heat take hundreds or thousands of years to cool (rock is a bad conductor of heat), this useful source of energy can be relied upon not only for heating buildings but also to produce steam for electrical generation. Such a plant, called a geothermal power station, has been built at Krafla to the north-east of Mývatn and large diameter pipes have been bored into Krafla's mountainside to tap the steam and transport it to the power station.

The most spectacular secondary volcanic features are geysers, which are deep cylindrical holes in the ground that periodically send columns of warm water high into the air. The best-known examples in Iceland are Geysir (after which all water spouts are named) and Strokkur (see p.110), both of which were probably formed in a great earthquake in 1294.

In a number of areas there are pits of boiling mud. These are formed when steam mixes with volcanic ash in underground cavities; the blue-grey colour of the mud is due to compounds of iron and sulphur. The consistency of the muds vary: the viscous ones let rising bubbles of gas move through them slowly, producing concentric rings on the surface when the bubbles escape; the more fluid ones throw blobs of the mud upwards and to the side of the pool (see p.134), building 'spatter cones' that may reach one metre in height. These should be approached with care as the surrounding clay surface can give way.

Altogether there are some 250-300 spring areas, many of them highly coloured due to the clays and other coloured rocks near them and to the deposits around the vents that have slowly built up. In a number of cases, they also allow vegetation to grow, giving life to otherwise barren ground. The most accessible solfatara areas are Námaskarð, Krafla (both near Mývatn), Krísuvík (Reykjanes peninsula) and Hengill (south of Thingvallavatn). The biggest are at Torfajökull (north of Mýrdalsjökull) and Grímsvötn (in Vatnajökull).

The Glaciers
DESPITE the name of the country, Iceland's ice-caps and glaciers only cover 11 per cent of the surface area (about 11,000 sq km). The beginning of this century saw the end of the 'little ice age' (c.1600-1900), a period during which Iceland's glaciers had grown, devouring farmlands and making communications more difficult. Since the turn of the century, however, the glaciers have been in retreat (perhaps by as much as 3 km), due to a warming of the climate.

The largest expanse is Vatnajökull (8,400 sq km) which is the biggest ice-cap in the world after

Antarctica and Greenland. Its central region is a plateau 1300 m-1700 m high with isolated summits, though most of its surface is fairly flat or undulating. The ice thickness is on average 420 m, up to a maximum of about 1000 m. To its south is the ice-cap Öræfajökull, within which is the country's highest mountain, Hvannadalshnúkur (2119 m). In the south and east of the Vatnajökull-Öræfajökull ice-mass there are valley glaciers, sending rivers of ice down towards the coast while to the north and west, where the slope of the ground is not so great, wide lobes of ice spread out.

The other important glaciers are Langjökull and Hofsjökull (both in the central highlands), and two in the south, Mýrdalsjökull and Eyjafjallajökull, which were joined together by a thin neck of ice until recently. There are other smaller glaciers that cap high mountains such as Snæfellsjökull, Snæfell and Drangajökull. But it is Vatnajökull, and the many glaciers that flow from it, that is the most important and impressive example of glaciation in the country, and at Skaftafell National Park the visitor will have a good opportunity to look at some of Vatnajökull's outflow glaciers at close hand (see p.117).

The ice-caps are basically mountains on which snow (later to become ice) gathers and then travels slowly downwards via the glaciers. During winter (the main, but not the only, season for snow), snow collects as layers of crystals on the surface of the ice-cap. With continual melting and freezing, ice layers form inbetween the snow layers; rain or meltwater that percolates downwards and later freezes also changes the structure of the now-compressed snow and over a period of years the gradual process of snow crystals becoming (denser) ice crystals takes place. So long as the yearly addition of snow is greater than the amount melted, then the glacier will grow. The ice-cap may increase its thickness by up to 10 metres each year, and the additional weight will push the ice downhill.

Glaciers often start their downward journey from an ice-cap by following a steep V-shaped valley cut by a stream. In many ways a glacier behaves like a river of water, but the main difference is that the ice is frozen to the sides of the valley and as it moves down the valley it rips stones and boulders from the walls, widening its path considerably. At its base, too, it rips up the floor of the valley, deepening it as it travels. In this way the glacier transports vast quantities of material downhill, from large boulders to the finest of sand, the latter coming from the scraping of rocks frozen in the ice against other rocks still in the ground.

Along the edge of the glacier, the ice has a pile of rubble on it and frozen within it; this is the rock that has been taken off the valley wall and is called the 'lateral moraine'. When two glaciers meet and travel down the valley beside each other, the region where their lateral moraines meet and join together is called the 'medial moraine'. This is often a long ridge of black ice standing above the rest of the ice and is one of the most noticeable features of a glacier.

The glacier's speed (perhaps less than a few metres a day) is not constant all the way from the ice-cap to its snout. If the steepness of the slope increases then it will travel faster. Its speed across the glacier is not constant either: beside the valley walls it moves very slowly while at the centre of the glacier it moves much more quickly. All these changes in speed crack the ice and form crevasses, which are most obvious in the summer when there is little fresh snow on the glacier. If the glacier changes its direction then the crevasses will be curved, and if the glacier slows down then the crevasses may close up again. They may also appear at the valley walls and at the snout (the front of the glacier) when the glacier is spreading out.

If a glacier is retreating (or is 'stagnant') then its snout will be jet black since it will contain a higher proportion of black sand to ice (which is melting). In front of the snout are the moraines, glacial lakes, glacial rivers and sand. Right at the front of the snout is the material that has most recently been dropped by the ice. This is usually a mixture of pebbles and sand and is called the

A valley glacier coming down from an ice-cap.

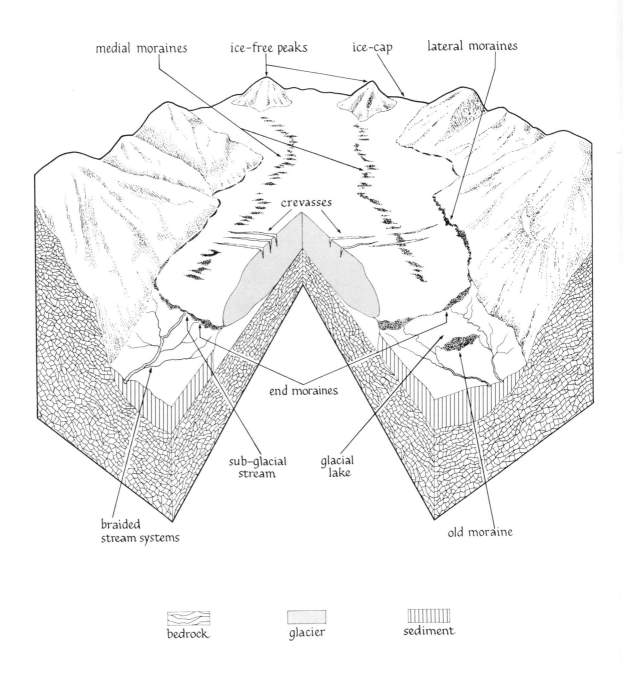

medial moraines   ice-free peaks   ice-cap   lateral moraines

crevasses

end moraines

sub-glacial stream

glacial lake

braided stream systems

old moraine

bedrock   glacier   sediment

'end moraine'. If the glacier is advancing then it will push this material in front of it and begin to ride above some of it. However, if it is receding, then the old moraines will mark the position of the glacier's snout in previous years. At the side of the glacier the lateral moraine will contain much larger boulders that have been torn away from the valley wall.

The space between the moraines may often be filled by small lakes that gather water from the melting snout and the subglacial streams. While only a few meltwater channels may flow out of the lakes and past the moraines, they soon break up and form a myriad of interwoven streams, heavy with suspended material. Many of the pebbles in these streams are well-rounded as a result of the grinding down that takes place at the edges and the base of the glacier; the smaller pebbles, and, finally, the sand, are washed away quite far from the snout and huge expanses of sand ('sandur') are formed. These often stretch into the open sea and around much of the south coast long sandbars have built up.

While the valley glaciers of the south produce these expanses of sand and sandbars, the rivers that carry Vatnajökull's meltwater to the north have to carry their load a greater distance to the sea. Great rivers like Jökulsá á Fjöllum and Jökulsá á Brú dump huge piles of grey gravel by their banks as they make their way through the surrounding lavafields.

In a number of places beneath the ice there are volcanoes which can erupt, melting vast quantities of ice and causing jökulhlaups ('glacier bursts'). Eruptions in Öræfajökull and Katla (in Mýrdalsjökull) have produced such bursts. Similarly, far up in the Vatnajökull ice-cap the subglacial solfatara area of Grímsvötn melts ice, the water from which then accumulates in lake Grímsvötn, which is formed in a depression in the mountains. About every five or six years, the water level rises sufficiently to lift up the surface ice, enabling the water to escape from the depression. A massive flood pours down, ending when the lake has dropped its level by as much as 200 m. Another area prone to jökulhlaups is

Grænalón, an ice-dammed lake to the west of Skeiðarárjökull. No volcanic or solfataric activity is involved here: it fills up with the meltwater of another small glacier and when its water level is more than nine-tenths of the thickness of the edge of the glacier, it lifts it up and sends a torrent of water into the river Súla.

The Climate

JUST A casual glance at a climatic map is enough to confirm one surprising fact about Iceland – it is much warmer than its latitude would imply. Cold water drifts south from Greenland, but its effect on the north and east coasts is offset by the passage of the warm Gulf Stream coming from the south-west. The warm current (about 4°C to 12°C) meets the submarine ridge that runs from the Faroes to Greenland and is forced to flow clockwise along the south and west coasts. This keeps the winters less severe than in other countries at the same latitude and while the sea temperature in the north may be about 1°C in February and 7°C in August, the temperature in the south may be 6°C and 11°C during the same months.

As well as bringing this warm water, the winds from the south-west bring a lot of rain and snow, much of it falling on the southern glaciers. The precipitation on Vatnajökull might be as much as 4,000 mm (160 inches) a year, but the ice-cap shelters the highlands to the north and these areas (including Mývatn) might only get 400 mm (16 inches) of precipitation each year. Snowstorms however, can occur at any time of the year, as can night frost.

Sometimes drift ice may come from Greenland, occasionally managing to get as far as the Westman Islands where it has even blocked Heimaey's harbour. The occurrence of drift ice (which appears first in the north-west) is very serious for, as well as affecting fish shoals and ships, its presence shortens the growing season for the crops, thus cutting the size of the harvest. However, this century's temperature increase (after the 'little ice age' of 1600-1900) has brought about a number of changes in the

33

country. The glaciers have receded between 2 km-3 km and, from 1919-1964, there was little sea-ice (although this trend was briefly reversed in the years 1965-1968). The growing season has also lengthened. Summer temperatures are now around 9°C-12°C on average during July, which is generally the warmest month, though the highlands are rather colder with the temperature falling by 0.5-0.7 degrees for each 100m of altitude. Winter temperatures on the coast can be relatively mild, ranging around 2°C-minus 2°C, although in the interior conditions are likely to be much more severe.

Towards Greenland and to the north-west of Iceland there is a region of semi-permanent low pressure which makes the country rather windy and its weather changeable, though thunderstorms are rare. Dust storms can occur over the open desert areas on the higher ground, the clouds of dust sometimes reaching 1,000m into the air and darkening the sky. In the fjords, sea-mist, brought in by gentle sea breezes, may drift in and blanket the water, settlements and hillsides. There may be strong winds in the area round Akureyri, which lies in a long northerly-facing fjord; these winds start in the afternoon but usually die away after a few hours.

Because of Iceland's latitude, the days are very long in the summer and can be exceptionally short during winter. In Reykjavík for example, the longest day is nearly 21 hours long, but the shortest is just under 4 hours. In the north, the summer sun hardly sets at all, with sunset after midnight in July. The amount of sunshine thus varies tremendously through the year; during the years 1931-1960, Reykjavík had on average 1,249 hours of sunshine each year, but while there were 189 hours in July, December only enjoyed 8 hours. The country's northerly position also means that the sun never rises more than 50 degrees above the horizon, so the length of the day to the north of hills can be very short, something that was often taken into consideration when settlements were being established. During autumn and the early winter, the 'northern lights' *(aurora borealis)* are often visible, usually as

bands of thin coloured rays that lighten the sky, although they can take other forms. The 'northern lights' are caused by charged particles from the sun entering the upper atmosphere near the Earth's magnetic pole.

Daytime visibility in the summer can be exceptionally good, with mountains visible which are 50-60 km away, though perhaps a little hazy. For example, from Reykjavík the Snæfellsjökull glacier, about 110 km away to the north-west, can often be seen quite clearly. The lack of industry, together with the change to geothermal energy from peat and coal burning for home heating, means that there is virtually no smoke in the atmosphere, even in the towns.

Visibility can be drastically reduced however by low cloud levels when it is raining or by dust storms which can take a long time to die out. In warm weather, persistent heat hazes can reduce visibility and also cause mirages in the form of a 'puddle' across the road or the 'flooding' of a valley in the distance.

The section on 'Camping and Walking' (p.77) suggests the type of clothes to wear and summer visitors should be prepared for rainy and cold conditions as well as pleasantly warm summer days. Those visiting outside the summer months should of course be prepared for wetter and much colder weather.

Fauna

DURING the last major ice age (c.11,000 years ago) 90 per cent of the land was covered by ice, and only the coast and a few ice-free peaks ('nunataks') provided some refuge for a small number of plants and animals. The sea level was rather lower than today (since a lot of seawater was trapped in the glaciers) and the wide coastal belts offered protection to the small number of species that could inhabit them. Birds such as rock ptarmigan and snow bunting were able to survive here and during the summer they were joined by auks, gulls, snipe and duck.

During subsequent cold winters, such as 1753-54 when the Greenland Sea froze, polar bears walked over; but once they landed they were killed, not only for the meat and fur, but also because of the danger they posed to such sheep as were left during winter. The arctic fox, too, came over on ice floes, and is now established as the only native land mammal. Nevertheless it is hunted for its pelt and to protect the eider duck. Reindeer were introduced as domestic animals in 1771, but have been free for a long time and now number about 3,000 in the north-east of the country. Mink, which were farmed in the 1930s, have escaped, bred quickly, and are now a nuisance. There are two species of indigenous seals (common and grey) and four other species that visit the island in the winter; they are often seen basking in the sun on the sandbars that have built up along the south coast. Small mammals brought in by man which have since become naturalised include the house mouse, wood mouse, brown rat and black rat.

Although insects are not very numerous due to the climate and the isolation, there are about 800 species, none of them poisonous. The most important ones are flies, gnats and midges, the last of which can be a nuisance, especially around Mývatn and near marshy ground.

Only five species of fish are found in the lakes and the rivers – salmon, trout, char, eel and the three-spined stickleback. There are no reptiles nor are there any amphibians.

But it is the bird life that is of greatest interest – in fact many ornithologists from all over the world come to Iceland to study its birds. It is not the vast numbers that are so important (though there are great numbers of some birds), but the mix that is present in such a small area. Iceland lies on the borders of four different geo-zoological regions and high arctic birds live alongside birds more commonly found much farther to the south. This is the only European home of the North American Barrow's goldeneye and the harlequin duck, while other birds are definitely European, the golden plover, for example. Altogether about 240 species are known with around 80 of them breeding in Iceland and this century's warmer climate has seen an increase in the numbers.

One of the most spectacular areas for birds is

Mývatn. As it is fed by warm springs, it never completely freezes over and its shallowness allows a luxuriant growth of aquatic plants. During the summer, this becomes one of the world's biggest concentrations of breeding ducks, with seventeen species making up a population of perhaps 15,000 breeding pairs. The most numerous are the tufted duck, common scaup, European widgeon and Barrow's goldeneye. The eider duck, Iceland's most common species, is farmed for its feathers in over two hundred colonies. The female grows very soft down between the breast and belly feathers which is shed at the beginning of the breeding season and used to line the nest. After breeding, these feathers are collected by the local farmers. The eiderdown is named after the feathers of these ducks, with which it is stuffed.

On the moors the most common – as well as the noisiest – birds are the golden plover and the whimbrel; the rock ptarmigan and common snipe also live there. In the rough lavafields on the central highlands snowy owls are found, feeding on field mice and small birds, while the short-eared owl lives on the lower moors and preys on rock ptarmigan. The best-known bird of prey is the gyr falcon: its speed and ability to hunt and catch a bird in flight made it much sought after. During the eleventh and twelfth centuries it was exported to Denmark and sent from there to many countries, but today its numbers are so few that it is protected by law and even photographing it on its nest is not allowed without a permit. The gyrfalcon is the only kind of falcon found in Iceland, and is the largest member of the falcon family.

The breeding sites of the predatory arctic skuas and great skuas are situated on the barren areas of the southern coast's glacial sands. These vicious birds will readily attack other birds carrying fish, even going to the extent of grabbing a bird's tail until it drops or disgorges its catch. They also fiercely attack any intruders daring to go near their breeding areas – so beware! Another bird that may attack people is the arctic tern, which is found in many parts of the island, both inland and near the sea. It is the most intrepid migratory bird found in Iceland, often spending winter in Antarctica.

Iceland is also the world's main breeding area for the pink-footed goose; the breeding site was only discovered in 1929, when 3,000 breeding pairs were found in an oasis in a desert area near the Hofsjökull glacier.

The sea cliffs are important breeding grounds for millions of sea birds; the most important coastal colonies are on the Westman Islands, on the south and west coasts of the Reykjanes peninsula, on the south coast of the Snæfellsnes peninsula, in the fjords of the north-west and the east, and on the islands of Drangey and Grímsey. Here, millions of kittiwakes, guillemots, razor bills, gannets and fulmars completely cover the narrow ledges of the high cliffs, while the puffins prefer the grassy slopes below.

Bird catching and the collection of eggs used to be of major importance to the Icelanders and men with large nets climbed down sheer cliffs, catching the birds as they flew off their nests. This form of hunting is still practised in the Westman Islands, although it is of little economic importance now.

The first record of a big bird colony was the vast number of fulmars recorded in Grímsey in 1640. By 1852 the farmers were taking 30,000 fledglings a year and in 1900 the number had increased to 56,000. This harvest was very important to the local economy and no part of the bird was wasted: the meat was salted or smoked and stored for the winter; the guts, head and wings were dried and used for fuel; the fat was used as lamp oil or as butter substitute and the feathers made warm bedding and clothing. Almost inevitably, the numbers of these birds dwindled. Ironically, they were saved by the colonies becoming infected with psittacosis, making their meat hazardous to eat. From this near-extinction in the 1930s, the fulmars have rapidly increased their numbers and are now crowding out other birds.

While the fulmar was saved from extinction, the flightless great auk was not so fortunate. The bird that was hunted by Neanderthal Man was finally killed off in June 1844 by some sailors on the southern island of Eldey.

Flora

ONE OF THE lasting effects of the last glacial age in Iceland was that many of the plant species were wiped out: it is known that only about half the present number of about 450 vascular plants (plants with stems) survived the onslaught of the glaciers; the others gradually arrived with driftwood, birds and man. More primitive plants are well represented and today about 450 species of lichen and 550 species of moss are found on the island. The flora is essentially North European; 97 per cent of the country's vascular plants are also found in Norway. The number of varieties found in the west is smaller than that found in the east as the west's climate is influenced by its proximity to Greenland.

At the time of the Settlement (874-930) as much as one-third of the country was covered with woodland. Since then, however, much of this has been destroyed by careless overgrazing and by tree-felling for ships, houses and for the charcoal needed by blacksmiths. For many centuries driftwood was an important source of timber for housebuilding following the destruction of many of the woods in the thirteenth and fourteenth centuries.

Volcanic eruptions have also ruined much land, both by lava and ash smothering vegetation and by poisonous fumes harming the remaining plant life. More recently the 'little ice age' between 1600 and 1900, meant that the glaciers' advance covered many of the wooded areas, and now these tracts of land are covered in huge piles of sand and gravel. These sands are almost completely bare, and the constantly shifting streams of meltwater make it very difficult for plants to establish themselves. Farther towards the sea, the surf lashes the land, and since the shoreline is usually made up of small, water-polished pebbles that are always on the move, the plants have a hard fight to get any kind of grip. All of these factors have meant that today only about one-fifth of the country has plant cover, while the huge gravel expanses of the highlands are exceptionally barren.

Little remains of the original woods, though these are being replanted, for example in Hallormsstaður near the eastern fjords. New trees (pines and spruces) are being imported from other mountainous northern countries where the flora is similar to that found in Iceland, but it will take time to make up for the centuries of misuse. At present birch is the most common tree and a stunted variety is found on many of the old lavafields where there is now some soil and a little shelter between the blocks of lava. These lavafields are very porous, so little surface water manages to gather, except perhaps where clay is brought down by meltwater streams and provides a non-porous bed on which some of the hardier plants can prosper. These vast expanses often have a thick carpet of moss on them, particularly in areas of block lava where there are many sheltered crevices in which the plants can take hold. Lichens too, are commonly found in this type of environment, especially since the air is free from any pollution.

In comparison, the areas covered with ashes cannot give as much protection to plant life, but some seeding from aircraft is being tried to help to stabilise the ground and develop some soil. If these plants can take root then they can take advantage of a soil that is poor in organic material, but rich in minerals that have come from the volcanoes.

The cold climate in the highlands means that the upper layer of continuous vegetation is very low, about 700 m, and the tree-line is no more than 300 m. Below the hills much of the land is desert or semi-desert with plant life exceptionally sparse in the exposed and wind-blown areas, however in some sheltered spots there are oases, often near warm springs. Some of today's deserts used to support some life, but over the centuries the soil has often been destroyed both by nature and by man; unfortunately it has only been in recent years that man's role in this has been fully recognized and even today overgrazing provides a continuing threat to the country's sparse vegetation.

THE ECONOMY AND INFRASTRUCTURE

The Traditional Economy: Agriculture and Fishing

FARMING used to be the single most important economic activity in Iceland, with 80 per cent of the population dependent upon it in 1860. Today, with the growth of the fishing industry and the development of other forms of employment, only 8 per cent of the population live off the land. The main agricultural areas are the lowlands of the south-west and the fjords of the north and east.

This century has seen a remarkable increase in productivity in agriculture, with tractors, ditch-digging equipment and grass-drying facilities all helping to expand production to the point where the domestic market is satisfied, allowing produce (mainly lamb and wool) to be exported. However, there is still overgrazing and because of the cold climate and the low level of organic material in the soil, heavy loads of fertiliser are often needed.

Up until the seventeenth century (at the onset of the 'little ice age'), grain was grown, but since then the main crop has been hay for winter feeding. Grass will only grow for about four months (mid-May to mid-September), so the size of the animal population depends to a great extent on the winter fodder available, since the cattle have to be fed for about eight months in the year and the sheep and horses for about six months.

Grazing land covers only about 20,000 sq km (out of approx. 103,000 sq km), but the amount of good quality land is being increased by draining large areas of wet meadows. These are usually the farm's outfields, the farmhouse normally being built on rising ground with its most fertile field, the home field ('*tún*'), around it. Most of the cattle and many of the sheep graze on the outer fields, the rest being moved onto common grazing lands in the uplands where they will stay from about July to September.

The cattle (c.60,000 of them in the early 1980s) are raised mainly for milk and butter products, though the production of beef is becoming more important. Most of the meat produced is mutton or lamb (there were c.800,000 sheep in the early 1980s) with about half of the sheep being slaughtered each year. Mutton, fleeces and various kinds of woollen goods are exported: Icelandic woollen goods are of excellent quality and are good souvenirs for visitors to take home.

One of the newest branches of agriculture, that of horticulture using natural warm water for heating the glasshouses, is expanding in a number of places. Some settlements (Hveragerði, for instance) specialise in this; in other areas horticulture is a subsidiary activity for the farmers. These glasshouses supply bananas, tomatoes, cucumbers and flowers.

For over a thousand years the Icelanders have relied on their horses for transport and today over 50,000 of them can be seen grazing on the farms. These are the direct descendants of the Vikings' horses as no other breed has been introduced since the Settlement. Although they are not very big, they are strong and able to carry a rider and provisions over rough ground for some distance, making them indispensable at the autumn round-up when the sheep have to be brought down from the highlands. During winter they grow a long shaggy coat as extra protection against the cold. They have five gaits: walk, pace, trot, gallop, and the *tölt*. The latter is a gait peculiar to Iceland: it is the equivalent of a running walk. On many farms the horses are being bred for export; this is an important activity in some areas in the south-west and in the north.

Fishing began as a supplement to the diet and income of farmers, starting in fjords where there was an existing farming community and where there was both shelter and suitable places for harbours, unlike the smooth, sandy south coast of the island. As the fishing activities increased, farmers were glad of the additional income during the winter months when there was less farm work to do, but not so happy in the late summer as the fishing season coincided with hay-making time. The higher wages won by fishing denied the farmers much of the extra help they needed at that time.

The waters around Iceland are very favourable for fish, with many spawning in the warm waters of the Irminger Current off the south and south-west coasts and later spending their maturity in the cold and highly oxygenated waters off the north and east coasts.

The use of first steam trawlers and, now, far more modern ships, has meant a complete change in the type of fishing. Nowadays many factory ships can freeze and even process their catch on board, enabling them to stay at sea for months at a time and therefore go to far-distant fishing grounds.

For many centuries other countries, especially Britain, fished off Iceland's coasts and since non-mechanised ships were used then, the fish stocks were never endangered. Up until 1901, Iceland had had fishing limits varying between 7 km and 60 km, with only Icelanders allowed to fish in fjords and bays. In 1901, however, Denmark made an agreement with Britain reducing the limit to 6 km, and opening up the fjords and bays. This agreement was ended by Iceland in 1951. In 1952, the fjords and bays were again restricted and a 6 km limit was enforced, this being raised to 22 km in 1958, and to 93 km in 1972. British opposition to these new limits resulted in two so-called 'cod wars' between the countries. When a 1973 agreement between them expired in 1975, a new limit of 370 km led to a third, and more serious 'cod war'. After a period when a limited number of British trawlers were allowed in the zone, no British vessels have fished inside this boundary since December 1976.

For Iceland, defence of the fishing stocks was crucial since fish and fish products amounted at that time to nearly 90 per cent of the country's exports. Since such earnings are the means of paying for most of the necessities of life which have to be imported, preservation of the previously overfished stocks is essential.

The types of fish that are caught have varied over the years, with the largest catches in 1981 being capelin (640,000 metric tons) and cod (460,000 metric tons), out of a total catch of 1,430,000 metric tons. There was a great expansion of the herring catch in 1960-1968, while the catch of capelin has forged ahead since then. Cod is a more valuable fish, however, and makes the greatest contribution to the fishing industry's total income. There are now fears over fish stocks and a 'quota' system has been introduced.

The great fluctuations in the catches have caused many problems in the Icelandic economy, not the least being the under-utilisation of the very expensive processing and freezer plants that have been built by many fishing co-operatives and other organisations in the larger ports. At full capacity these plants provide a major source of employment.

While only a small proportion of the fish is for home consumption, much is exported frozen or reduced to meal and fish oil. All over the fishing districts there are racks of fish drying and these are exported all over the world with cod's heads being particularly popular in West Africa and South America. While the larger ports will have trawlers operating out of them, the smaller fishing communities will have their own fleet of small boats which catch fish for local consumption or for transportation to a processing plant prior to export.

In some parts of the country, scallops, shrimps, and lobsters are caught but the quantities are not very large. There is only one whaling station in the country, which is in Hvalfjörður, north of Reykjavík. Whaling has been carried out since the Settlement but is now permitted for only a few summer months each year and will be phased out in 1986; the only two types of whale now caught are the fin-back and the sei. Much of the meat is exported to Japan for human consumption; the remainder is used for meat extract and pet food. The blubber is processed into oil and the bones into meal.

The Modern Economy: Industry and Energy

ICELAND'S industrial revolution came some 200-300 years after that of most other European nations, but already the Icelanders enjoy a very high standard of living. However, with virtually no natural fuels, one of the greatest economic problems has been how to get and pay for the energy needed for industry and transport, for fuelling fishing boats and heating buildings. Peat and coal were the two major fuels earlier this century; peat supplied 30 per cent of the energy needs in 1918, but by 1948 had become uneconomic, while coal's share was a massive 80 per cent in the 1930s, however it was effectively exhausted by the late 1960s. It was oil that filled the energy gap and by the time of the huge oil price rises in 1973-74 it satisfied 60 per cent of the energy demand, a share that was rising dangerously. The price increases threatened the whole economy and so a major effort was needed to speed up the development of the country's two great natural assets: hydroelectric and geothermal energy.

While oil products are used for road, sea and air transport, hydroelectric sources now supply 19 per cent of the country's total energy needs and geothermal sources 37 per cent. In a country lying at so northerly a latitude, keeping buildings warm is obviously important and about 40 per cent of the total energy is used for this. Today, 80 per cent of Iceland's homes are heated by geothermal energy, with only 13 per cent using electricity and 7 per cent oil.

With only about 12 per cent of the economically exploitable hydroelectric power presently being used (the corresponding figure for geothermal energy is 5 per cent), the last few years have seen the establishment of large-scale

39

energy-dependent industries. By far the largest is the aluminium smelter at Straumsvík (south of Reykjavík) with its electricity being supplied by the new Búrfell hydroelectric power station on the Thjórsá. The Swiss-owned smelter produced its first ingots in 1969, and is now making enough aluminium to account for 10 per cent of the country's total exports. A ferro-silicon plant was set up in Hvalfjörður in 1979, and the other energy-intensive plants that may be set up in future years will most probably also be in the metals industry.

Near Mývatn, geothermal energy in the form of steam is used in the diatomite plant. This factory sucks up the microscopic skeletons (diatoms) that make up a 5-10m layer on the lake bed and dries them with steam, the finished product being exported for use in filtering equipment in the chemical and brewing industries. Geothermal energy will probably be used in the future for seaweed drying and the production of chemicals from sea-water.

Iceland has few valuable minerals to exploit. Sulphur, which is a byproduct of volcanic activity, is found in a number of areas and, indeed, was mined from the thirteenth to nineteenth centuries. Iceland was once the world's main producer of the mineral 'Iceland spar', which is used in optical instruments. Today, shellsand is used in the production of cement and volcanic slag is an important insulating material that is used in the building industry.

Although Icelanders enjoy a high standard of living, the economy has been subject to many fluctuations in past years, due mainly to the increase in oil prices and the variation in the size and value of the fish catches. Inflation has been one of the greatest recent problems, causing frequent devaluations in the króna, and increasing the price of imported goods (although currently the rate of inflation has been lower). In 1981 the value of the króna had fallen by so much that there was a full currency reform, with the new króna worth 100 of the old ones. Despite these problems, between 1969 and 1979 the national income rose at an average annual rate of 5 per cent and unemployment was much lower than in other European countries.

With membership of EFTA in 1970 and a trade agreement with the EEC in 1972, the tariff barriers, previously erected mainly for fiscal reasons, have been brought down, causing some problems in home industries. The development of industry has inevitably led to a concentration of population, with over half of the country's population of c.235,000 living in Reykjavík and the surrounding towns.

Transport

FOR ABOUT a thousand years after the Settlement, there was little real progress in building and maintaining a network of tracks between the settlements. Rivers were the main obstacles to travellers and the first big bridge was only opened in 1891. Until the age of the motor vehicle, the only means of transport was the horse, which proved remarkably good at crossing the highland areas, rivers and even the glaciers.

The first vehicle was imported in 1913, but by 1924 there were still only three hundred of them, travelling on roads that were usually tracks strewn with rubble and deeply rutted. This situation lasted for quite some time as the main consideration was to increase the extent of the road system rather than to improve its quality and even today most of the ring road has a gravel surface which is often badly rutted. The three main roads out of Reykjavík (to Hvolsvöllur, Keflavík and Hvalfjörður) have a modern highway surface, and there are some good stretches in other places. In addition, the settlements usually have a reasonable surface. Today the road network is about 9,000 km long with another 4,500 km of roads that are open in summer only. The Icelandic bus routes cover some 7,000 km of this total.

The southern coast of the country was where the last stretch of the ring road was completed. Such is the formidable might of the river Skeiðará that it was only bridged in 1974. This has made a great difference to the road distance between towns; for example, Höfn to Reykjavík used to be

971 km round the northern coast, but now this has been shortened to 476 km by travelling along the southern route. The completion of the ring road, which is 1414 km long, means that the tourist industry can now really begin to grow as visitors can bring their own vehicles and travel right round the island.

Iceland has never had a railway system, though a locomotive was used earlier this century to help in the building of the Reykjavík harbour. There was once, however, a plan to build a railway line from the capital to Thingvellir, with lines going to Selfoss and the Thjórsá.

Before 1914, almost all the imports and exports were carried in foreign ships, mainly Danish and Norwegian. Today, nearly all the ships are Icelandic-owned, although they are not always Icclandic-built; it was not until about 1965 that shipbuilding really developed in the country. The main port is Reykjavík, which has frequent sailings to many foreign ports.

Coastal shipping carries a high proportion of the heavy freight round the country, but the completion of the ring road has reduced the coastal passenger service. The coastline is very inhospitable especially in winter when gales lash the island. The first lighthouse was built on Reykjanes as late as 1878 and the second one some twenty years later, although now numerous lighthouses and navigation masts provide information to passing ships. Should shipwrecks occur, there is a chain of rescue huts dotted along the coast, especially on the southern sandur where there is little shelter.

Iceland's first aeroplane was imported in 1919, and Icelandair, the national airline, was founded in 1938. The international airport of Keflavík at the western end of Reykjanes peninsula is very large for such a small country, since it is the site of a NATO base as well as a refuelling stop between America and Europe.

Reykjavík and most towns have airports, while there are many unmanned airstrips around the country. These landing sites are very important in the winter, since many communities become snowbound when the roads are impassable and doctors, mail and food supplies are often lifted in during these dark and dangerous months. The small aircraft are put to very good use during the rest of the year as they provide a fast and efficient network of services round the country. While in other European countries flying might only be used for longer distances, Icelanders will often fly between towns as it is faster and more comfortable, and there are now some forty regular internal air routes operated by Icelandair and some smaller firms.

PART TWO

THE
PRACTICAL
GUIDE

How to go, where to stay, what to take

INTRODUCTION

ALTHOUGH visitors have been going to Iceland for a long time, the 'tourist industry' is still in its infancy – that is one of the country's attractions. However, it means that the type of information a visitor wants and needs can be difficult to obtain and lists of hotels, campsites, tours and places to see are not always easy to obtain. This part of the Guide gives details of the accommodation, transport, trips and other facilities that are normally available.

The average travel agent outside Iceland knows little about the country as it is not, as yet, a major tourist destination and there are only a few tour operators in any country that can give expert advice on Icelandic conditions and the facilities available. A selected number of tour operators are listed on pp.98-99: these may be usefully approached. They are in contact with agencies, tour operators and hotels in Iceland and should be able to help you decide how to plan your visit. Leaflets, brochures, price lists and so on can be obtained from them. In addition, they can organise all your requirements – transport to and in Iceland, accommodation and trips – into a 'package' which can work out much cheaper than buying the individual services yourself.

The tourist season is rather short (usually mid-June to mid-September); many facilities are not available or are curtailed outside the main season. The Guide refers to examples where hotels are closed, roads are impassable and so on, but you are recommended to contact a tour operator for up-to-date information on the availability of particular services outside the holiday season. This slack period in the tourist trade means, however, that trips can be much cheaper and some good 'package deals' are usually available then.

CHOOSING A HOLIDAY
What Kind of Visit?

THIS SECTION describes briefly some of the main types of activity that can be undertaken on an Icelandic holiday. The country lends itself particularly well not only to general touring holidays, but also to more specialised visits by enthusiasts of pursuits such as skiing, mountaineering, bird-watching, fishing, and geology. Some of the most popular categories of holiday are briefly discussed below. If you want to have your holiday organized for you, details of the tours available can be obtained from the tour operators listed on pp.98-99, or mentioned below. Many tour operators specialize in particular 'special interest' activities, and a 'tailor-made' package can sometimes be organized to fit your particular requirements.

The availability and itinerary of tours will vary widely from year to year and for this reason details are not provided here.

General touring holiday
ICELAND's unique scenery and its tranquillity are the reasons why the majority of visitors seek its shores. It remains unspoiled by tourism and

visitors wanting peace and quiet will not be disappointed.

Tours may be by bus or car (the latter will have to have four-wheel drive to visit a number of places off the ring road). Bus tours can range from taking a seat in a coach with a specific itinerary and a guide organized by a tour operator, and staying at pre-designated hotels, hostels or campsites, to travelling around yourself as you wish, using local bus services (see pp.50-56 for details of bus tours and services).

Car tours can be undertaken either in your own vehicle which can be ferried or freighted over (see pp.48-49 for details) or by hiring a car (see p.60). General driving information, which may be of use in either case, is provided on pp.57-68.

Those who are walking can plan their own routes or join up with well-organised groups that trek through the highlands. Treks may be arranged by Icelandic tour operators or by clubs or tour operators in other countries. Those who are walking and camping will find information and advice on pp.77-83.

Special interest holidays
Skiing
The snow-covered wilderness of Iceland's interior provides cross-country and alpine skiing far away from centres of population. Organised tours in late winter/spring, by when there is a reasonable amount of daylight, take skiers into breathtaking mountain scenery. For those wanting to stay in or close to Reykjavík, there is skiing on Bláfjöll (to the south-east of the city) and at Skálafell (on the road to Thingvellir). The other main skiing centres are at Akureyri, Ísafjörður and Siglufjörður. Iceland's skiing facilities are not widely publicised abroad as the weather conditions are very variable and bad weather can easily curtail or cancel a winter sports holiday.

Summer skiing is possible in the Kerlingarfjöll mountains, which are between the Langjökull and Hofsjökull glaciers. There are also snowmobile tours during the summer on Vatnajökull. Those staying in Reykjavík can fly out to Fagurhólsmýri (south of Vatnajökull) and from

there join the tour's starting point, which is at Breiðamerkurjökull (to the south-east of Vatnajökull).
Cruises
Just over a dozen cruise ships sail to Iceland each summer, usually with stops at Reykjavík and Akureyri. Passengers can either use the ship's short stay at one of the ports for sight-seeing or take a longer trip through the country, rejoining the ship when it stops at the next port of call.
Expeditions/Scientific Parties
Iceland's rugged nature has always attracted expeditions and groups of scientists. Permission has to be sought for any serious undertaking. Regulations have been drawn up by the Iceland National Research Council (see p.97) and research permits must be obtained from them, after detailing what kind of work is to be undertaken. A 'clearing house' for expeditions from Britain is operated by the Iceland Unit of the Young Explorers' Trust which is based at the Royal Geographical Society (see p.102). Any groups in Britain intending to mount an expedition or a research project should contact the Iceland Unit for help and advice.

The Bibliography (see pp.256-259) contains a number of entries that may prove useful.
Climbing/Mountaineering
Any trip through the highlands or onto the mountains needs careful planning and preparation. The advice offered in 'Camping and Walking' (see pp.77-83) is only intended for those going on a 'walk' rather than a 'trek' and anyone intending climbing/mountaineering/crossing glaciers must be well-briefed beforehand. In Britain, you should seek advice from Dick Phillips (see p.99) or the Iceland Unit of the Young Explorers' Trust (see p.102); in other countries your tour operator should be able to put you in contact with experts. In Iceland, you can seek advice from one of the touring clubs (for instance Ferðafélag Íslands or Útivist, see p.96).
Fishing
Iceland is rightly proud of its rich freshwater fishing. Salmon, char, brown trout and sea trout are found in both lakes and rivers. Sea fishing is

also available. Special fishing lodges have recently been built and farm accommodation is often available near good fishing. Brochures listing the fishing available in different parts of the country can be obtained from tour operators. Fishing tours can also usually be arranged through them.

Four books (in Icelandic) have been published by Landssamband Veiðifélaga; these books *(Vötn og veiði)* describe the most important fishing lakes and rivers. Freshwater fishing is licensed.

Pony trekking

The Icelanders have long used their ponies for transport over deserts, lavafields, rivers and glaciers; now these sturdy animals can be hired for tours or just for a day. Farms in the southwest, north, east and Snæfellsnes are amongst the places now operating this service.

Brochures that give details of farms from which pony trekking is available can be obtained from tour operators.

Ornithology

Iceland's teeming birdlife offers fascinating scope for study, both for the interested layman and the more serious naturalist. Bird cliffs are found in numerous parts of the country: some are mentioned in the section on 'Fauna' (see p.36). Tours visit some of the important bird colonies.

Geology

Geologists from all over the world come to Iceland, to see the North Atlantic Rift in action and to study the island's volcanoes and glaciers.

Many of the country's best-known landmarks have been studied by scientists and the Guide describes many of them. For those with a particular interest in geology, special tours are sometimes available that visit the important sites.

Photography

Not surprisingly, photographic tours pass through some of the most splendid scenery Iceland has to offer. A professional photographer is on hand to offer advice, and some major camera companies now offer prizes for the best pictures taken on the tour.

Business

Iceland's geographical position in the North Atlantic makes it well placed as a venue for international conferences, especially as there are flights to and from so many large cities throughout the world (see p.47). Reykjavík is the main conference centre, but Akureyri, Húsavík and Höfn also provide facilities, albeit on a smaller scale. The well-organised day-tours by bus that are listed in the section 'Tours and Trips' (see pp.54-56) offer a break from other activities. Conferences, as well as business travel, can be organised by a tour operator (see pp.98-99).

A list of useful addresses is included in the Guide (see pp.95-102). Useful information for UK businessmen visiting Iceland is contained in a booklet 'Hints to Exporters, Iceland', published by the Department of Trade, Sanctuary Buildings, 16-20 Great Smith Street, London SW1P 3DB.

GETTING TO ICELAND

A NUMBER of factors influence the choice between air or sea travel: (a) the cost of fares (taking a car by ferry becomes relatively cheaper as the number of passengers in the car increases); (b) time available (the ferry takes a few days); (c) whether you want to take a car with you. This may be a matter of balancing the cost of air fare plus car hire against the time wasted on the boat.

Air Services

ICELANDAIR is the national carrier and it operates an extensive network of flights, together with hotels, car rental and other tourist services available in Iceland. SAS (Scandinavian Airlines System) has a smaller range of flights but has a large number of offices and agents throughout the world. The third airline, Eagle Air (Icelandic owned), has a small number of flights, but also operates other services, such as tours within Iceland. The table below shows the cities which are connected to Reykjavík from April-October (inclusive); winter timetables are issued separately. International flights land at Keflavík International Airport (48 km) from Reykjavík. There are also services between Reykjavík and Greenland, and between the Faroe Islands and Egilsstaðir.

Flights to Reykjavík

The table below gives the cities from which the three carriers fly during the summer.

Country	Icelandair	SAS	Eagle Air
Belgium	Brussels	—	Brussels
Denmark	Copenhagen	Copenhagen	—
England	London (Heathrow)	—	—
The Faroes	Vagar	—	—
Finland	Helsinki	—	—
France	Paris	—	Paris
Greenland	Narssarssuaq	—	—
Holland	Amsterdam	—	Amsterdam
Italy	Milan	—	Rome
	Rome	—	—
Luxembourg	Luxembourg	—	—
Norway	Bergen	—	—
	Oslo	Oslo	—
Scotland	Glasgow (Abbotsinch)	—	—
Sweden	Stockholm	Stockholm	—
	Gotenburg	—	—
Switzerland	Zürich	—	Zürich
West Germany	Düsseldorf	—	Düsseldorf
	Frankfurt	—	Frankfurt
	Hamburg	—	Hamburg
	Münich	—	Münich
USA	Chicago	—	—
	Detroit	—	—
	New York	—	—
	Washington (Baltimore)	—	—

Travelling by Air

ARRIVING early at the airport's check-in desk will help you get a good seat; most planes coming from Europe fly along the south coast of Iceland from the Westman Islands, so a window seat on the right-hand side should give an excellent view of the spectacular coast and the mountains. Flights from the USA usually approach Iceland from the south-west, so views are limited. The luggage limit is 20 kg but luggage can be pooled by passengers arriving at the check-in at the same time. Skis can be taken, as can bicycles so long as the wheels are separate. Fuel containers (eg GAZ cylinders) are prohibited.

Alcohol is not always easy to find in Iceland (see p.94); you may therefore wish to take duty-free with you. Alternatively, there is a duty-free shop at the Keflavík terminal. Keflavík is Iceland's international airport and is situated 48 km south-west of Reykjavík.

The present air terminal is rather small considering the number of passengers it handles and a replacement terminal is now being built.

Arrival

The terminal bus takes fare-paying passengers as well as those who have bus transit tickets as part of a package deal. Major international currencies are accepted in payment for the fare. This bus takes you to the Loftleiðir Hotel, which is the airport's terminal in Reykjavík (45-minute journey, see p.155). The bus may then take you on to your hotel or guesthouse. Alternatively your tour operator might have arranged a special bus for you. Taxis are also available; cars can be hired from Icelandair Car Rental at the airport, but should be ordered in advance.

Departure

You should reconfirm your return booking three days before you are due to fly home, unless you know that your tour operator is going to do this for you. Telephone numbers for the three major airlines are given on p.97. The airport bus will leave the Loftleiðir Hotel 2 hours before flight departure. Bus tickets are available from the hotel lobby. A cafeteria, a duty-free shop and a currency exchange kiosk are situated in the departure lounge.

The Ferry Service

THE FERRY SERVICE to Iceland has undergone major changes recently. Iceland can only be reached by ferry via the Faroes. To reach the Faroes, UK visitors take a ferry from Aberdeen to Lerwick in Shetland, and then take another from Lerwick to Tórshavn in the Faroes.

Visitors from the European mainland may either travel via Aberdeen, from Hanstholm in Denmark or from Bergen in Norway.

The m/s 'Norröna' currently plies the route between Tórshavn and Seyðisfjörður in the eastern fjords of Iceland, as well as making the Lerwick-Tórshavn, Hanstholm-Tórshavn and Bergen-Tórshavn crossings mentioned above. The round trip between these ports is as follows and takes a week to complete: Tórshavn – Hanstholm (Denmark) – Tórshavn – Lerwick (Shetland) – Bergen (Norway) – Lerwick – Tórshavn – Seyðisfjörður – Tórshavn. A tour operator will have current details of the time of arrival at and departure from each port of call.

Soon after the ferry lands, a bus takes passengers from Seyðisfjörður to Egilsstaðir (see pp.155-156).

As this itinerary shows, there may be an enforced stay in the Faroes for some passengers while the ship sails to the other ports, prior to crossing to Iceland; Part 4 of the Guide has a section on the Faroes (section 45) which suggests a number of interesting places that can be visited (see pp.252-254).

Various types of accommodation are available on the ship, but this should be checked once you are on board to ensure there is no double booking (this was a not uncommon problem in the past). Those with roof-racks should enquire about increased fares for vehicles over a certain height and drivers may have to unpack the roof-rack in order not to incur a surcharge.

There is an entry tax for diesel vehicles brought into the country. The tax payable depends on the duration of the visit.

At present there is no ferry service from the USA. US visitors who want to drive round Iceland can freight their cars to Reykjavík (see below) or buy a fly/drive package.

Freighting a vehicle

SHIPPING a vehicle can be expensive, but it is relatively straightforward. Ships sail to Reykjavík from the following ports: Immingham (UK), Felixstowe (UK), Antwerp (Belgium), Hamburg (Germany) and Rotterdam (Holland). These ports are served by a roll-on/roll-off service, while at other ports a vehicle will have to be lifted onto the ship by crane. The shipping arrangements are made by a shipping agent, the address of one at the port of your choice can be obtained from a tour operator or from an Icelandic Embassy or Consulate (see pp.99-101).

The shipping charge is based on the 'overall volume' (length × breadth × height) of the vehicle so it may be advisable to take high things off the roof-rack for the duration of the voyage. Cover all valuable equipment and leave any special instructions about burglar alarms and starting. Lock the vehicle, leave one set of keys at the docks and keep the spares with you.

In Reykjavík, take your 'bill of lading' (which you get from the shipping agent) to the shipping company. They will tell you where the vehicle is and give you the forms required by the Customs. At the Customs building you present these forms and complete a Customs declaration. The vehicle can then be collected from the docks (Sundahöfn is closed from 12.00-13.00). Hand in the forms from the Customs and a label showing the date of your departure will be put on the windscreen. Then check the vehicle's exterior as well as the contents. Any damage or loss should be reported immediately.

You will probably have to take out a special marine insurance policy that will be quite separate from your normal travel insurance. You will also need a new bill of lading for the return journey. It is best to try to get this when you first arrive if you may only have a short time in Reykjavík just before your journey home.

SCHEDULED TRANSPORT WITHIN ICELAND

THE TRANSPORT SYSTEM is well organised and can be relied upon; unfortunately the weather is not equally reliable and so for this reason flights may be cancelled. Ferries can save a great deal of driving round long coastal routes; they can often be busy so arrive well in advance of sailing (it is also advisable to book). Details of ferry and air services should be obtained from your tour operator. Winter schedules may differ markedly from those in operation during the summer (June to September).

Internal Air Services

BY FAR the biggest carrier is Flugleiðir (Icelandair) with its two regional off-shoots: Flugfélag Norðurlands (Akureyri) and Flugfélag Austurlands (Egilsstaðir). Even quite small settlements are connected by the air services and this is now one of the major means of travelling around the country, especially in winter. Both summer and winter schedules of the three airlines should be available from your tour operator and these give the frequency of the flights together with details of stops and connecting flights.

Flugleiðir's services are as follows:

Reykjavík to: Akureyri, Bakkafjörður, Borgar-
fjörður eystri, Breiðdalsvík, Egilsstaðir, Grímsey,
Höfn, Húsavík, Ísafjörður, Kópasker, Norðfjörður,
Ólafsfjörður, Patreksfjörður, Raufarhöfn,
Sauðárkrókur, Siglufjörður, Westman Islands,
Vopnafjörður, Thingeyri, Thórshöfn.
Akureyri to: Egilsstaðir, Grímsey, Húsavík,
Ísafjörður, Kópasker, Ólafsfjörður, Raufarhöfn,
Reykjavík, Siglufjörður, Vopnafjörður, Thórshöfn.
Egilsstaðir to: Bakkafjörður, Borgarfjörður,
Breiðdalsvík, Höfn, Norðfjörður, Reykjavík,
Vopnafjörður.

Poor ground or air conditions can cause flights to
be postponed or cancelled (especially in winter),
so be prepared to spend time waiting at an airport if the weather is bad. If you think that there
may be problems, phone the airport or ask your
hotel or travel agent to do it for you (the telephone numbers are listed on p.97). Check-in time
is usually thirty minutes before departure.

There are often taxis or a bus waiting at the
airport when a plane lands and some airports
may also have direct telephone lines to taxi
services (Reykjavík airport has four). If your
destination is some distance from the airport, it is
best to check the availability of taxis or buses
before you fly; this is especially important in the
winter time and at small airfields.

As with international flights, you should reconfirm your return flight.

There are a number of special reduced fare
tickets available for the domestic services:

1. An 'Air Rover' round trip ticket connecting
Reykjavík, Ísafjörður, Akureyri, Egilsstaðir, Höfn
and Reykjavík. The round trip can be made in either
direction.
2. A 'Triangular Air Rover' ticket which connects
Reykjavík to any of the following sets of towns:
Ísafjörður/Akureyri; Akureyri/Egilsstaðir;
Akureyri/Egilsstaðir/Höfn; Höfn/Egilsstaðir. (The
journey can start at any of the named towns.)
3. An 'Air Traveller's Bonus' ticket: three return
flights at a cheap rate if they are all taken within the
four day period Monday-Thursday.

4. Family fares.
5. Student fares.
6. Discounts on internal flights are also often
available with package deals involving Icelandair's
international flights.

Eagle Air's services from Reykjavík go to
Bíldudalur, Blönduós, Flateyri, Gjögur,
Grundarfjörður, Hólmavík, Rif, Siglufjörður,
Stykkishólmur and Suðureyri.

Ferries
The main ferries are as follows:
1. Reykjavík-Akranes. The 'Akraborg' is a very
frequent ferry, with usually four return journeys
each day.
2. Stykkishólmur-Flatey-Brjánslækur. The
'Baldur' has six crossings a week; the journey is
described in section 31 of the Guide.
3. Thorlákshöfn-Westman Islands. The bus
from Reykjavík connects with the daily sailings of
the 'Herjólfur'.
4. Akureyri-Grímsey. The 'Drangur' makes only
two return journeys a month.
5. Ísafjörður-Hornstrandir-Ísarfjarðardúp.
The 'Fagranes' plies this route twice a week (June-
Aug; see section 30). Other places in Ísafjarðardúp
called at all year round include: Vigur, Hvítanes,
Ögur, Æðey, Bær, Melgraseyri, Vatnsfjörður,
Reykjanes, Arngerðareyri, Eyri.
6. Litli-Árskógur-Hrísey. The small ferry 'Sævar'
sails a few times daily to the small island of Hrísey in
Eyjafjörður from a point south-east of Dalvík.

Cargo boats going round the island may also
take passengers in cabins but these services will
depend on what cargo has to be carried. Since a
ship's schedule may only be known a few days
before sailing, this form of travel cannot be
planned far in advance.

Scheduled Bus Services
THE RUGGED NATURE of the Icelandic
roads has encouraged a special breed of bus to be
built, rather different to the buses found elsewhere! Those on the long-distance routes have a
high body to give them good ground clearance
and often have a two-way radio in order to get
advance warning of adverse road or weather

conditions. Some buses have four-wheel drive if they are expected to cross very rough terrain.

Whatever your main mode of transport in the country, a bus trip is definitely worth considering, even if only to get a rest from driving. On many routes the experienced Icelandic drivers can cover distances much more quickly than a foreign motorist and for many visitors a bus trip is the only way they are able to see Askja, Sprengisandur and Landmannalaugar, as they are in the interior and so accessible only with four-wheel drive.

Apart from the buses run by the towns of Reykjavík and Akureyri (which have 68 and 5 buses respectively), the buses are owned by a large number of relatively small companies that are grouped into two organisations. The Icelandic Bus Routes Union (BSI) runs the scheduled service as well as operating tours and hiring out buses. The Touristbus Union deals mainly with tours and bus hire. Members of BSI have 169 buses between them and the members of the Touristbus Union have 153.

At present BSI operates about 40 routes covering a distance of about 4,000 km, with the main centres from which the buses are run being Reykjavík, Akureyri, Egilsstaðir and Höfn. The list on pp.52-53 details all the routes, together with the basic information that will enable a visitor to begin planning journeys. The frequency quoted is to be taken only as a guide to what is available. The complete timetable *('leiðabók')* is available only in Icelandic (nevertheless it is quite easy to understand) and a (free) English-language summary is published. Both should be available through a tour operator. If you intend to base your holiday on travelling by bus then it is advisable to get the *leiðabók* before you go as many connections may involve a lot of waiting, so that journeys must be well planned in advance.

As well as the scheduled services shown in the list, during the summer BSI also have buses on the following routes which pass through or go into the interior:

1. Kjölur mountain track north of Gullfoss and

between Langjökull and Hofsjökull. This route is usually open in the first week of July. The service operates in a southward direction only and stops at the end of August.
2. mountain track through Sprengisandur. This goes past Hekla and Goðafoss (northwards only) and is usually open in July but closes at the end of August.
3. track via Herðubreið to Askja and back.
4. track behind Hekla through Landmannalaugar to the ring road (both directions). This is usually open at the beginning of July.
5. track to Thórsmörk; daily, June to August.

The weather and surface conditions obviously determine when the buses can actually run. Even the ring road between Höfn and Akureyri (especially the part just east of Akureyri) may not be completely opened until mid-May and may be closed again early in September. So if a trip is planned outside the summer season it is best to find out first what journeys can be undertaken.

Apart from tickets for particular journeys, there are some special tickets that allow a fair degree of freedom in choosing routes. The 'Omnibus Passport' lasts 1, 2, 3 or 4 weeks and allows unlimited travel on the scheduled routes (this does not include the 5 mountain routes listed above). You can get on or off the bus anywhere (even between scheduled stops). This ticket is available throughout the year but is not recommended outside the May-September period.

Alternatively, the 'Full-Circle Passport' lasts between June and mid-September and enables the passenger to travel (clockwise or anti-clockwise) once round the ring road in as many stages as is wished. The journey can be started at any place on the ring road. Holders of either of the two Passport tickets can also use them to go on the mountain routes or on a BSI tour for a reduced price. Finally, a 'Fly-Drive' ticket lets you fly from Reykjavík to Akureyri, Egilsstaðir, Ísafjörður or Höfn and take a bus back. Tickets can be bought from tour operators abroad, or from travel agents in Iceland.

There are no group fares on (contd on p.54)

Scheduled Bus Routes operated by BSI

Route No.	From	To	Route (all operate in both directions)	Distance (km)	Duration (hrs.min)	Frequency in Summer (approx.)
1	Akureyri	Dalvík	west shore of fjord	44	1.05	2 per weekday
2	Akureyri	Egilsstaðir	ring road, east	275	5.20	6 per week
3	Akureyri	Grenivík	east shore of fjord	48	1.10	5 per week
7	Akureyri	Mývatn	ring road, east	100	2.30	1 per day
8	Akureyri	Ólafsfjörður	west shore of fjord	62	1.20	4 per week
9	Ísafjörður	Bolungarvík	coastal road, north	15	0.15	2 days per week
16	Egilsstaðir	Eiðar	north	15	0.15	1 per week
17	Egilsstaðir	Hallormsstaður	south, by lake	28	0.30	3 per week
18	Egilsstaðir	Neskaupsstaður	south-east via Búðareyri	75	1.30	1 per weekday
19	Egilsstaðir	Eskifjörður	south-east via Búðareyri	49	1.10	1 per weekday
20	Egilsstaðir	Stöðvarfjörður	south via Búðareyri	129	3.45	3 per week
21	Egilsstaðir	Seyðisfjörður	east	27	0.30	1 per weekday
30	Akureyri	Húsavík	north-east	91	1.35	6 per week
35	Höfn	Djúpivogur	ring road, north-east	105	2.30	4 per week
36	Höfn	Egilsstaðir	ring road, north	249	5.30	5 per week
36	Höfn	Egilsstaðir	coastal road via Búðareyri	308	7.30	1 per week
40	Keflavík	Grindavík	across Reykjanes	23	0.30	2 per weekday
47	Reykjavík	Akranes	coastal road, north	108	2.00	1 per week
49	Reykjavík	Akureyri	ring road, north	436	9.00	1 per day
50	Reykjavík	Gullfoss	via Selfoss and Geysir	125	3.15	1 per day
51	Reykjavík	Borgarnes	coastal road, north	117	2.00	2 per day
52	Reykjavík	Mosfell	via Brúarland and Reykjalundur	17	0.20	many each day
53	Reykjavík	Króksfjarðarnes	ring road north then via Búðardalur	286	5.30	2 per week
54	Reykjavík	Ísafjörður	ring road north, then via Búðardalur then clockwise round NW fjords	543	13.00	1 per week
57	Reykjavík	Grindavík	west	52	0.50	1 or 2 per day

Route No.	From	To	Route (all operate in both directions)	Distance (km)	Duration (hrs.min)	Frequency in Summer (approx.)
58	Reykjavík	Hafnarfjörður	west	12	0.15	many each day
60	Reykjavík	Drangsnes	ring road north, then via Borðeyri and Holmavík	371	6.00	2 per week
61	Reykjavík	Búrfell	ring road east then west bank of Thjórsá after Selfoss	124	2.30	3 per week
61	Reykjavík	Flúðir	ring road east then west bank of Thjórsá after Selfoss	103	1.55	3 per week
63	Reykjavík	Stokkseyri	ring road east via Hveragerði then south from Selfoss and via Eyrarbakki	71	1.30	4 per day
63	Reykjavík	Úlfljótsvatn	ring road east via Hveragerði then north from Selfoss	78	1.30	2 per week
64	Reykjavík	Thorlákshöfn	ring road east then south-west from Hveragerði	52	1.00	2 per day
65	Reykjavík	Sandgerði	west to Keflavík then to smaller settlements	56	1.00	1 per day
66	Reykjavík	Gullfoss	ring road east then north from Selfoss via Laugarvatn and Geysir	125	3.40	1 per day
67	Reykjavík	Hellisandur	coast road north to Borgarnes then north-west via Búðir and Ólafsvík	249	4.15	1 per day
68	Reykjavík	Hvolsvöllur	ring road east	106	2.00	1 per day
69	Reykjavík	Höfn	ring road east	476	10.30	1 per day
70	Reykjavík	Húsafell	ring road north to Borgarfjörður, then east to Reykholt, Húsafell; then return to Borgarfjörður via Síðumúli and Varmaland	190	3.30 to Varmaland	1 per week
71	Reykjavík	Stykkishólmur	coastal road north to Borgarnes, then north-west to Vegamót	217	4.00	1 per day
71A	Reykjavík	Grundarfjörður	as above, then west	245	5.00	1 per day
72	Reykjavík	Garðabær	south-west	10	0.15	many each day
74	Reykjavík	Thingvellir	north-east route	52	0.50	1 per day

scheduled services and children 4-8 years old pay half-fare and those 9-12 years old pay 75% of the normal fare. Seats do not normally have to be booked, but turn up in good time if you want a window seat. If you wave down a bus between two settlements, you will be charged the cost of travelling the distance you are carried. The BSI office is in the long-distance coach terminal immediately to the north of Reykjavík's airport.

There is no country-wide bus livery so look out for green/white buses on the Reykjavík-Höfn-Egilsstaðir section, blue/white between Egilsstaðir and Akureyri, and red/white between Akureyri and Reykjavík. Scheduled buses should carry the letter 'S'; other buses may carry the letter 'H'. Scheduled buses can carry bicycles.

TOURS AND TRIPS

A GREAT NUMBER of well-organised tours and short trips are now available – they might even be too 'organised' for some. The bus tours are described and dealt with in some detail as they offer an excellent opportunity to see the country. The current trips by bus, plane and boat are then given, but it should be borne in mind that some may be subject to change from year to year; however, a tour operator should have information on what is currently available. Be warned, however, that the weather may determine whether a particular journey takes place, especially at the beginning and end of summer.

Bus Tours
IF YOU THINK that Icelandic bus tours are the same as those found elsewhere in Europe then you are in for a shock. You can forget your tie, smart jacket and shiny shoes; instead you are travelling 'on safari'!

These tours are for those who want to see and enjoy the countryside but wish neither to drive nor to stay in one place all the time. There are numerous tours starting from Reykjavík which are arranged by the Icelandic operators and sold abroad by tour operators and travel agents. Depending on the type and length of tour there is usually some time when you can go for a walk instead of being driven about and some tours combine a travelling and trekking holiday. But generally speaking, as you might expect, you will have much less time to wander about on a tour than on an independent camping or motoring holiday, and you will have to follow a more rigid itinerary.

Your tour operator should have details of all the tours. The main points to be considered in choosing and planning a tour are looked at in detail below:

1. Time
The tours vary from between three days to around three weeks, with the most popular period being about two weeks. Beware of rather long routes being covered in a short time as this means you will not have much time in each stopping place.

2. Cost
The airfare to Iceland is often included in the tour's quoted price and this (and perhaps two or three nights in Reykjavík) accounts for a significant proportion of the price. This means that a three-week tour is not much more expensive than a two-week tour, and in terms of value for money, a one-week tour is rather expensive. The tour's price is dictated by its length, popularity, the type of vehicle and the accommodation offered.

3. Vehicle
Sometimes a four-wheel drive bus is used, but normally a very rugged and specially adapted two-

wheel drive vehicle is adequate. A few tours are by Land Rover; these are relatively expensive as fewer passengers are carried.

4. Routes
There are many different routes but they are usually based on one of the following routes out of Reykjavík (see map at front of book).
a) round the ring road
b) south-west Iceland then behind Hekla, returning by the ring road
c) ring road to eastern fjords and Mývatn, then on one of the interior routes back to Reykjavík
d) ring road north then return to Reykjavík by an interior route
e) south-west Iceland then Snæfellsnes and/or north-west fjords

Tours that include the south-west usually stop at Thingvellir, Laugarvatn, Geysir and Gullfoss. If Mývatn is en route then the usual detours are to Askja and Ásbyrgi (and Dettifoss). The choice is thus very wide, but those based on c) above probably give the visitor the best chance to see the many different types of magnificent scenery (fjords, glaciers, volcanoes, deserts) that the country has to offer.

5. Accommodation
This can either be in hotels, huts or tents. Some of the hotels are comfortable (for instance the Edda chain, see p.69), others are a little more spartan. Sleeping bag accommodation is available in some hotels. Camping is definitely the way to see and enjoy the countryside. Most tour operators use the main 'tourist' sites. A few may not, however, and the facilities offered in that case may be rather primitive. Most tours include tents and meals but some 'budget' ones do not. The meals may be cooked in a special kitchen bus that is part of a two-bus 'convoy'. You may be required to help with cooking/washing up.

These tours are sold all over Europe and America (and sometimes elsewhere) so there will probably be a mixture of nationalities and languages on the bus. All the guides speak English and often Danish or another Scandanavian language. If a tour has been booked from one particular country then a guide who speaks the appropriate language will accompany it.

A few 'specialist' tours have recently been developed. These include photography, nature study, geology, geothermal energy study, glasshouse and floral study and a 'classical Saga tour'. It is also possible to go on a tour that combines a visit to Greenland (see pp.250-251) with one to Iceland.

There are also tours operated by the Icelandic touring clubs which are designed primarily for Icelanders. Some of these tours will visit places not usually frequented by the commercial tour operators and may be suitable for non-Icelanders wanting to go walking in the highlands.

Short trips by bus, plane and boat
THERE ARE numerous short trips organized by Icelandic tour operators (see pp.95-96) and the choice is widening every year. They are particularly useful to visitors outside the summer period when travelling and accommodation is more restricted. No matter what type of visit you have, try to keep a couple of days free for these trips as this may be the only way you will see the wilderness of the interior. Most of the places visited in these trips are described in Part 4 of the Guide.

The actual itinerary should be checked with the tour operator. A guide is provided for most trips and some include lunch. They are divided into 5 groups: **A.** by bus from Reykjavík; **B.** by air from Reykjavík; **C.** from Akureyri; **D.** from Mývatn; **E.** from Ísafjörður. The approximate duration of each tour is given in brackets.

A. By bus from Reykjavík
  1. City sightseeing (2½ hours)
    – main 'tourist' sights; including Árbær Museum
  2. Modern Reykjavík (3 hours)
    – industrial sights (October to April only)
  3. Cultural Reykjavík (3 hours)
    – museums, galleries and architecturally interesting buildings (October to April only)
  4. Reykjavík by night
    – includes meal and visit to night club
  5. Hveragerði (4 hours)
    – glasshouses heated by natural hot water (October to April only)
  6. Golden Circle tour (9 hours)

– Geysir, Gullfoss and Thingvellir
7. Whaling station (4 hours)
   – this is to Hvalfjörður and is 'whale permitting'
8. Highland road 'Between the glaciers' (11 hours)
   – north to Hvalfjörður, to Reykholt, between the glaciers Ok and Thörisjökull and past Thingvellir
9. Thjórsárdalur (10 hours)
   – Hekla, Búrfell power station and excavated farmhouse at Stöng
10. Grindavík and Krísuvík (4½ hours)
    – Bessastaðir (President's residence), fishing village of Grindavík and solfatara field at Krísuvík
11. 'South Shore Adventure' (10 hours)
    – along the coast to Sólheimajökull, one of Mýrdalsjökull's outlet glaciers
12. Pony trekking (3 hours)
    – just outside the city
13. To Akureyri via Sprengisandur (15 hours one way)
    – through the interior desert, spend night in Akureyri
14. Sea angling (5-7 hours)
15. Trout fishing (half or full day)
16. 'Snowcat adventure' (5 hours)
    – in the Bláfjöll area (December to March/April only)
17. 'Behind the mountains' (10-11 hours)
    – round Hekla to warm spring area of Landmannalaugar. See Eldgjá, Ófærufoss and finish at Kirkjubæjarklaustur
18. Gullfoss, Geysir
19. Thingvellir
20. Thórsmörk (5 hours one way)
    – behind Eyjafallajökull, spend the night at Thórsmörk
21. to Mývatn via Sprengisandur (13-14 hours one way)
    – spend night at Mývatn

B. By air from Reykjavík

1. Akureyri
   – visit to fish processing and wool factories, Folk Museum
2. Heimaey
   – tour of island and boat trip
3. Volcanoes and glaciers (2 hours)

– Reykjanes, Surtsey, Heimaey, southern glaciers, Hekla and Thingvellir
4. Midnight sun (5 hours)
   – land at Grímsey (on Arctic Circle) (June to August only)
5. Mývatn (12 hours)
   – fly to Akureyri or Húsavík then coach to Mývatn. Tour of lake, mud pools, lava formations
6. Eastern fjords
   – flight to Egilsstaðir then bus to Eiðar, south to Hengifoss and round Lögurinn to Hallormsstaður (groups only)

C. Trips from Akureyri

1. Tour of town (2 hours)
   – botanic gardens, Folk Museum
2. Mývatn (10 hours)
   – via Goðafoss then a tour round the lake
3. Pony trekking (4 hours)
4. Eyjafjörður valley cruise (5 hours)
5. 'Midnight picnic' (4 hours)
   – late evening, north to Ólafsfjörður
6. to Reykjavík via Kjölur (14-15 hours one way)
   – through the interior, spend night in Reykjavík
7. 'Five small towns'
   – Akureyri, Dalvík, Ólafsfjörður, Hofsós and Sauðárkrókur

D. Trips from Mývatn

1. Grand Mývatn tour (7½ hours)
   – the lake, Námaskarð, Krafla. This tour can also be done in 2 separate halves (morning and afternoon)
2. 'Northern Highlights' (10 hours)
   – Dettifoss, Jökulsárgljúfur Canyon, Ásbyrgi, Húsavík
3. Askja (15 hours)
   – past Herðubreið to Askja
4. to Reykjavík via Sprengisandur (13-14 hours one way)
   – spend night in Reykjavík
5. 'Dettifoss Waterfall Tour' (10 hours)

E. Trips from Ísafjörður

1. Ísafjörður and Bolungarvík (4 hours)
2. Ísafjarðardjúp – land and sea (11 hours)
3. 'The spectacular Westfjords from the air' (2 hours)
4. Boat trip to Grunnavík

VEHICLES AND DRIVING

THERE ARE several distinct advantages to touring Iceland by car: it gives you greater independence and flexibility; it allows you to carry more equipment for camping or photography and, depending on the vehicle, it may also provide you with free accommodation. This part of the book tries to put the conditions of Icelandic roads into perspective and to suggest how common pitfalls can be avoided. Since road conditions will provide the biggest problem facing many visitors, some aspects of using a vehicle are dealt with in detail.

The Road System

THE RING ROAD (number 1) goes all the way round the country. For the purpose of numbering the roads, the country is split into 8 sections (numbered 2-9) starting at the south and going clockwise. The two-digit roads get their number from the district they are in (eg 21, 31, 41 etc). The three-digit roads branch off the two-digit roads and take their prefix accordingly (eg 211, 212 etc). They are less important but it does not necessarily follow that their condition is worse than a more important road. Mountain tracks have two digits and the prefix 'F'. Road signs are not all that numerous, however most farms and rivers are signposted, and the information in Part 4 of the Guide and on the 1:500 000 map should enable the visitor to get around the country without too many problems.

The ring road that circles the country has a number of stretches of highway surface that give a smooth, comfortable journey and the Icelanders are hoping to resurface the whole road over the next few years. Meanwhile the rest of the road system can be rough; in many places the road is built with sand and gravel, often with an oil to bind everything together. This surface can soon develop pot-holes, ruts, corrugations and a line of gravel running down the middle of the road. When it is built, the road often ȿ metre above the surrounding land and from time to time a large earth-moving scraper smoothes off the surface. The roads by the fjords (where the rocks are much older and harder) often have many sharp stones, so punctures are more common here; on the southern glacial sands the gravel is rounded and may loosen more easily, producing ruts that can affect steering badly.

The roads are very bumpy and suspensions will take a lot of punishment if care is not taken on the worst sections. Visitors with two-wheel drive vehicles should stay on the (numbered) roads; Part 4 of this Guide keeps the driver to these roads and specifically states where a (safe) track may be taken. Only four-wheel drive vehicles should go on the mountain tracks and, even then, they are advised to keep to the ones described in the Guide, since these are the ones most frequented by Icelanders.

Scare stories about the road conditions may deter some would-be visitors from going to Iceland; it is hoped that this first real attempt to describe road conditions will help potential visitors to make decisions on the basis of facts. It must be remembered, however, that bad weather and the infrequency of road maintenance may drastically change the conditions on any stretch of road from those described.

Winter driving

THE WHOLE of this part of the Guide refers to conditions likely to be experienced during the summer – winter driving is another matter altogether! From October to June (or perhaps even longer) the interior routes will be closed and around November, Icelanders will fit studded tyres to their cars.

Snow ploughs are used to try to keep all the major routes passable. The south coast is usually clear but the ring road's northern section can be badly affected by snow, especially between Egilsstaðir and Akureyri, so the coastal roads are usually used instead. No attempt is made to clear many other roads if they are blocked; tracked vehicles are employed instead. Winter visitors unused to driving in such conditions should stick to public transport and taxis.

Preparation and Maintenance

Preparation of a vehicle

1. The vehicle should be thoroughly checked and serviced before leaving, since the cost and delay of a breakdown can be disproportionate to the cost of avoiding it. The biggest problem is vibration so pay particular attention to the following: springs, shock absorbers, exhaust, exhaust hangers, wheel nuts, roof-rack clamps.

2. Loose stones are often thrown up and many Icelanders put grilles over their headlights. Sticky transparent tape may help to stop stones from smashing lights.

3. Tyres are all-important: worn tyres are prone to punctures and this is the most common form of breakdown. Your spare should be in very good condition.

4. A roof-rack will enable you to store (light) items but as it will also be subject to vibrations it must be strong. This is dealt with more fully on p.59.

5. Anti-freeze should be put in the radiator.

6. If your spare tyre is usually kept underneath the vehicle, it should be moved to a more accessible place.

7. Spare fuel cans should be carried in the boot or on the roof-rack, not in front of the vehicle.

8. UK drivers should ensure that their lights dip to the right.

Recommended spares and tools

Two checklists are given: the list below is suggested for normal cars on numbered roads; that on p.59 is suggested in addition to the first for four-wheel drive vehicles spending some time in the interior, although there may be some items on this that drivers of normal vehicles may also wish to take. The lists are based on the author's own experiences of driving a Volkswagen 'Beetle' and a six-cylinder petrol Land Rover. Those taking a diesel vehicle may omit certain electrical items and should consider taking spares for the pump and injectors instead. Taking spare parts with you will save expense and delay should the worst happen and a breakdown occur, as spares can be both expensive and difficult to obtain.

adhesive tape	pliers
bulbs	points
cloths	roof-rack
elastic bands	rotor arm
emergency windscreen	scissors
(US: windshield) –	screwdrivers
usually available at	sheets of rubber or old
roadside shops	inner tubes (for damping
engine oil	vibration)
fire extinguisher	shovel
first-aid kit	socket set
hammer	spanners (US: monkey
handbook	wrenches)
hand cleanser	spare fan belt
inner tube	spare fuel can
insulating tape	spare tyre (in good
jack and block of wood	condition)
jump leads	spark plugs
keys	spark plug spanner
knife	(US: wrench)
long tow rope	string
lubricating oil	torch (US: flashlight)
luggage restraints	tyre pressure gauge
(elastic)	tyre pump
nuts, bolts, washers,	warning triangle
clips, pins, screws etc.	water
nylon rope	wrench

Hints for equipping four-wheel drive vehicles

As frequently stressed in the Guide, motoring in the interior is for four-wheel drive vehicles only.

The four-wheel drive vehicle most commonly available in Iceland is probably the Russian-made Lada – this can be hired and is usually adequate for most trips through the interior. Japanese vehicles are becoming popular, and there are many Land Rovers. The latter is the most popular four-wheel drive vehicle amongst visitors to Iceland for although it is less comfortable than many other vehicles, it is strong and is able to carry heavy loads. Its layout behind the driver is useful, too; it is a straightforward job to build cupboards in the rear and fit a sink and cooker, making it into a (rather cramped) motor caravan. The Bibliography lists books and pamphlets that may be of use to those wanting to kit out a vehicle, while visitors wanting a ready-made caravanette based on a Land Rover or Range Rover can get one supplied by Carawagon of 11 Welbeck Street, London W1.

Roof-racks

If you are going into the interior with a number of passengers, you will probably need a roof-rack. The choice and use of a roof-rack generally receives less thought than it should, so the following points are worth considering:

1. A heavy duty roof-rack is needed if fuel cans or wheels are to travel on it. One with a lot of bolts can be troublesome as their tightness may need frequent checking, something that is avoided when using a welded roof-rack.
2. A rail around the roof-rack helps to keep the load secure.
3. Check tightness after loading and after a bad track.
4. A wheel can be tied down, but thin rope gets frayed, and loosening ropes is very time-consuming. Consider bolting it down.
5. Wooden slats or a wooden board makes walking on the roof-rack easier.
6. Weight should be distributed properly, taking into account the manufacturer's recommendations. This probably means keeping the weight to the back – and never over the windscreen.

7. Tarpaulins, nets, elastic luggage restraints and nylon rope are all useful when securing the load.
8. The roof-rack should be secured to the back of the roof so that it cannot slide forward when travelling on corrugated tracks.
9. Many visitors carry too much spare fuel in jerrycans. Use the information on pp.66-68 and in Part 4 to calculate your fuel needs and then find out if jerrycans are needed at all. If you do need them they should be carried in their holders (which should be bolted down) and strips of inner tube should be used to ensure that the can does not rub against the holder. Use a tube and a funnel for filling the tank – this means that you need never lift the jerrycan off the roof.
10. A ladder up the back of the vehicle makes access much easier, especially if you want to get up quickly to take photographs.

Recommended spares and tools for four-wheel drive vehicles

The following items are suggested for four-wheel drive vehicles crossing the interior, in addition to those listed on p.58 for normal cars on numbered roads. Other suggestions can be found in the Land Rover publication listed in the Bibliography (see p.257).

adhesive	G-clamp
air filter	glass fibre repair kit
Allen keys	grease
axle stand	hacksaw, blades
blocks of wood	heavy duty gloves
brake fluid	jerrycans (plus holder,
brass brush	funnel, tube)
coil	light guards
cold chisels	multimeter
condenser	oil for gearbox, overdrive
crow bar	oil solvent
disposable gloves	snow chains (also for
electrical cable	mud)
electrical connectors	spot lamps
emery paper	starting handle
exhaust hangers	tarpaulin
extension tube for wheel	tweezers
brace	vehicle manual
extra inner tubes	windscreen (US:
feeler gauges	windshield) sealant
files	wire brush
fuses	wire strippers

Maintenance

The following list sets out those parts of the vehicle that will need most frequent checking during a trip. The tyres and roof-rack should be checked each day and items 3-8 inclusive should be looked at at least twice a week. If you are crossing the interior (or are about to do so) you should check all the items each day.

1. Tyres – check pressure when cold and look for stones in the tread;
2. Roof-rack supports and framework;
3. Wheel nuts;
4. Exhaust and exhaust hangers;
5. Coolant;
6. Engine oil;
7. Lights;
8. Shock absorbers, springs;
9. Air filter (especially after desert);
10. Linkages, doors, connections (after corrugated tracks);
11. Under the body, sump (after a track with boulders).

After the journey

The vehicle should be checked upon returning home and the following points may be of use:

1. UK drivers should readjust the direction of the lights;
2. If rivers have been forded then the engine oil should be changed. If a lot of deep rivers were crossed then the gearbox and axles may need an oil change too;
3. The air filter may need changing;
4. Linkages, hinges etc should be oiled;
5. Wheels, steering, tyres should be checked for damage;
6. Shock absorbers, springs and exhaust system should also be checked for damage;
7. Brakes and breather valves on axles (for example) should be cleaned if clogged with silt from glacial rivers.

Services and Facilities

Car Hire

YOUR TOUR OPERATOR should be able to arrange this for you. A car can be hired for the whole of your visit or just for a day should you only want it for a short trip; most car-hire firms require the vehicle to be returned to the place from which it was hired, so 'round trips' have to be planned. The vehicles that are available include the Lada Sport, Subaru (saloon), Land Rover and Mitsubishi L2000 (all four-wheel drive), the Volkswagen Golf and the Volkswagen Microbus.

When you take over the vehicle you should check the following: distance travelled; marks, bumps or scrapes on the bodywork; condition of seat belts and spare wheel and the whereabouts of the jack and the wheel brace. Ensure that you know what to do if you have a breakdown or an accident. To minimise any claims against you in the event of an accident you are advised to pay an accident damage waiver. Find out just what the insurance covers you for; in particular whether it covers accidents/breakdowns when you are off the road and on a track or going through water. Ensure that you know exactly how the final hire charge will be calculated; the usual method of charging is based on a daily rate with a distance charge on top of that. In Iceland these two rates are often quoted exclusive of a sizeable sales tax, but tour operators abroad may have this tax included in their prices.

Towns and settlements with car-hire firms include: Reykjavík, Akranes, Akureyri, Bolungarvík, Egilsstaðir, Hafnarfjörður, Höfn, Húsavik, Ísafjörður, Keflavík, Kópavogur, Sauðárkrókur, Selfoss, Súðavik (and see p.255).

Car Importers, Dealers and Garages

All the main dealers are in the Reykjavík/Kópavogur district and they have a good network of contacts in the larger settlements. Obviously large quantities of spares cannot be kept in the outlying garages, so a speedy service is operated from the capital (it is not at all unusual to airfreight parts). If you phone a dealer on the list below, he should be able to tell you which garage near you holds the spare parts you need. If the spare part is not kept in Iceland, it will have to be flown in for you. The delays and costs that a breakdown involves therefore make it that much

Car Importers and Dealers

Name	Tel no	Address	Makes of vehicles
Bifreiðar og landbúnaðarv hf	91-38600	Suðurlandsbraut 14, 105 Reykjavík	Gaz 69, Lada, Moskovich, UAZ 450, Volga
Bílaborg hf	91-81299	Smiðshöfði 23, 110 Reykjavík	Mazda, Hino
Brimborg hf	91-685870	Ármúli 23, 105 Reykjavík	Daihatsu
David Sigurðsson hf	91-77220	Smiðjuvegur 4, 200 Kópavogur	Fiat, AMC, Concord, Gremlin, Hornet, Wagoneer, Cherokee, Javelin, Jeep, Matador, Pacer, Rambler, Willys
Globus hf	91-81555	Lágmúli 5, 105 Reykjavík	Citröen, Hyundai
Gunnar Bernhard	91-38772	Suðurlandsbraut 20, 105 Reykjavík	Honda
Hafrafell hf	91-685211	Vagnhöfði 7, 110 Reykjavík	Peugeot, Talbot
Hekla hf	91-21240	Laugavegur 170-172, 105 Reykjavík	Audi, Auto Union, British Leyland, Caterpillar, Colt, Galant, Land Rover, Range Rover, Mitsubishi, Lancer, Porsche, Volkswagen, Austin, Morris
Ingvar Helgason	91-33560	Vonarland, Sogamýri 6, 108 Reykjavík	Barkas, Datsun, Subaru, Trabant, Wartburg
Ísarn hf	91-20720	Reykjanesbraut 10-12, 105 Reykjavík	Scania Vabis
Jöfur hf	91-42600	Nýbýlavegur 2, 200 Kópavogur	Alfa Romeo, Chrysler, Commer, Dodge, Skoda, Valiant
Kraftur hf	91-685235	Vagnhöfði 3, 110 Reykjavík	MAN
Kristinn Guðnason hf	91-686633	Suðurlandsbraut 20, 105 Reykjavík	Renault, BMW
P. Samúelsson	91-44144	Nýbýlavegur 8, 200 Kópavogur	Toyota
Ræsir hf	91-19550	Skúlagata 59, 105 Reykjavík	Mercedes Benz, Bedford, Cadillac, Blazer
SÍS	91-38900	Ármúli 3, 105 Reykjavík	Buick, Chevrolet, GMC, International, Oldsmobile, Opel, Pontiac, Vauxhall

Name	Tel no	Address	Makes of vehicle
Sveinn Egilsson hf	91-685100	Fordhúsið, Skeifan 17, 108 Reykjavík	Ford, Lincoln, Mercury, Suzuki
Töggur hf	91-81530	Bíldshöfði 16, 110 Reykjavík	Auto Bianchi, Lancia, Saab
Veltir hf	91-35200	Suðurlandsbraut 16, 105 Reykjavík	Daf, Volvo

more important to have the vehicle fully serviced before departure.

A list of selected major car dealers is given above. The 1:500 000 Touring Map also shows some garages, although it gives no indication of the facilities these may offer. Labour charges are usually quite reasonable but spare parts can be very expensive. Cost can therefore be reduced by taking these with you.

Garages are normally open from 08.00-18.00 or 19.00 during weekdays, but few are open at weekends. Because of this, and the distance between garages, it is advisable to seek help as soon as you are aware that the vehicle may need attention.

Fuel

Petrol stations are quite numerous (except of course in the interior) and are normally open from 07.15-21.15. They are usually open during the weekends except during the middle of Sunday. All the petrol stations sell one grade of petrol (93 octane) and diesel fuel, but there is no LPG (low pressure gas) available in Iceland. The price of fuel is the same everywhere in the country; diesel is about half the price of petrol, which is expensive.

The 1:500 000 Touring Map (see p.85) indicates where many of the petrol stations are − some are in settlements, others by hotels or major junctions, or by farms in the remoter places.

FIB

The FIB is the Icelandic Motoring Club, which is a member of the international motoring organiz-ation 'L'Alliance Internationale de Tourisme' (AIT), and its services are available to members of any motoring club also affiliated to AIT. The Club has 10,000 members and, given the nature of the problems faced, it can only offer limited assistance. During summer weekends (Friday night to Sunday night) and public holidays (see p.94) their part-time road patrols operate out of the following 10 places:

South-west: Thingvellir; Thrastalundur (south of Thingvallavatn); Hvalfjörður (fjord on west coast); Hella. **North-west:** Viðigerði. **West:** Hvítárbakki (Borgarfjörður). **North:** Vaglaskógur (east of Akureyri). **East:** Egilsstaðir; Höfn; Vík.

In their respective areas the patrols are on the main roads and can be contacted through a petrol station, a roadside cafe or a police patrol. If you have a breakdown during the week (when the patrols do not operate) phone FIB's office in Reykjavík to get advice. The telephone number is listed on page 96.

Driving Hints

THE FOLLOWING POINTS should be borne in mind by anyone driving in Iceland.

1. Vehicles drive on the right.
2. Outside the settlements, the road may be of single-lane width, with a line of gravel up the middle and along the sides.
3. Driving through the gravel cuts down vibrations but also reduces traction and control over steering.
4. Slow down near bridges as both ends often have very big potholes; cattle grids are not affected so badly.

5. Look out for any changes in the colour of the road as this may mean a change in surface conditions.
6. After a downpour, parts of the road may get washed away, so keep away from the side of the road.
7. Blind summits are marked 'blind hæð' – so keep to the right if you see this sign.
8. Icelandic drivers often announce their wish to overtake by sounding their horn.
9. Slow down when being overtaken and let the vehicle get past quickly to lessen the chance of flying pebbles striking the windscreen.
10. The speed limit in the settlements if 50 kph (30 mph) and outside it is 70 kph (45 mph).
11. Do not drink and drive. The punishment is very severe, and the limit, at 0.5% alcohol in the blood, is much lower than in many other countries.
12. Keep lights on when driving, even in daylight.
13. Seat belts should be worn by drivers and front seat passengers. This is compulsory if seat belts are fitted.
14. At a junction where there are no give-way signs, give way to a vehicle coming from the right.
15. Traffic signs are similar to those found in the rest of Europe.

Crossing the Interior (four-wheel drive vehicles only)
The central highlands are dominated by the main glaciers (Langjökull, Hofsjökull and Vatnajökull) and the vast areas of gravel that lie between them. Driving conditions vary considerably and are really dependent on the time of year and weather conditions. In good weather the journey through the two main routes (Kjölur and Sprengisandur) can be breathtaking, with views stretching over long distances. However, in poor conditions, the journey can be tedious as the cloud level may obscure the scenery, and in bad weather the tracks will be difficult or downright dangerous as the rivers and soft sandy areas can be treacherous.

While many visitors will manage a crossing without too much difficulty, the vehicle must be checked carefully before and during the journey. Only a few vehicles might cross the interior each day and no-one will (or should) start a crossing in the afternoon.

There are no farms, settlements or garages in the interior, so all provisions, including extra fuel, must be carried. Part 4 mentions where the fuel can be bought and the distance to the next fuel station. There are a number of 'tourist huts' on or near the main routes offering primitive accommodation; the 1:500 000 map shows their positions and the descriptions of the interior routes covered in Part 4 (sections 36–43) detail the huts that are passed. For emergencies, there are small shelters (equipped with radios) and a few small buildings used by farmers during the autumn round-up. Some buildings in both these categories are also mentioned in Part 4, and the 1:500 000 map shows the emergency rescue huts.

While each of the main features (such as side-tracks, rivers and signposts) of all the major cross-country tracks are described in Part 4, it must be stressed that these are subject to change, often for the following reasons: drifting sand, rockfalls, changing river courses, new tracks to power stations, late snow etc. So before setting off check at an hotel or fuel station near to the start of the route to determine if extra difficulties are likely to be encountered.

Side tracks leading off the main tracks may be closed and in any case are probably more difficult than the main ones; they have even less traffic (perhaps only one or two cars on a fine summer day) and may pose far more problems, especially to a single vehicle.

A number of points to bear in mind when driving in the interior are listed below.

1. Do not attempt too great a distance in one day (see Part 4 for suggested journeys). Progress may be slower than you anticipate.
2. Calculate how much fuel is needed (see Part 4 for petrol stations *en route*) then add 30-50 per cent as fuel consumption is high in the interior.
3. Make sure you take the appropriate 1:250 000 map.
4. On sections where there are hills, rivers or loose surfaces, keep in four-wheel drive.
5. The surface is very loose, so to avoid skidding use gears rather than the brake for slowing down.

6. Yellow stakes usually mark the main tracks.
7. Puddles may conceal deep holes.
8. No warnings will be given of blind summits.

River Crossings

River crossing is discussed in some detail as this type of driving (through fast rivers of up to 50 cm deep) can be dangerous. If the river is fast then wait for another vehicle to come so that you can help one another if necessary. If an Icelander comes, invite him to cross first so that you can see where to go and what angle and speed to take.

Kjölur and Sprengisandur have a number of rivers which are described in Part 4; south of Landmannalaugar there are many rivers and the route to Askja has three. As long as there has not been a lot of rain then these rivers will probably be passable without too much difficulty. In that case not all of the following points apply. Thórsmörk is a very different proposition and every one of the following points should be considered. It may be advisable to try one of the other routes before you attempt Thórsmörk so that you get practice.

The interior routes may not be open until July if there has been a bad winter; check with your tour operator if this may affect your plans.

Dos and Don'ts

1. Glacial rivers are highest in the afternoon and evening, especially after a warm day. This can make an enormous difference over a period of only a few hours, so try to cross in the morning if possible.
2. Spray electrical equipment (plugs, distributor, condenser, coil) with water-repellent and put a plastic bag over the distributor, fastened with an elastic band. This should stop water from shorting the electrics.
3. If the water is very deep then loosen the fan belt to stop the fan spraying water all over the engine.
4. Have your tow rope fixed to the front of the vehicle, but you should be able to take it off and put it on the rear in case you have to be hauled out backwards.
5. Water may get in the vehicle so lift luggage, food etc off the floor and tie everything down.

6. Do not assume that the narrowest crossing is the easiest. The river is probably deepest and fastest at this point. Look for the wider crossings where it will be shallower and slower.
7. Try wading the river (with a safety rope if necessary) to see how deep it is and where the boulders are. Examine all alternative crossings.
8. You can expect to be carried downstream by a fast river so aim slightly upstream of a suitable landing place.
9. Try to cross by heading downstream, so that you are not fighting against the current.
10. Keep in lowest gear (using low ratio gear/transfer box).
11. Go as slowly as possible so as not to build up a bow wave or splash water over the engine. This is the most common mistake that people make.
12. Do not stop in the river!
13. There will probably be hidden boulders in the river, especially at its edges, so be prepared for the wheels suddenly lurching upwards.
14. Test your brakes after crossing, especially if you have drum brakes. Once these get thoroughly soaked, you can expect the steering to snatch when the brakes are applied.
15. If you get stuck in a river for an extended period, then the engine will almost certainly need an oil change – and probably much more.

Accidents

SHOULD YOU HAVE an accident the procedure to follow is similar to that in many other countries. If possible, the vehicles should be left in the position of the accident until the police arrive. You should contact the following: **1.** Police (road patrols are on the main road); **2.** FIB (if you are in a motoring club affiliated to AIT); **3.** Insurance company (by telegram) about car; **4.** Personal Insurance company (by telegram) if hurt.

The accident should be reported to the police as soon as possible and you may be asked to make a statement which you will probably not be required to sign. Insurance companies recommend that no admission of liability should be made.

Road Distances

THE COMPLETION of the ring road revolutionised road travel in 1974. While the previous road distance between Reykjavík and Höfn (via the north coast!) was 971 km, the new road cut this dramatically to its present figure of 476 km. Further improvements, such as the bridge over Borgarfjörður at Borgarnes, are bringing settlements much nearer to each other and making travelling less tiring. The distance chart that follows will be useful for planning your itinerary.

It is based on the ring road's length of 1414 km and gives the shortest distance from many settlements to Reykjavík, to six other major settlements on the ring road and to Ísafjörður in the north-western fjords. The chart gives the road number and location of each settlement, which have been grouped together according to the general map they are on. (For further information on maps, see pp.85-87.) None of the settlements listed are located on general map 5, as this covers the interior: there are therefore no entries for map 5.

Note: Remember that on some maps that are available 'Th' may be represented by the Icelandic letter 'Þ'. Thus Thorskafjörður may appear on the map as 'Þorskafjörður', and so on.

Road Distances Between Major Settlements

Map 1: North-west

Place	Road no.	Location	Reykjavík	Selfoss	Vík	Höfn	Egilsstaðir	Akureyri	Borgarnes	Ísafjörður
			Distance (km) to:							
Hólmavík	68	W coast of Steingrímsfjörður, in Húnaflói	322	365	500	784	625	350	205	315
Ísafjörður	61	W coast of Skutulsfjörður, off Ísafjarðardjúp	543	586	721	1005	944	669	426	—
Vatneyri	62	N coast of Patreksfjörður, W coast of NW fjords	470	513	648	932	871	596	353	192
Flókalundur	60	N coast of Vatnsfjörður, S coast of NW fjords	408	451	586	835	809	534	291	135
Bjarkarlundur	60	E of Thorskafjörður, SE corner of NW fjords	279	322	457	741	680	405	162	264

Map 2: West

Place	Road no.	Location	Reykjavík	Selfoss	Vík	Höfn	Egilsstaðir	Akureyri	Borgarnes	Ísafjörður
Brú	1	S of Hrútafjörður	204	247	382	666	507	232	87	397
Búðardalur	60	E coast of Hvammsfjörður	198	241	376	660	599	324	81	345
Stykkishólmur	56	N coast of Snæfellsnes	217	260	395	679	642	367	100	432
Ólafsvík	574	N coast of Snæfellsnes (to the west)	241	284	419	703	697	422	124	489
Borgarnes	54	N coast of Borgarfjörður	117	160	295	579	594	319	—	426
Reykholt	518	NE of Borganes	129	172	307	592	598	323	44	430

Map 3: South-west

Place	Road no.	Location	Reykjavík	Selfoss	Vík	Höfn	Egilsstaðir	Akureyri	Borgarnes	Ísafjörður
Akranes	51	E coast of Faxaflói	108	151	286	570	631	356	37	463

Place	Road no.	Location	Distance (km) to:							
			Reykjavík	Selfoss	Vík	Höfn	Egilsstaðir	Akureyri	Borgarnes	Ísafjörður
Reykjavík	1	E coast of Faxaflói	—	57	192	476	711	436	117	543
Keflavík	41	S coast of Faxaflói	48	99	234	518	753	478	159	585
Grindavík	43	SW corner of Iceland	52	103	238	522	757	482	163	589
Thorlákshöfn	38	S coast, SE of Reykjavík	52	32	167	451	692	474	155	581
Selfoss	1	S of Thingvallavatn	57	—	135	419	660	479	160	586
Thingvellir	36	N shore of Thingvallavatn	52	46	181	465	703	428	109	535
Map 4: North										
Húsavík	85	E coast of Skjálfandi	527	570	705	478	229	91	410	760
Akureyri	1	W coast of Eyjafjörður	436	479	614	524	275	—	319	669
Siglufjörður	76	N coast, NNW of Akureyri	449	492	627	717	468	193	332	682
Sauðárkrókur	75	W coast of Skagafjörður	366	409	544	644	395	120	249	603
Varmahlíð	1	SSE of Sauðárkrókur	341	384	519	619	370	95	224	574
Blönduós	1	W coast of Húnaflói	290	333	468	670	421	146	173	523
Hvammstangi	72	E coast of Miðfjörður, in Húnaflói	242	285	420	704	479	204	125	435
Map 6: South										
Hvolsvöllur	1	SW of Hekla	106	49	86	370	611	528	209	635
Skógár	1	S of Eyjafallajökull	160	103	32	316	557	582	263	689
Vík	1	S of Mýrdalsjökull	192	135	—	284	525	614	295	721
Kirkjubæjarklaustur	1	NE of Mýrdalsjökull	273	216	81	203	444	695	376	802
Laugarvatn	37	E of Thingvallavatn	93	40	175	459	700	515	196	622
Gullfoss	35	S of Langjökull	125	72	183	467	708	547	228	654

Map 7: North-east

Place	Road no.	Location	Distance (km) to:							
			Reykjavík	Selfoss	Vík	Höfn	Egilsstaðir	Akureyri	Borgarnes	Ísafjörður
Grímsstaðir	1	E of Mývatn	577	620	659	383	134	141	460	810
Reykjahlíð	1	NE corner of Mývatn	541	584	700	424	175	100	419	775
Kópasker	85	E coast of Axarfjörður	628	671	741	455	206	192	511	861
Raufarhöfn	85	NW coast of Thistilfjörður	681	724	800	524	275	245	564	914
Vopnafjörður	85	W coast of Vopnafjörður	676	719	704	428	179	240	559	909
Bakkagerði	94	in Borgarfjörður	789	732	597	321	72	347	666	1016

Map 8: East

Place	Road no.	Location	Reykjavík	Selfoss	Vík	Höfn	Egilsstaðir	Akureyri	Borgarnes	Ísafjörður
Djúpivogur	1	E coast, opposite island of Papey	573	516	381	105	146	421	676	1090
Breiðdalsvík	1	E coast, N of island of Papey	649	592	457	181	84	359	678	1028
Búðeyri	1	in Reyðarfjörður	745	689	554	278	34	309	628	978
Neskaupstaður	955	N coast of Norðfjörður	782	728	593	317	71	346	665	1015
Egilsstaðir	1	N shore of Lagarfljót	717	660	525	249	—	275	594	944
Seyðisfjörður	93	W coast of Seyðisfjörður, E of Egilsstaðir	744	687	552	276	27	302	627	971

Map 9: South-east

Place	Road no.	Location	Reykjavík	Selfoss	Vík	Höfn	Egilsstaðir	Akureyri	Borgarnes	Ísafjörður
Skaftafell	1	S of middle of Vatnajökull	343	286	151	137	378	653	446	872
Höfn	99	SE of Vatnajökull	476	419	284	—	249	524	579	1005

ACCOMMODATION

Hotels, guesthouses and youth hostels

THE STANDARD of accommodation varies tremendously through the country, from the modern hotels in the capital to the rather more modest buildings in the country where you can use your own sleeping bag. With such a short tourist season, there has been no need for a substantial number of year-round hotels, so many of the district schools at which pupils stay during the rest of the year are opened as summer hotels. Nineteen of the largest of these, known as the 'Edda' hotels, are run by the Iceland Tourist Bureau. This is the only chain of hotels and they offer good accommodation, meals and other facilities (ten of them have swimming pools). There is no chain of youth hostels as such, but there are a total of 15 of them which are included in the list below. A brochure, 'Hostelling in Iceland', is published annually by the Icelandic Youth Hostels Association.

Each year the Tourist Board publishes a list of the prices of the most popular hotels and guesthouses and a tour operator should have these details. Prices are usually quoted exclusive of breakfast, but taxes are always included in the prices. Few hotels outside Reykjavík have bars.

The list on pp.71-76 gives details of various types of accommodation in each of the areas covered by the nine general maps (see pp.85-86). As far as possible entries have been listed according to the order in which they would be encountered by travelling anti-clockwise round the country starting at Reykjavík. Some of the places that are listed can be rather tricky to find, so fairly detailed information is given to get you near the hotel. Then ask.

Should you wish to write to an hotel or hostel, then the name of the settlement it is in or near will suffice for a postal address; except for Reykjavík or Akureyri, where the full address is needed.

Farmhouse Accommodation

AN INCREASING NUMBER of farms offer board to visitors. The number of these is still small as catering for foreign visitors is a new concept to many farmers in the outlying districts. However, a holiday based in a farmhouse is an excellent way of getting to know the countryside and the people. Tour operators should have details of what is available; the brochure 'Farm Holidays in Iceland' lists some 42 farms around the country that take visitors. It is well laid out and gives detailed information about each place.

Summer Homes

SUMMER HOMES are often built near beauty spots; some of them are privately owned while others have been built by organisations such as trade unions for their members' use. Sometimes they are available for renting – check with your tour operator.

Huts

THE Icelandic Touring Club (Ferðafélag Íslands) operates a number of huts in the remoter parts of the country. These can be used by visitors but members of the Club have priority. They are usually quite basic. Some may have wardens in the summer who will receive payment; in the others, money should be left for the facilities used. They cannot be booked. Other huts are owned by individuals and by other clubs and organisations. Because of the ferocity of the winter seas around the island, there are a number of rescue huts dotted along the coast (mainly on the southern sandur and in the NW fjords); these are not for casual use. The 1:500 000 map shows both types of huts.

Never rely on using a hut but check at a roadside cafe, garage, hotel or campsite as to whether a hut marked on the map is likely to be available. Alternatively, phone Ferðafélag Íslands (91-

19533) for information.

Three huts on the main cross-country routes (Kjölur, Sprengisandur and Landmannalaugar) are described in Part 4.

How to use the accommodation list
Location: this is the name of the town, settlement or farm the hotel is in or near.
Name: the accommodation may be advertised as an hotel, guesthouse, school, youth hostel or just listed under someone's name. The same place may operate under a number of different names.
  'Félagsheimili' is a community centre.
  'Skóli' is a school building.
Road Number: this is the numbered road nearest to the location: it is not necessarily the road that the hotel is on. Road number 1 is the ring road. Road numbers are on the 1:500 000 touring map and on the reverse of the 1:750 000 tourist map.
Directions: this gives compass directions from the nearest fjord (coast of . . . fjörður), glacier (. . . jökull), lake (shore of . . . vatn), large settlement or other important place on the 1:250 000 map. Often a settlement in a fjord shares the fjord's name.
Time of Opening: S = summer only; A = all year; S&A = part is open all year, extra facilities in summer. These designations are given where known. For youth hostels this is usually given in months. Very few visitors travel to Iceland in the winter and the hotels can be quiet during the Christmas and New Year period, so even though an hotel is listed (and advertised) as 'open all year', the normal services may be curtailed during mid-winter. Winter visitors should check this prior to their arrival.
Number of Rooms: this is given where known. This will also give some idea of the extent of the facilities that may be offered.
Sleeping Bag Accommodation: many places offer dormitory accommodation where you can use your own sleeping bag. This type of accommodation is called *'svefnpokapláss'* but unlike youth hostels, these places may not always have kitchen facilities for visitors' use. You may therefore have to buy meals.
Telephone Number: if you are travelling a long distance it is advisable to book in advance, especially out of season, during a holiday weekend or if you are going somewhere where there is no alternative accommodation. Some of the youth hostels may be completely booked up by walking parties. If no telephone number is given, dial -02 to get help from the operator – but be warned that not all operators speak English. If you are dialling from outside Iceland, the prefix '9' is needed.

Some telephone numbers will inevitably have changed since the Guide went to press: in these cases, the correct number can be obtained from the operator.

Inevitably these lists are incomplete; nevertheless they are probably the most extensive lists of accommodation available anywhere. Various tour operators, agencies in Iceland and the Icelandic Tourist Board publish lists but these do not cover as many establishments.

The availability of accommodation in many of the 'summer hotels' listed here, such as schools or community centres, depends on the willingness of the individual schoolmasters and wardens to provide rooms. Availability may therefore alter at short notice.

There are no entries for map 5, as this covers the interior where there is no accommodation available. Campsites in this area are listed on p.80. In some entries blanks have been left where information is currently not available.

Separate and more detailed lists of hotels and guesthouses in Reykjavík and Akureyri can be found in their respective sections in Part 4 (see p.168 and p.197).

Accommodation List of Hotels, Guesthouses and Youth Hostels

Map 1: North-West

Location	Name	Road No.	Directions	Time of Opening	No. of Rooms	Sleeping Bag Acc.	Tel. No.
Hólmavík	Guesthouse Hólmavík	68	W coast of Steingrímsfjördur, in Húnaflói	A	10	—	95-3185
Hólmavík	Barnaskólinn Hólmavík	68	W coast of Steingríms-fjördur, in Húnaflói	S	—	yes	95-3129
Bjarnarfjödur	Hotel Laugarhóll	643	W coast of Húnaflói	S	4	yes	95-3111
Árnes	Barnaskólinn Finnbogastaðir	643	E coast of NW fjords, near northern limit of road	S	—	yes	—
Ísafjördur	Hotel Hamrabær	61	W coast of Skutulsfjördur, off Ísafjarðardjúp	A	8	—	94-3777
Ísafjördur	Skiðheimar	61	W coast of Skutulsfjördur, off Ísafjarðardjúp	winter ski hotel	—	yes	94-3581
Ísafjördur	Youth Hostel/Guesthouse	61	W coast of Skutulsfjördur, off Ísafjarðardjúp	A	(42 beds)	yes	94-3043
Ísafjördur	Hotel Edda	61	W coast of Skutulsfjördur, off Ísafjarðardjúp	S&A	31	—	94-4111
Bolungarvík	Primary Shcool	61	NW of Ísafjördur	S	—	yes	94-7530
Thingeyri	Guesthouse Höfn	60	S coast of Dýrafjördur, W coast of NW fjords	A	3	—	94-8151
Bíldudalur	Hotel Vegamót	63	S coast of Arnarfjördur, W coast of NW fjords	A	3	—	94-2232
Vatneyri	c/o Erla Haflidadóttir	62	N coast of Patreksfjördur, W coast of NW fjords	—	—	—	94-1235
Vatneyri	Grunnskóli Patreksfjardar	62	N coast of Patreksfjördur, W coast of NW fjords	—	—	yes	94-1257
Breiðavík	Youth Hostel	612	W tip of NW fjords	A	(40 beds)	yes	94-1100
Flókalundur	Hotel Edda	60	N coast of Vatnsfjördur, S coast of NW fjords	S	14	—	94-2011
Bjarkalundur	Hotel Edda	60	E of Thorskafjördur, SE corner of NW fjords	S	12	yes	93-4762

Map 2: West

Location	Name	Road No.	Directions	Time of Opening	No. of Rooms	Sleeping Bag Acc.	Tel. No.
Staður	Staðarskáli	1	SW of Hrútafjörður	S	4	—	95-1150
Reykir	Hotel Edda	1	E coast of Hrútafjörður, NE of Borðeyri	S	28	yes	95-1003/1004
Reykhólar	Bær í Króksfirdi	607	W coast of Berufjörður, NE coast of Breiðafjörður	S	—	yes	93-4757
Reykhólar	Grunnskólinn Reykhólum	607	W coast of Berufjörður, NE coast of Breiðafjörður	S	—	yes	93-4731
Svarfhóll		605	N coast of Gilsfjörður, NE coast of Breiðafjörður	A	—	yes	—
Sælingsdalur	Hotel Edda, Laugar	589	N of NE corner of Hvammsfjörður	S	27	yes	93-4265
Búðardalur	Hotel Bjarg	60	E coast of Hvammsfjörður	A	7	—	93-4322
Búðardarlur	Félagsheimilið Dalabúð	60	E coast of Hvammsfjörður	—	—	yes	93-4126
Stykkishólmur	Hotel Stykkishólmur	56	N coast of Snæfellsnes	A	26	yes	93-8330
Ólafsvík	Guesthouse Sjöbúðir/Hotel Nes	574	N coast of Snæfellsnes (to the west)	A	38	yes	93-6300
Arnarstapi	Félagsheimilið Snæfell	574	S coast of Snæfellsnes (to the west)	—	—	yes	93-7102
Búðir	Hotel Búðir	54	S coast of Snæfellsnes (to the west)	S	20	—	93-7102
Vegamót	Félagsheimilið Breiðavík	54	S coast of Snæfellsnes due S of Stykkishólmur	—	—	yes	93-7690
Borgarnes	Hotel Edda	54	N coast of Borgarfjörður	A	35	yes	93-7119/7219
Hreðavatn	Hotel Bifröst	1	SW of junction with road 60	S	31	—	93-5000/5005

Location	Name	Road No.	Directions	Time of Opening	No. of Rooms	Sleeping Bag Acc.	Tel. No.
Hreðavatn	Hreðavatnsskáli	1	SW of junction with road 60	—	—	—	93-5011
Reykholt	Hotel Edda	518	NE of Borganes	S	64	yes	93-5260
Map 3: South-west (excluding Reykjavík)							
Svartsengi	Guesthouse Bláa Lonið (Blue Lagoon)	43	near Grindavik, S coast of Reykanes peninsula	A	10	—	92-8650
Akranes	Hotel Akranes	51	E coast of Faxaflói	A	11	—	93-2020/2144
Hveragerði	Hotel Ljósbra	1	S of Thingvallavatn	S	12	—	99-4588
Selfoss	Hotel Selfoss	1	S of Thingvallavatn	—	—	yes	99-1970
Selfoss	Hotel Thóristún	1	S of Thingvallavatn	A	17	—	99-1633
Thingvellir	Hotel Valhöll	36	N shore of Thingvallavatn	S	37	—	99-4080
Map 4: North (excluding Akureyri)							
Garður	School	85	S coast of Axarfjörður	—	—	—	—
Húsavik	Barnaskóli	85	E coast of Skálfandi	S	—	yes	96-41307
Húsavik	Skílagarður	85	E coast of Skalfandi	—	—	yes	96-41111
Húsavik	Hotel Húsavik	85	E coast of Skálfandi	A	34	—	96-41220
Laugar	Hotel Laugar	846	E of Ljósavatn, NW of Myvatn	S	70	yes	96-43120
Stórutjarnir	Hotel Edda	1	by Ljósavatn, E of Akureyri	S	24	yes	96-43221
Dalvík	Guesthouse Víkurröst	82	W coast of Eyjafjörður	S	20	yes	96-61354
Ólafsfjörður	Hotel Ólafsfjörður	82	W coast of Eyjafjörður	A	6	—	96-62400
Siglufjörður	Hotel Höfn	76	N coast, NNW of Akureyri	A	14	—	96-71514
Siglufjörður	Íþróttamiðstöðin Höll	76	N coast, NNW of Akureyri	—	—	yes	96-71284

Location	Name	Road No.	Directions	Time of Opening	No. of Rooms	Sleeping Bag Acc.	Tel. No.
Varmahlíð	Hotel Varmahlíð	1	S of Skagafjörður	A	17	yes	95-6170
Tungsveit	Steinstaðaskóli	1	S of Varmalið	S	—	yes	95-6033
Miðfjörður	Hotel Edda, Laugabakki	1	3 km S of junction with road 72	S	15	yes	95-1904
Húnavellir	Hotel Edda	724	S of Blönduós	S	23	yes	95-4370
Lýtingsstaðir	School	762	S of Mælifell	—	—	yes	95-5100
Sauðárkrókur	Hotel Mælifell	762	S of Skagafjörður	A	25	yes	95-5265
Blönduós	Youth Hostel/ Hotel Blönduós	1	W coast of Húnaflói	A	(30 beds)	yes	95-4126
Grímsey	Félagsheimilið Múli		island off N coast, N of Akureyri	—	—	yes	—

Map 6: South

Location	Name	Road No.	Directions	Time of Opening	No. of Rooms	Sleeping Bag Acc.	Tel. No.
Hella	Guesthouse Mosfell	1	SW of Hekla	A	20	yes	99-5928
Hvolsvöllur	Hotel Hvolsvöllur	1	SW of Hekla	A	20	yes	99-8351/ 8187
Fljótsdalur	Youth Hostel	261	N bank of Markarfljót, N of Eyjafjallajökull	Apr-Oct.	(15 beds)	yes	99-8498
Skógar	Hotel Edda	1	S of Eyjafjallajökull	S	34	yes	99-8870
Vík	Hotel K.S./ Guesthouse Vík	1	S of Mýrdalsjökull	A	10	yes	99-7193
Vík	Félagsheimilið Leikskálar	1	S of Mýrdalsjökull	—	—	yes	99-7184
Reynisbrekka	Youth Hostel	214	NE of Vík	Jun-Oct	(14 beds)	yes	99-7106
Kirkjubæjarklaustur	Hotel Bær	1	NE of Mýrdalsjökull	—	—	yes	99-7614
Kirkjubæjarklaustur	Hotel Edda	1	NE of Mýrdalsjökull	A	32	yes	99-7626
Laugarvatn	Hotel Edda (ML)	37	NW shore of Laugarvatn, E of Thingvallavatn	S	88	yes	99-6118

Location	Name	Road No.	Directions	Time of Opening	No. of Rooms	Sleeping Bag Acc.	Tel. No.
Laugarvatn	New Edda Hotel (HSL)	37	NW shore of Laugarvatn, E of Thingvallavatn	S	27	—	99-6154
Flúðir	Summerhotel Flúðir	30	Between rivers Hvítá and Thjórsá	S	27	—	99-6630
Flúðir	Motel Skjölborg	30	Between rivers Hvítá and Thjórsá	A	8	—	99-6624
Árnes	Félagsheimilið Árnes	32	Stórinúpur, by W bank of Thjórsá, W of Hekla	—	—	yes	99-6044
Skálholt	Guesthouse Skálholt	31	SE of Apvatn	S	10	—	99-6870
Leirubakki	Youth Hostel	26	W of Hekla, E of Skarð	Jun-Sept	(15 beds)	yes	99-5591
Heimaey	Hotel Gestgjafinn		Westman Islands, off S coast	A	14	—	98-2577
Heimaey	Guesthouse Heimir		Westman Islands, off S coast	A	22	—	98-1515
Heimaey	Youth Hostel		Westman Islands, off S coast	Jun-Sept	(30 beds)	yes	98-2315

Map 7: North-east

Location	Name	Road No.	Directions	Time of Opening	No. of Rooms	Sleeping Bag Acc.	Tel. No.
Reykjahlíð	Hotel Reykjahlíð	1	NE corner of lake Mývatn	S	12	—	96-44142
Reykjahlíð	Hotel Reynihlíð	1	NE corner of lake Mývatn	A	44	—	96-44170
Skútustaðir	School	848	S shore of Mývatn	S	—	yes	96-44279
Kópasker	Guesthouse Kaupfélags	85	E coast of Axarfjörður	A	3	yes	96-52121
Raufarhöfn	Hotel Norðurljós	85	NW coast of Thistilfjörður	S	30	yes	96-51233
Vopnafjörður	Hotel Tangi	85	W coast of Vopnafjörður	A	12	—	97-3224
Húsey	Youth Hostel	926	Héraðsflói	Jun-Sept	(20 beds)	yes	97-3010
Bakkagerði	Hotel Borg	94	in Borgarfjörður	A	2	yes	97-2943
Bakkagerði	Félagsheimilið Fjarðaborg	94	in Borgarfjörður	S	—	yes	97-2920

Map 8: East

Location	Name	Road No.	Directions	Time of Opening	No. of Rooms	Sleeping Bag Acc.	Tel. No.
Djúpivogur	Hotel Framtíð	1	E coast, opposite island of Papey	A	9	yes	97-8887
Berunes	Youth Hostel	1	N coast of Berufjörður	Jul-Sept	(30 beds)	yes	97-8988
Staðarborg	Hotel Edda	96	W of Breiðdalsvík	S	9	yes	97-5683
Breiðdalsvík	Hotel Bláfell	96	Breiðdalsvík	A	8	—	97-5770
Reyðarfjörður	Guesthouse KBH	92	Búðareyri, in Reyðarfjörður	A	3	—	97-4200
Eskifjörður	Hotel Askja	92	N coast of Reyðarfjörður	A	7	—	97-6261
Neskaupstaður	Hotel Egilsbúð	955	N coast of Norðfjörður	A	5	—	97-7321
Egilsstaðir	Hotel Egilsstaðir	1	N shore of Lagarfljót	S	15	—	97-1114
Egilsstaðir	Menntaskólinn Egilsstöðum	1	N shore of Lagarfljót	S	—	yes	97-1485
Egilsstaðir	Hotel Valaskjálf	1	N shore of Lagarfljót	S&A	24/13	yes	97-1261
Hallormsstaður	Hotel Edda	931	E shore of Lagarfljót	S	22	yes	97-1683
Eiðar	Hotel Edda	94	N of Egilsstaðir	S	60	yes	97-3803
Seyðisfjörður	Vesturveg 4	93	W coast of Seyðisfjörður, E of Egilsstaðir	—	—	—	97-2126
Seyðisfjörður	Youth Hostel	93	W coast of Seyðisfjörður, E of Egilsstaðir	Jun-Sept	(36 beds)	yes	97-2239

Map 9: South-east

Location	Name	Road No.	Directions	Time of Opening	No. of Rooms	Sleeping Bag Acc.	Tel. No.
Höfn	Hotel Höfn	99	SE of Vatnajökull	A	40	—	97-8240
Höfn	Youth Hostel	99	SE of Vatnajökull	May-Sept	(30 beds)	yes	97-8571
Nesjaskóli	Hotel Edda	99	before Höfn is reached	S	30	yes	97-8470

CAMPING AND WALKING

CAMPERS who are going by ferry will probably be taking their own equipment with them; those who are flying can hire all the necessary camping equipment (see p.96), although this must be arranged well before you leave (note that a sizeable sales tax may be added to the hire charge). Although frame tents are quite popular with Icelandic families because they can accommodate so many people, they can blow about a lot in the windy conditions. The best tent is probably a ridge tent, especially one with an extension that can be used for storage and for cooking when it is windy or raining. Since many of the sites are on stony ground with little or no soil, take a good number of long, strong pegs and a claw hammer or a hook to get them out of the ground. The wind may suddenly rise at night, so peg the tent down well. The tent should have a sewn-in groundsheet; this helps to keep out dust and water. The groundsheet can easily be damaged by stones lying on the hard ground, so take some thick polythene sheets to lay down underneath the tent; on cold nights this will also give some insulation.

The night temperature can vary a great deal in the Icelandic summer and a good sleeping bag is essential. If you think you might be cold at night, one solution is to take two bags – one to be used by itself most nights, and the other to fit over the first when it is very cold, windy or when camping near glaciers. The first bag should have a draw cord and both should be stored in waterproof stuff-bags. While some may want to take a camp bed or an air mattress, a closed-cell mat is probably more serviceable. If you hire equipment you will probably be supplied with a mattress.

If you take your own vehicle and are camping it is advisable to take as much food as possible with you as food prices are high. Those on an extended visit may be affected by the 10 kg food limit mentioned in the section on Customs (p.85); dried food provides a lightweight alternative to tins. The section on Customs also mentions those foods that cannot be taken into the country. Do not rely on being able to stock up at every settlement, always take advantage of a supermarket when you find it. Shops are closed on Sundays and not all are open on Saturdays; the only campsites with a shop are at Skaftafell and Thingvellir.

Bread is easy to get and so are various kinds of milk packaged in different coloured cartons – try the sour milk with muesli as a quick midday snack; you should also taste the uniquely Icelandic dish of *skyr* (made from curdled milk), either by itself or with fruit. There are few foods that will be new to most visitors, apart from *skyr* and the different ways of cooking and presenting lamb and fish dishes.

Keep your food in polythene bags or containers to protect it from sand.

As far as cooking is concerned, paraffin can often be bought at petrol stations as can small GAZ containers. Big GAZ cylinders and other bottled fuels may be more difficult to find, but the larger roadside shops sometimes stock them. A good first-aid kit should be carried, bearing in mind that chemists, doctors and hospitals are few and far between. Spring water is clean, so that stomach upsets are uncommon, but sediment in the glacial streams can cause irritation; these should not be used for drinking water.

Campsites

WHILE MANY of the camp sites are being upgraded as the tourist industry grows, some of them are still just open spaces set aside for tents; signs may be non-existent or not very obvious. Look out for tents or the 3m-high black triangular boxes that are the toilets. Not all the sites have WCs, but nearly all have some form of toilet. Tents can usually be erected anywhere away from settlements as long as they are not within fenced or on cultivated ground; but permission should be sought. In protected areas like Mývatn and Skaftafell, camping is restricted to organised camping sites.

Some sites have wardens on them and others may have someone who comes round in the evening to collect the (very reasonable) fees. The sign 'Tjaldstæði' means that camping is allowed; 'Tjaldstæði bönnuð' means that it is not.

The following list is not exhaustive as camping is normally allowed at the tourist huts in the interior and many small settlements will have a place set aside. These are not publicised, so visitors are often not aware of their existence.

The lists of campsites that are published in Iceland can be very confusing and may not readily differentiate between sites of varying quality. Most lists of sites are written in Icelandic and the few that have been translated into English have only included a few sites. The following list covers all the sites whose details are published and others that the author has stayed

at or seen. Swimming pools, shops, main roads and so on may be far away and that is why Part 4 goes into a lot of detail about sites – where to find them and what facilities there are on the site.

The list is arranged in nine parts – corresponding to the general map (see pp.85-86) which the sites are on. The sites are listed under the section number in which they appear in Part 4. The information is as follows:

Section: the number of the Part 4 section is given. If the site is off the author's route then this number is in brackets.

Listed: To assist in gauging the popularity of the sites, there is an asterisk beside each one that was listed in the most recent camping list produced by the Iceland Tourist Board.

Place: this is the name of the site; sometimes an alternative name is given in brackets.

Road: this is the numbered road (or track) nearest the site although the site is not necessarily on that road.

Location: this gives the position of the site relative to fjords, lakes, glaciers etc.

List of Campsites

Map 1: North-west

Section	Listed	Place	Road	Location
28		Bjarkalundur	60	near Berufjörður, at SE corner of NW fjords.
30	*	Ísafjörður	61	town at north of NW fjords.
(31)		Flateyri	64	settlement on NW of NW fjords.
31	*	Brjánslækur	62	settlement in Vatnsfjörður, on south side of NW fjords.

Map 2: West

Section	Listed	Place	Road	Location
13	*	Staður	1	SE shore of Hrútafjörður
13	*	Hreðavatn	1	by lake, NE of Borganes
(13)		Munaðarnes	1	NE of Borgarnes, SW of Hreðavatn.
13	*	Borgarnes	531	town in Borgarfjörður.

Section	Listed	Place	Road	Location
28	*	Búðardalur	60	settlement on E side of Hvammsfjörður.
28	*	Laugar	589	in Sælingsdalur, at NE corner of Hvammsfjörður.
28		Bær	60	in Króksfjördur, NW of Breiðafjörður.
32	*	Stykkishólmur	56	town on N coast of Snæfellsnes.
(32)	*	Kverná	57	near Grundarfjörður, N coast of Snæfellsnes.
32		Ólafsvík	574	settlement NW coast of Snæfellsnes.
32		Hellisandur	574	settlement on NW coast of Snæfellsnes.
32		Arnarstapi	574	settlement on SW coast of Snæfellsnes.
32	*	Búðir	38	on S coast of Snæfellsnes.
(33)		Laugagerðisskóli	567	NE corner of Faxaflói.
34	*	Húsafell	518	NE of Borgarnes and N of the Ok glacier.

Map 3: South-west

Section	Listed	Place	Road	Location
1	*	Reykjavík	1	capital, E side of Faxaflói.
2	*	Selfoss	1	town, SE of Reykjavík, S of Thingvallavatn.
(14)	*	Akranes	51	town on E side of Faxaflói.
16	*	Thingvellir	36	N shore of Thingvallavatn.
20		Kleifarvatn	42	S shore of lake, SW of Reykjavík.
(21)		Thrastalundur	35	S of Thingvallavatn, E of Ingólfsfjall.

Map 4: North

Section	Listed	Place	Road	Location
11	*	Laugar	846	S of Húsavík, E of Akureyri.
(11)	*	Vaglaskógur	836	near Háls, E of Akureyri.
12	*	Akureyri	1	W side of Eyjafjörður, N coast.
(13)		Dalvík	82	N of Akureyri.
(13)	*	Ólafsfjörður	82	NW of Akureyri, N coast.
(13)		Siglufjörður	76	NNE of Akureyri, N coast.

Section	Listed	Place	Road	Location
(13)	*	Fljót	76	in Fljótavík, SW of Siglufjörður, N coast.
(13)	*	Sauðárkrókur	75	SW of Skagafjörður, N coast.
13	*	Varmahlíð	1	S of Sauðárkrókur.
13	*	Blönduós	1	E side of Húnafjörður, N coast.
13	*	Stóra Giljá	1	E of Hóp, S of Blönduós.
(13)		Hvammstangi	72	E side of Miðfjörður.
27	*	Húsavík	85	E side of Skjálfandi, N coast.

Map 5: Central highlands

Section	Listed	Place	Road	Location
36	*	Hveravellir	F37	between Langjökull and Hofsjökull.
38	*	Nýidalur	F28	SW of Tungnafellsjökull.

Map 6: South

Section	Listed	Place	Road	Location
2	*	Hella	1	SW of Hekla.
3		Hvolsvöllur	1	SE of Hella.
3	*	Skógar	1	S of Eyjafjallajökull.
3	*	Vík	1	S of Mýrdalsjökull.
4	*	Hrífunes	1	E of Mýrdalsjökull.
4	*	Kirkjubæjarklaustur	1	SW of Vatnajökull.
17	*	Laugarvatn	37	E of Thingvallavatn.
17	*	Geysir	35	S of Langjökull.
17		Gullfoss	35	S of Langjökull.
18		Flúðir	30	between Hvítá and Thjórsá rivers.
18		Árnes	32	N of river Thjórsá, W of Hekla.
18	*	Thjórsárdalur	32	W of Búrfell, which is W of Hekla.
19		Galtalækur	26	W of Hekla.
19		Leirubakki	26	W of Hekla.
23	*	Heimaey		on Westman Islands, off S coast.
(39)	*	Veiðivötn	off F28	SE of Thórisvatn.
41	*	Landmannalaugar	F22	E of Hekla.
42		Eldgjá	F22	NE of Mýrdalsjökull.
43	*	Thórsmörk (Básar, Langidalur, Húsadalur)	249	N of Eyjafjallajökull.

Section	Listed	Place	Road	Location
		Map 7: North-east		
(9)		Vopnafjörður	85	Vopnafjörður, fjord in NE.
10	*	Reykjahlíð (Mývatn)	1	N side of Mývatn.
10	*	Skútustaðir	848	S side of Mývatn.
26	*	Ásbyrgi	85	SE of Axarfjörður, N coast.
(26)		Raufarhöfn	85	on very NE of coast.
(26)	*	Thórshöfn	85	in Thistilfjörður, NE coast.
27	*	Vesturdalur	862	S of Ásbyrgi, W side of Jökulsá á Fjöllum.
(27)		Skúlagarður	861	S of Axarfjörður, N coast.
		Map 8: East		
7	*	Thórisdalur	1	near Stafafell, NE of Höfn.
7	*	Djúpivogur	1	Berufjörður, E fjords.
7	*	Berunes	1	Berufjörður, E fjords.
7	*	Breiðdalsvík	97	Breiðdalsvík, E fjords.
8	*	Stöðvarfjörður	96	Stöðvarfjörður, E fjords.
8		Búðir	96	Fáskrúðsfjörður, E fjords.
(8)	*	Búðareyri (Reyðarfjörður)	92	Reyðarfjörður, E fjords.
(8)		Eskifjörður	92	Reyðarfjörður, E fjords.
(8)	*	Neskaupstaður	92	Norðfjörður, E fjords.
8	*	Egilsstaðir	1	N shore of Lögurinn, just inland from E fjords.
(9)	*	Hvannalindir	F98	N of Vatnajökull, E of Jökulsá á Fjöllum.
24	*	Seyðisfjörður	93	Seyðisfjörður, E fjords.
25	*	Atlavík (Hallormstaður)	931	E shore of Lögurinn, just inland from E fjords.
40	*	Herðubreiðalindir	F88	E of Herðubreið, NE of Askja.
		Map 9: South-east		
5	*	Skaftafell	1	W of Öræfajökull.
6		Kvíárjökull	1	SE of Öræfajökull.
6	*	Höfn	1	E of Vatnajökull.

Walking

WARM CLOTHING is essential as the wind can bring the temperature down very quickly, and those venturing into the highlands have to be prepared for very cold conditions. Waterproofs (jacket and leggings) are also needed, as are good walking boots, a warm jacket, gloves and a hat. Rubber boots are often useful in marshy areas or by rivers. In general the ground drains very quickly as the water percolates through the lava, except in those places where there is a lot of clay and here the wet clay can stick to your boots and clog up the treads, making walking hazardous. The sharp rock can also rip boots apart. Glacial rivers can run quickly and are often difficult and dangerous to cross, especially during warm weather (and during the afternoon) when more ice will melt. Much of the rock is loose and the hillsides are often covered with scree, making walking slow and tricky at times. The scree is very sharp so a ready supply of sticking plaster is handy as the sharp stones can easily cut hands or knees. But the greatest danger in the hills is isolation; if you are alone and injured it may be a long time before anyone else sees or hears you.

Since many of the lavafields have few individually recognisable features it is easy to get lost in them; a compass should therefore be carried as well as a whistle and torch for safety, but be aware that compass deviation may be high. These remarks might give the impression of some danger; in fact going for a walk or trek in the lowlands poses problems that are similar to those encountered in the Scottish Highlands and experienced walkers who take sensible precautions will be able to enjoy some breathtaking scenery. A final word about lowland glaciers: in spring, snow has covered many of the crevasses making them potentially lethal traps; in summer the snouts can be walked on, but this should only be done with crampons and an ice-axe. Long walks on the glaciers should only be attempted by those with proper equipment and experience. Icelandic glaciers are temperate, thus their surfaces are often wet, slippery and dangerous. Attempts on Vatnajökull and the other highland glaciers should only be made by full-scale expeditions.

Those attempting long walks, especially through the interior, must be aware of the special dangers they are letting themselves in for – fast rivers, snow/sand storms, high winds and an absence of shelter are the main hazards. For advice on particular routes, a touring club (see p.96) should be contacted, while large groups and expeditions from the UK should seek assistance from the Young Explorers' Trust (see p.101).

One problem that is mentioned several times in Part 4 is that posed by overaggressive birds, particularly skuas. The author made his own 'anti-skua device' by attaching a nylon 'flag' to a long bamboo pole which could be hand-held or fastened by elastic bands to a rucksack. This worked well and the skuas wheeled away before getting too near. Those venturing onto the glacial sands on the south coast should make one of these or be prepared for an unnerving experience!

Conservation

FOR A WHOLE NUMBER of reasons, such as low temperature, winds, eruptions, and over-grazing, the Icelandic soil is poor and in many places is non-existent, and the country's ecology is correspondingly delicate. In the past not enough was done to conserve the environment. However, many of the past mistakes, especially over-grazing, are now being recognised. The country's scenery is its main attraction to the visitor – whether it is in the richness of the valleys or the barren wastes of the interior and the following points should be borne in mind to help conserve this unique environment:

1. Keep to the roads and tracks. Motorcyclists (both Icelandic and foreign) are probably the worst culprits as tyre marks can destroy plants and remain as significant scars on the poorly constituted ground for years to come.
2. Plants should not be uprooted.
3. Do not light open fires near vegetation, or use plants as kindling.
4. Rubbish should not be buried or thrown away.
5. Do not disturb birds' nests or eggs. Photography

of eagles, falcons, snowy owls and little auks on their nests is forbidden without a permit.

The Nature Conservation Council has been established to ensure protection of the natural heritage (such as landscapes, rock formations and endangered species) and a great number of places are now protècted. Some of these are small, perhaps just a waterfall, while others are massive, for instance the peninsula of Hornstrandir in the north-west fjords. Within certain protected areas, Mývatn, for instance, camping is restricted to recognised sites and further regulations may be made to protect the delicate environment. In some cases, these new regulations have come too late; the area of wilderness has been increasing, and expensive methods of conservation have had to be employed, such as using light aircraft to seed deserts. The next few years may see more regulations aimed at protecting the country's natural beauty. Unfortunately its almost impossible to stop selfish and lazy people from driving everywhere: visitors to places like Lúdent and Askja will see tracks going right up to the rims of these craters.

DOCUMENTS AND CURRENCY

Passports and Visas

VISITORS are divided into 3 groups for passport and visa purposes.

Group 1

Visitors from the following countries require neither passports nor visas: Denmark, Faroes, Finland, Greenland, Norway, Sweden.

Group 2

Visitors from the following countries require a passport (or else an equivalent acceptable document) but not a visa: Australia, Austria, Bahamas, Barbados, Belgium, Botswana, Brazil, Bulgaria, Canada, Chile, Cyprus, Dominica, Fiji, France, Gambia, Greece, Grenada, Guyana, Holland, India, Ireland, Israel, Italy, Jamaica, Japan, Lesotho, Liechtenstein, Luxembourg, Malawi, Malaysia, Malta, Morocco, Mauritius, Mexico, Monaco, New Zealand, Portugal, Romania, San Marino, Singapore, South Korea, Spain, Swaziland, Switzerland, Tanzania, Trinidad and Tobago, Tunisia, UK (see note), USA, West Germany, Vatican, Yugoslavia.

Note

A UK Visitor's Passport is acceptable. The following colonies and territories are treated as British for visa purposes: Bermuda, British Honduras, Cayman Islands, Falkland Islands, Gibraltar, Hong Kong, Leeward Islands (Antigua, St Kitts-Nevis, Anguilla, Montserrat and Virgin Islands), New Hebrides, St Helena, Seychelle Islands, Turks and Caicos Islands, West Pacific Islands (Gilbert and Ellice Islands and British Solomon Islands), Windward Islands (Dominica, St Lucia and St Vincent Islands).

Group 3

Visitors from all other countries must carry a visa in their passports. These can be obtained from Icelandic representatives abroad (see pp.99-101).

Visitors may be asked to show upon arrival that they have adequate funds for their stay; that their passport has a valid permit back to their country of origin or another country and that they have a valid return travel ticket. Entry is for a period of 3 months and if an extension is required, an application should be made to the police for the necessary permission.

Research permits

THOSE INVOLVED with expeditions will have to ensure that they have obtained all the necessary documentation, including a research permit from the Iceland National Research Council. Expeditions or educational groups who have the permit or an 'Announcement' from the Council will usually be exempted from the 10 kg food limit. However, this exemption should be arranged well before your arrival.

Vehicle documentation

THE FOLLOWING ITEMS are required by those taking a car into the country:

1. Driving licence (This is also needed by anyone hiring a car).
2. International Driving Permit (1926 Convention). This can be issued by a motoring club (for instance, AA in US or UK). It is also needed by anyone hiring a car.
3. Insurance Certificate from your insurance company.
4. International Motor Insurance Certificate ('Green Card'). If you are travelling via the Faroes then this must be valid for Denmark as well.
5. Vehicle Registration Certificate.
6. Nationality Identification Plate or sticker.

While some of these documents might not be asked for at the Customs, they may be necessary if you have an accident.

When you arrive you will be given a Customs declaration form to complete. Keep your copy as you will need it when you leave the country. A label is attached to the vehicle's windscreen showing the date on which the vehicle is leaving. Should you want to keep the vehicle in the country past this date then contact the Customs. No spare fuel should be carried in fuel cans and the total limit of fuel that can be brought in is 200 litres (44 Imperial gallons or 37 US gallons).

Miscellaneous documents

THE FOLLOWING is a checklist of other items that may be needed:

1. Travel insurance. This is essential and should cover personal belongings, sickness, repatriation, vehicle, hire of an alternative vehicle after a breakdown, etc. Take the policy with you so you know what you are covered for and who to contact should you need help. Your insurance company will probably have an agent in Iceland; find out their name before you go. In the event of an accident the agent should be contacted and it will obviously save some problems if the travel and vehicle insurances are dealt with by the same company/agent/broker at home. If you are taking a car, check that it is covered for the voyage.
2. Camping carnet. This is not required for campsites but its insurance (third party cover while on a campsite) may be useful if this is not covered by your travel (or household) insurance.
3. Vaccination Certificates. Generally speaking, there are no specific requirements for vaccination certificates, but this may change according to any outbreaks of particular diseases. At present, visitors who have lived in or have passed through Djibouti, Ethiopia, Kenya or Somalia within fourteen days of arriving in Iceland must have a valid smallpox vaccination certificate.
4. Motor club membership card. This is needed if you wish to use the services of the FIB.

Currency

THE MAJOR UNIT of Icelandic currency is the Króna (kr), which is divided into 100 Aurar. There are banknotes of 10kr, 50kr, 100kr, 500kr and 1,000kr.

Do not buy Icelandic currency before you leave home as the rate of exchange will probably be bad. Instead, currency can be obtained on board the ferry or at Keflavík airport; many hotels in Reykjavík (and elsewhere) will change money for you as well. Banks can be found in the towns but in the smaller settlements they may only be open a couple of afternoons each week so it is best to keep a reasonable amount of cash on you. This is especially important if you have a vehicle as you may need cash for fuel or repairs. Once a bank has been found, there is no difficulty in cashing cheques (with an international cheque card), or travellers' cheques (although you may need your Passport as proof of identity). Credit cards may not be accepted in the country areas but many hotels (including the Edda hotels) will accept the major cards as may other firms who deal with tourists (such as car hire and bus companies, bookshops and restaurants). There is no limit to the amount of foreign currency that can be taken into Iceland. Your currency exchange receipts should be kept as you may be asked to show them when you re-exchange your Icelandic currency.

Customs Regulations

RECENT (1983) regulations limit the amount of food that can be taken in to 10 kg per person. The following foods are not allowed in: uncooked meat and meat products, eggs, poultry products, butter and uncooked milk.

Other restricted items are: live animals and birds, medicines (except for personal use), narcotics, poisons, firearms and ammunition. Those with flares should make enquiries about whether they are regarded as 'firearms'.

Visitors aged 15 or over may bring in 250 g of tobacco (200 cigarettes) duty free. The duty-free limit for alcohol (for those over 20 years old) is one litre of spirits and either one litre of wine or 12 bottles of imported or 24 of Icelandic beer.

Up to 3000kr can be taken through Customs (either way), in denominations of 100kr or less.

Fishing equipment (waders, boots, rods and so on) and horse-riding equipment will have to be disinfected at the Customs if you have not got a certificate of disinfection from a vet. This does not apply to unused equipment.

MAPS

THE COUNTRY is well covered by the various series of maps produced by the Iceland Geodetic Survey. However, maps can be very difficult to obtain outside Iceland; specialist travel book and map stockists may well not have them but your tour operator may have limited stocks. In Britain, Dick Phillips specialises in supplying maps; Sonicworld also supply maps from their Crawley office (see p.99).

1. Road Maps

Touring Map (1:500 000), 1984.

Whole island on 2 sides with the following shown: garages, huts, petrol stations, airfields, road numbers, type of road/track and a number of other details. Very suitable for general touring but obviously limited in amount of detail that can be included at such a scale. All drivers should take this map.

Little Touring Map (1:1 000 000), 1982.

One side shows relief, the other just roads (and their numbers), rivers, lakes, towns and glaciers. Useful for general route planning, but not much else.

Tourist Map of Iceland (1:750 000), 1981.

This is published by the Touring Club of Iceland. Similar to the Little Touring Map but with rather more detail.

2. General Maps Series 1:250 000

These are very useful for touring the country and give a mass of detail; indeed the amount of this can sometimes be confusing. The 9 maps show contours, types of land surface, roads, settlements, farms and so on. Nearly all farms and rivers are marked and since there are often signs outside farms and on bridges, it is easy to use these maps to find out exactly where you are.

In the Guide the lists of hotels, camping sites and road distances refer to these maps. On the back of each map there is an excellent index listing settlements, rivers, farms, hills and their position within a grid system; these indexes are invaluable. If you are not venturing into the north-western fjords or the highlands then maps 1 and 5 respectively are not needed. The only overlap between the maps is with maps 4 and 5. References in the Guide to places that are in this overlap area are listed under map 4.

Anyone driving over one of the interior tracks should, without fail, always have the appropriate general map.

The list below gives the most recent editions (the main changes made in new editions are in the road system, especially any modifications to the ring road). Those travelling through the interior may find new roads or tracks going to power station sites which may not be shown on the maps.

Map no.	Area covered	Most recent edition
1	north-west	1979
2	west	1981
3	south-west	1979
4	north	1980
5	central highlands	1981
6	south	1980
7	north-east	1970
8	east	1980
9	south-east	1976

Eight of the above-mentioned maps are also available printed back to back (ie 1 and 2, 3 and 6, 4 and 7, 8 and 9). These are cheaper than the single-sided sheets but omit the useful index.

3. Special Maps
These cover the following places:

Area	Scale	Date
Thingvellir (double-sided)	1:25 000	1969
Hekla	1:50 000	1979
Mývatn	1:50 000	1974
Hornstrandir (northern part of NW fjords)	1:100 000	1982
Öræfajökull	1:100 000	
(Skaftafell on reverse)	1:25 000	1979
Westman Islands and Surtsey	1:50 000	1978
Reykjavík (double-sided street map of city and suburbs, with index)	1:15 000	1977

Care has to be taken over the designation of 'road' and 'track' and their suitability for the vehicle you have. Roads are usually shown by a continuous line on the maps and should (in summer) be passable to all vehicles. Tracks (for four-wheel drive vehicles only) are shown in dotted lines or in different colours and have to be treated with care as the various maps available show some variation in their classification. One good example is the track running to the north-east of Hofsjökull in the central highlands which is given a higher classification on the Little Touring Map and the 1:750 000 Tourist Map than on the 1:500 000 Touring Map. Since the bus service does not run on this track it is best not followed anyway, but the moral is that you should seek local advice before attempting roads or tracks that you think may be tricky, and the maps should be interpreted in the light of this advice. Pre-planning a route before you leave is all very well, but road conditions can easily change for better or worse after the map has been published.

The 1:500 000 map is probably the most reliable as far as road and track designations are concerned.

Unless you have a particular interest in one area, the 1:250 000 General Map Series and the 1:500 000 Touring Map should be sufficient for travelling through the country. Free tourist maps of Reykjavík and Akureyri are available from their respective Tourist Offices. Small free maps of the Jökulsárgljúfur and Skaftafell National Parks and of Mývatn can be obtained from the campsites there. A comprehensive list of other maps available, including school, geological and vegetation maps, is provided in the Bibliography (see p.259).

LANGUAGE AND VOCABULARY

THE COUNTRY'S physical isolation has meant that the language has changed little since it was taken to the island. It is difficult to learn and most visitors are soon glad to discover that English, Danish, Norwegian and German are understood by many of those working in Reykjavík's tourist trade.

Pronunciation: consonants and vowels
THE LANGUAGE is based on the Latin alphabet and has two extra consonants:

'þ', pronounced like 'th' in 'thin' eg Þingvellir.
'ð' (capital: 'Ð'), pronounced like 'th' in 'that' eg Hveragerði.

In this book 'þ' has been written 'th'.

Other consonants that often give problems are:

j pronounced 'y' as in Langjökull.
ll pronounced 'dl' as in Hella.
hv pronounced 'kv' as in Hvolsvöllur.

The vowel sounds are pronounced approximately as follows:

a as in 'bath'
á as in 'now'
e as in 'each'
é as in 'yet'
i as in 'hit'
í as in 'seen'
o as in 'hot'
ó as in 'toe'
ö as in 'turn'
u as in 'earn'
ú as in 'soon'
æ as in 'I'

Vocabulary
THE FOLLOWING English-Icelandic and Icelandic-English lists of words are intended to help visitors read leaflets, brochures, timetables and maps as well as make themselves understood in matters concerning transport, accommodation, and shopping. Most Icelanders in regular contact with visitors, for instance those working in hotels, big shops, car hire and banks, are likely to speak English. It is really only out in the countryside that communicating may be difficult. In general, young people have a reasonable to good understanding of English.

English-Icelandic Vocabulary
Places in towns

alcohol shop	*áfengisbúð*
bank	*banki*
barber shop	*hárgreiðslustofa* or *rakarastofa*
bookshop	*bókabúð*
bridge	*brú*
chemist	*apótek*
church	*kirkja*
cinema	*bíó*
college	*menntaskóli*
community centre	*félagsheimili*
conference	*fundur*
dentist	*tannlæknir*
doctor	*læknir*
dry cleaning	*hreinsun*
exhibition	*sýning*
fishing permit	*veiðileyfi*
golf course	*golf völlur*

hairdresser	*hárskeri* or *rakari*		restaurant	*veitingastaður*
harbour	*bryggja*		room	*herbergi*
hospital	*spítali*		shower	*sturta*
house	*hús*		sleeping bag	*svefnpoki*
information office	*upplýsingaskrifstofa*		sleeping bag	
laundry	*thvottahús*		accommodation	*svefnpoka gisting*
lavatory	*salerni*		tent	*tjald*
library	*bókasafn*		waiter	*thjónn*
museum	*safn*		warden	*vörður*
opera house	*óperuhús*		youth hostel	*farfuglaheimili*
optician	*augnlæknir*			
park	*garður*			

Documents, customs

police station	*lögreglustöð*		beer	*bjór*
post office	*pósthús*		briefcase	*skjalataska*
river	*á* or *fljót*		camera bag	*myndavélataska*
road	*vegur*		cash	*reiðufé*
roundabout	*hringtorg*		cheque	*ávísun*
sauna	*gufubað*		cigarettes	*sígarettur*
school	*skóli*		credit card	*kredit kort*
shop	*búð*		customs	*tollur*
stadium	*leikvöllur*		driving licence	*ökuskírteini*
street	*gata*		duty-free	*tollfrjáls*
supermarket	*stórmarkaður*		handbag	*handtaska*
swimming pool	*sundlaug*		luggage	*farangur*
telegram	*skeyti*		parcel	*böggull*
telephone	*sími*		passport	*vegabréf*
theatre	*leikhús*		perfume	*ilmvatn*
travel agent	*ferðaskrifstofa*		photograph	*mynd*
university	*háskóli*		present	*gjöf*
viewdial	*útsýnisskífa*		signature	*undirskrift*
			spirits	*alkohól* or *áfengi*
			suitcase	*ferðataska*

Accommodation, eating out

bath	*bað*		tobacco	*tóbak*
bathroom	*baðherbergi*		travellers cheque	*ferðatékkar*
bed	*rúm*		visa	*áritað vegabréf*
bedroom	*svefnherbergi*		wine	*vín*
breakfast	*morgunmatur*			
cafeteria	*kaffitería*			

Numbers

campsite	*tjaldstæði*		0	*núll*
dining room	*borðstofa*		1	*einn*
evening meal	*kvöldmatur*		2	*tveir*
guest house	*gestahús*		3	*thrír*
hotel	*hótel*		4	*fjórir*
hotel bill	*reikningur*		5	*fimm*
hotel manager	*hótelstjóri*		6	*sex*
hut	*kofi*		7	*sjö*
kitchen	*eldhús*		8	*átta*
mattress	*dína*		9	*níu*
meal	*máltið* or *matur*		10	*tíu*
menu	*matseðill*		11	*ellefu*
night	*nótt*		12	*tólf*

13	*threttán*
14	*fjórtán*
15	*fimmtán*
16	*sextán*
17	*sautján*
18	*átján*
19	*nítján*
20	*tuttugu*
21	*tuttugu og einn*
22	*tuttugu og tveir*
30	*thrjátíu*
40	*fjörutíu*
50	*fimmtíu*
60	*sextíu*
70	*sjötíu*
80	*áttatíu*
90	*níutíu*
100	*hundrað*
1,000	*thúsund*
1,000,000	*milljón*

Calendar

January	*Janúar*
February	*Febrúar*
March	*Marz*
April	*Apríl*
May	*Maí*
June	*Júní*
July	*Júlí*
August	*Ágúst*
September	*September*
October	*Október*
November	*Nóvember*
December	*Desember*
Sunday	*Sunnudagur*
Monday	*Mánudagur*
Tuesday	*Thriðjudagur*
Wednesday	*Miðvikudagur*
Thursday	*Fimmtudagur*
Friday	*Föstudagur*
Saturday	*Laugardagur*
month	*mánuður*
week	*vika*
year	*ár*

Time

morning	*morgunn*
afternoon	*síðdegi*
evening	*kvöld*
midday	*hádegi*

midnight	*miðnætti*
today	*í dag*
tomorrow	*á morgun*
yesterday	*í gær*

Expressions

good day	*góðan daginn*
goodbye	*bless*
yes	*já*
no	*nei*
please	*gerið svo vel*
thank you	*takk fyrir*
how much?	*hversu mikið*
how many?	*hversu mörg*
how long?	*hversu langt*
why?	*af hverju*
what?	*hvað*
who?	*hver*
how?	*hvernig*
when?	*hvenær*
where?	*hvar*
how far?	*hve langt*

Transport

aeroplane	*flugvél*
airport	*flugvöllur*
bicycle	*hjól*
boarding pass	*brottfarar spjald*
bus	*rúta*
bus station	*rútustöð*
car hire	*bílaleiga*
car park	*bílastæði*
fare	*fargjald*
ferry	*ferja*
passenger	*farthegi*
pony	*hestur*
rowing boat	*árabátur*
ship	*skip*
taxi	*leigubíll*
ticket	*miði*
timetable	*tímatafla*

Vehicles

accident	*slys*
alternator	*altonator*
brake	*bremsur*
breakdown	*bilaður*
broken	*brotinn*
car	*bíll*
car battery	*geymir*
carburettor	*carburretor*

clutch	*kúpling*
diesel	*dísel*
dynamo	*dínamór*
engine	*vél*
exhaust system	*púströr*
fan belt	*viftureim*
fuel can	*bensínbrúsi*
fuel tank	*bensín (or dísel) mælir*
garage	*verkstæði*
gear box	*gírkassi*
grease	*feiti*
hammer	*hamar*
headlamps	*aðalljós*
horn	*flauta*
inner tube	*slanga í dekki*
lights	*ljós*
motor cycle	*mótorhjól*
oil	*olía*
petrol	*bensín*
petrol station	*bensínstöð*
pump	*pumpa*
puncture	*sprungið*
roof rack	*grind*
screwdriver	*skrúfjárn*
spade	*skófla*
spanner	*skiptilykill*
suspension	*dempari*
tyre	*dekk*
water	*vatn*
wheel	*felga*
windscreen	*framrúða*
windscreen wipers	*thurkublöð*

Food

bread	*brauð*
butter	*smjör*
cereal	*kornmatur*
cheese	*ostur*
chicken	*kjúklingur*
chocolate	*súkkulaði*
coffee	*kaffi*
egg	*egg*
jam	*sulta*
margarine	*smjörlíki*
meat	*kjöt*
milk	*mjólk*
pepper	*pipar*
potatoes	*kartöflur*
rice	*hrísgrjón*
salt	*salt*

soup	*súpa*
sour milk	*súrmjólk*
sugar	*sykur*
tea	*te*
tomatoes	*tómatur*
yoghurt	*jógúrt*

Topographical

The words listed below are often used as suffixes in the names of physical features and in Icelandic place names, eg:

rivers: *Hvítá, Thjórsá* ('*á*' means 'river')
valleys: *Kaldidalur, Bárðardalur* ('*dalur*' means 'valley')
mountains: *Hverfjall, Ingólfsfjall* ('*fjall*' means 'mountain')
lakes: *Mývatn, Thingvallavatn* ('*vatn*' means 'lake')

á	*river*
austur	*east*
bær	*farm*
bakki	*river bank*
bjarg	*cliff*
borg	*town*
botn	*valley bottom*
brekka	*slope*
brú	*bridge*
dalur	*valley*
djúp	*long inlet (to fjord)*
drangur	*rock column*
dyngja	*shield volcano*
ey	*island*
eyri	*sand spit*
eystri	*eastern*
fell	*hill*
fjall	*mountain*
fjörður	*fjord*
fljót	*large river*
flói	*large bay*
foss	*waterfall*
gígur	*crater*
gil	*gorge*
gjá	*fissure*
heiði	*moorland*
hellir	*cave*
hlíð	*hillside*
höfði	*promontory*
höfn	*harbour*
hóll	*rounded hill*
hólmur	*small island*
hraun	*lavafield*
hver	*hot spring*

hvoll	*hill*		strönd	*coast*
innri	*inner*		suður	*south*
jökull	*glacier*		syðri	*southern*
jökulsá	*glacial river*		thing	*assembly place*
kirkja	*church*		tindur	*summit*
klettur	*rock*		tjörn	*small lake*
kvísl	*river*		vatn	*lake*
laug	*hot spring*		vegur	*road*
lækur	*stream*		vestri	*western*
lón	*lagoon*		vestur	*west*
mörk	*woodland*		vík	*bay*
múli	*headland*		vogur	*inlet*
mýri	*marsh*		völlur	*plain*
nes	*headland*		ytri	*outer*
norður	*north*			
núpur	*peak*		**Notices and Signs**	
nyrðri	*northern*		vinstri	*left*
öræfi	*wasteland*		hægri	*right*
ós	*estuary*		karlar	*men*
reykur	*smoke*		konur	*women*
rif	*reef*		einstefna	*one way*
sandur	*glacial sands*		bannað	*not allowed*
skarð	*mountain pass*		varúð	*be careful ('danger')*
sker	*reef*		ýta	*push*
skógur	*woods*		draga	*pull*
slétta	*plain*		tjaldstæði	*camping is allowed*
staður	*parish*		tjaldstæði bönnuð	*no camping*

PHOTOGRAPHY

Choice of Equipment

ALMOST every visitor to Iceland will want to take a camera. While most types of modern cameras will perform adequately, the most adaptable is certainly the 35mm single lens reflex. The great advantages of this camera are that it records whatever is seen in the viewfinder and that it is compatible with a great variety of interchangeable lenses. The most useful lenses will obviously depend on the user's particular interests, but a 35mm (or 28mm) focal length for landscapes will probably get most use. A stan-dard lens (50mm focal length) and a short tele-photo may be wanted for shots of more distant objects and a lens of 400mm or more is needed for bird photography. The author found a macro lens valuable for close-ups of cinders, plants and silica deposits, but the good depth of field and close focusing ability of a wide-angle lens can manage quite a number of these photographs.

Before leaving home the camera and lenses should be thoroughly cleaned with a blower brush. If the camera or any of the lenses are new then run a film through and check that everything is working properly. Above all, make sure that you know how all the equipment works: film is cheap, but a repeat holiday to retake photographs is an expensive business. For those taking bird photographs, a motor drive or an autowinder is a useful addition, as well as coming in handy when photographing Strokkur and the pits of boiling mud (and an eruption if you manage to see one!).

As the sun never gets very high, the brilliance of the light is not comparable to that found in countries to the south, so whether print or slide film is taken, medium-speed film (eg Kodachrome 64) will cover most needs, but a faster film (eg Ektachrome 200) may be required on duller days or for some action shots. Visibility is normally very good as there is no air pollution, but will be very poor should clouds come down. Grey, cloudy days may need an amber filter to warm up the pictures. The sky is not as blue as in southern countries so if you want deep blue skies then take a polarising filter. Buy all the film that you think you will need – then buy some more – as film is prohibitively expensive in Iceland. It is probably not worth sending film away for processing until you get home as there is virtually no chance of a vehicle being broken into and equipment being stolen.

Protecting Equipment
ONE OF THE great dangers to photographic equipment is vibration, especially when travelling on tracks. Equipment should never be able to roll about on a car or bus seat, so keep it in a bag or, best of all, in a box lined with foam rubber. Lens hoods are very useful as apart from shielding the lens from unwanted light (especially directly from the sun) they also protect the lens from small sideways knocks that might otherwise break the skylight filter. Dust is the other great enemy. Whenever possible keep the camera in its case, and unless you are using a tripod or an autowinder keep the part of the case that fits over the back of the camera on all the time as this gives it some protection against both dust and vibration. The easiest way to protect gear and to transport a number of items is by using a soft shoulder bag, with the lenses in cases or pouches in this. Just walking about in a lavafield or over moraines can kick up a great deal of dust, so only open the bag when necessary and clean it out every few days. The dust can easily get into the camera or the lenses, so protect both when changing lenses; keep a skylight filter and a lens cap on the lens and clean both periodically. The camera should also be cleaned out frequently by using a blower brush and by firing the shutter a few times every time a film is changed as this dislodges dust from around the mirror box. Battery contacts can be fouled up by dust so these should be wiped occasionally. Make sure that the blower brush, tissues and cloths are kept in a polythene bag away from the sand.

In cold weather keep the camera under your jacket when not in use and keep a spare battery in a pocket where it will be warm. When the weather is very cold the film can become brittle and the fast winding-on speed of an autowinder or motor drive can snap it.

When indoors, keep the camera in a bag and let it reach room temperature slowly; if you expose the cold camera body to warm moist air it will get covered by condensation.

Film should never be left on a car window ledge as it can easily be damaged by excessive heat; this is even more important after the film has been exposed. If you want to protect film (especially fast film or infra-red film) from the summer heat in a car then take an insulated 'cool-box' normally used to keep food cool, or make your own container using foam rubber or polystyrene. If film is taken by plane, then carry it on your person or in personal luggage and ask for the films (and cameras if they have films in them) to be hand-searched. In case you cannot get a hand-search then you can use a lead-lined pouch that will protect film from low-dosage X-ray machines; however the pouch offers no protection from high-dosage X-ray machines. Finally, do not take film marked 'Professional' as this is meant to be refrigerated before use and processed immediately after exposure.

Exposure

THE MAIN picture-taking difficulty will be on or by the glaciers, especially with an automatic camera, as the large area of white ice or snow in the viewfinder will 'fool' the camera into under-exposing the picture, so that the white ice or snow becomes a mid-grey and the surroundings quite dark. This is inevitable with an automatic camera, but manual cameras and those with manual override can be adjusted easily: either take a meter reading from another part of the scene or go by the film manufacturer's own instructions which tell what shutter speed and aperture to use for different strengths of sunlight. Another way to solve the difficulty is to use an 'incident light' meter. Lastly, the author's own method is to take a light reading 'off the hand' (ie with the palm held a few centimetres in front of the meter) and then open the lens up a stop to get an 'average' exposure setting.

During the winter the sun is seen for a short time (if at all) and on the shortest day of the year, December 22nd, Reykjavík has its sunrise at 11.20 and its sunset at 15.30. Akureyri, Húsavík, Ísafjörður and many other northern towns and settlements do not see the sun at all in mid-winter, but Mývatn (because of its altitude) may get around an hour of sunlight then. Even in places where the sun is seen, much of the light comes from the open sky and so the moment of sunrise or sunset might not affect light levels a great deal. With little direct sunlight, the landscape can be bathed in an eerie pale-blue light with no (or only very weak) shadows, so contrast is greatly reduced.

It is probably best to take fast film (400 ASA) during mid-winter, especially in the north; at Easter and in autumn slower film (perhaps 64 or 100 ASA) can be used, but some faster film should be taken as well. Fast film will certainly be needed with long (and heavy) lenses and a light tripod may be useful. The blueness of winter light can be 'warmed-up' by using an amber filter, but some photographers may want to use the colour to convey the feeling of cold.

Purchase and Repair

PHOTOGRAPHIC shops are only found in Reykjavík, Akureyri and Húsavík, though film can be bought in most settlements, but be prepared to spend a lot of money as spares can cost a great deal. As an insurance against camera failure, it is best to take a second camera. Remember to take at least one extra battery.

Should you need to buy film, the most commonly available 35mm types are: colour print: Kodak VR 100; colour transparency: Kodachrome 25; monochrome: Ilford FP4.

The makes of film that are available are: Agfa, Fuji, Ilford, Kodak (including instant picture), Polaroid, Vericolour, 3M.

The most common camera makes are: Canon, Kodak, Konica, Nikon, Olympus and Pentax. These and the following can normally be repaired in Reykjavík: Fujica, Minolta, Polaroid, Vivitar and Yashica. The only other types found are Bronica, Chinon, Hannimex, Hasselblad, Mamiya, Praktica, Ricoh and Topcon.

MISCELLANEOUS INFORMATION

Shopping

The most popular Icelandic goods to buy as presents are undoubtedly the splendid woollen goods: jumpers, cardigans, hats, blankets and so on. They are expensive but are of high quality and are good-looking. Many shops in Reykjavík stock them so it is worth shopping around.

The cost of living is very high, with prices often two to three times those found elsewhere in the West. Food grown in Iceland (such as milk, meat and fish) may be quite cheap but anything that is imported is probably expensive. Prices are not stable so check with your tour operator for up-to-date information.

Alcohol

Alcohol can be difficult to obtain in Iceland as there are no 'pubs' and licensed hotels are few in number outside the capital. The section on Reykjavík in Part 4 lists the hotels with bars and gives the names of some of the licensed restaurants.

The only retail outlets for strong alcohol are in Reykjavík (Lindargata 46, Laugarásvegur 1 and Snorrabraut), Akranes, Akureyri, Heimaey, Ísafjörður, Keflavík, Sauðárkrókur, Seyðisfjörður, Siglufjörður.

Icelanders living some distance away from these retail outlets often get their drink by post. The difficulty of getting alcohol today stems from the time of total prohibition (1915-1922); local beers are available but they are much weaker than beers from the rest of Europe. The national drink is a spirit called *brennivín* – sometimes called 'the black death' on account of the colour of the label on the bottle.

Time

Iceland is on Greenwich Mean Time throughout the year, so during the summer it is one hour behind British Summer Time. New York is five hours behind Iceland from November-April, four hours behind from May-October.

Electricity

The electrical system supplies 220v at 50Hz. Two-pin continental-type plugs are used.

Public holidays

New Year's Day, Maundy Thursday, Good Friday, Easter Monday, first day of summer, Labour Day (May 1st), Ascension Day, Whit Monday, National Day (June 17th), August Bank Holiday, Christmas Eve, Christmas Day, Boxing Day, New Year's Eve.

Icelandic names

Icelanders do not have a system of family names as in many other countries and a child takes his/her surname from the father's forename. Thus the son of Jón Pálsson might be called Magnús Jónsson while the daughter might have the name Auður Jónsdóttir. On marrying, women keep their own names. You will be addressed by your forename and in return you should address Icelanders in a similar fashion. The telephone directory is arranged according to forenames, not surnames.

Telephone system

There are few public telephone boxes, but telephones are found in hotels, roadside shops, bus stations and post offices. Not all exchanges are automatic and the manual ones may only be open during office hours. If you go to a manual exchange in a post office you will be asked to write down the name and number of the person you want and the operator will dial the number. Coin boxes only take money when your call is answered. They accept 5kr coins.

There are dialling codes to the various parts of the country. Reykjavík's prefix is 91; Akureyri's is 96. For any other town or settlement you wish to phone, look up the code that is given against the hotel's telephone number in the accommodation list (see pp.71-76). Some establishments can only be reached through the operator, so if a telephone number is not given then dial 02 to enlist the operator's help. Overseas calls can be made by dialling 09.

The telephone directory (*'símaskrá'*) covers the whole country and has four main sections in it: Reykjavík and suburbs; other towns and settlements in alphabetical order; miscellaneous postal information; a commercial directory. Inside the front cover is a list of the dialling codes (*'svæðisnúmer'*) for the main towns and settlements and inside the back cover there are street maps of the capital and its suburbs.

Swimming
One of the Icelanders' most civilised habits is their enjoyment of outdoor swimming pools, heated by natural hot water. These are found all round the country (wherever there are warm springs) and many are mentioned in Part 4; the one beside Reykjavík's campsite is very large. You are expected to shower before entering the water. Some pools, called 'hot pots' have rather warmer water – perhaps 40°C.

USEFUL ADDRESSES

THE FOLLOWING LISTS give names and addresses of organisations, agencies and shops that may be of use to the visitor to Iceland. Addresses of hotels are given in the 'Accommodation' section on pp.71-76 or in the sections dealing with Reykjavík and Akureyri. The main garages in Reykjavík are listed on pp.61-62.

The street names given in these lists are in the form that will be found on the maps in this book, on other published maps and on street signs. These lists will therefore help visitors physically to locate the buildings they are looking for. Unfortunately in Icelandic many (but not all) street names change their endings when the word is used as part of a postal address. For example building number 34 on Borgartún has the address Borgartúni 34. Thus the correct postal address on an envelope or in a brochure will be spelt slightly differently to the corresponding map entry or street sign. Examples are given below of how addresses may be written in Icelandic brochures and leaflets; it is also the form that should be used when addressing a letter.

name of street	name used in address
Hverfisgata	Hverfisgötu
Grundarstígur	Grundarstíg
Boltholt	Boltholti
Borgartún	Borgartúni
Laugavegur	Laugavegi
Súðarvogur	Súðarvogi

The following names give examples of some endings that do not change when used in an address:

Ármúli
Reykjanesbraut
Sundaborg
Skeifan

Icelandic addresses are written with the number of the building written after the name of the street eg. Austurstræti 9.

Addresses in Reykjavík
Tourist information and services
1. Iceland Tourist Board, Laugavegur 3, Reykjavík
2. Tour Operators:
   a) Úlfar Jacobsen Travel, Austurstræti 9, Reykjavík.
   b) Iceland Tourist Bureau, Skógarhlíð 6, Reykjavík.
   c) Úrval Travel, Pósthússtræti 23, Reykjavík.
   d) Samvinnuferðir-Landsýn, Austurstræti 12, Reykjavík.
   e) Guðmundur Jónasson, Borgartún 34, Reykjavík.
   f) Útsýn, Austurstræti 17, Reykjavík.

g) Reykjavík Excursions, Hotel Loftleiðir, Reykjavík.

3. Clubs:
   a) Ferðafélags Íslands, Öldugata 3, Reykjavík.
   b) Útivist, Lækjargata 6, Reykjavík.
   c) Bandalag Íslenzkra Farfugla (Youth Hostels), PO Box 1045, Reykjavík.
   d) The Association of Icelandic Anglers, Hotel Saga, v/Hagatorg, Reykjavík.

4. Travel: *planes and buses*
   a) Icelandair, Reykjavík Airport, Reykjavík.
   b) SAS, Laugavegur 3, Reykjavík.
   c) Eagle Air, Lágmúli 7, Reykjavík.
   d) Bifreiðastöd Íslands (BSI, scheduled buses), Umferðarmiðstöðin, v/Hringbraut, Reykjavík.
   Travel: *car hire*
   a) Bílaleiga Akureyrar, Skeifan 9, Reykjavík.
   b) Bílaleiga Flugleiða, Reykjavíkurflugvöllur, Reykjavík.
   c) Vík Bílaleiga, Grensásvegur 11, Reykjavík.
   Travel: *shipping companies*
   a) Eimskipafélag Íslands, Pósthússtræti 2, Reykjavík.
   b) Hafskip h.f., Hafnarhúsið, Tryggvagata, Reykjavík.
   c) Skipaútgerð Ríkisins, Hafnarhúsið, Reykjavík.

5. Félag Íslenzkra Bifreiðaeigenda (FIB – Icelandic Automobile Association), Borgartún 33, Reykjavík, tel. 91-29999.

6. Farm holidays:
   Ferðathjónusta bænda, Búndaðarfélag Íslands, Bændahöllinn, Hagatorg, Reykjavík.

7. Fishing holidays:
   Landssamband veiðifélaga, Bolholt 6, Reykjavík.

8. Embassies and consulates

Austria	consulate	Austurstræti 17, Reykjavík.
Belgium	consulate	Hverfisgata 6, Reykjavík.
Brazil	consulate	Hverfisgata 4, Reykjavík.
Canada	consulate	Skúlagata 20, Reykjavík.
Chile	consulate	Ármúli 16, Reykjavík.
China	embassy	Viðimelur 29, Reykjavík.
Cyprus	consulate	Ármúli 8, Reykjavík.
Czechoslovakia	embassy	Smáragata 16, Reykjavík.
Denmark	embassy	Hverfisgata 29, Reykjavík.
East Germany	embassy	Ægissída 78, Reykjavík.
Finland	embassy	Kringlumýrarbraut, Reykjavík.
Finland	consulate	Hafnarstræti 5, Reykjavík.
France	embassy	Túngata 22, Reykjavík.
France	consulate	Grundarstígur 12, Reykjavík.
Greece	consulate	Vesturgata 42, Reykjavík.
Holland	consulate	Hafnarstræti 20, Reykjavík.
Ireland	consulate	Thverholt 19-21, Reykjavík.
Israel	consulate	Sundagarðar 4, Reykjavík.
Italy	consulate	Skúlatún 4, Reykjavík.
Japan	consulate	Síðumúli 39, Reykjavík.
Luxembourg	consulate	Víðigrund 11, Reykjavík.
Mexico	consulate	Ægisgata 10, Reykjavík.
Norway	embassy	Fjólugata 17, Reykjavík.
Norway	consulate	Ánanaust, Grandagarður, Reykjavík.
Peru	consulate	Suðurlandsbraut 16, Reykjavík.
Portugal	consulate	Sundaborg 42, Reykjavík.
South Africa	consulate	Austurstræti 18, Reykjavík.
South Korea	consulate	Lágmúli 5, Reykjavík.
Spain	consulate	Laugavegur 172, Reykjavík.
Sweden	embassy	Lágmúli 7, Reykjavík.
Switzerland	consulate	Austurstræti 6, Reykjavík.
Tunisia	consulate	Lyngás 1, Reykjavík.
UK	embassy	Laufásvegur 49, Reykjavík.
Uruguay	consulate	Vesturgata 17, Reykjavík.
USA	embassy	Laufásvegur 21, Reykjavík.
USSR	embassy	Garðastræti 33, Reykjavík.
West Germany	embassy	Túngata 18, Reykjavík.
Yugoslavia	consulate	Hafnarstræti 20, Reykjavík.

9. Shops
Camping and skiing equipment
   a) Sportval, Laugavegur 116, Reykjavík.
   b) Útilíf, Álfheimar 74, Reykjavík.
   c) Skátabúðin, Snorrabraut 60, Reykjavík.
Hire of camping equipment:
   Tjaldaleigan, Umferðarmiðstöðin, v/Hringbraut, Reykjavík.
Bookshops:
   a) Bókaverslun Sigfúsar Eymundssonar, Austurstræti 18, Reykjavík.
   b) Bókaverslun Snæbjarnar ('The English

Bookshop'), Hafnarstræti 4, Reykjavík.
c) Bókábuð Máls og Menningar, Laugavegur 18, Reykjavík.
d) Bókábuð Lárusar Blöndal, Skólavörðustígur 2, Reykjavík.

Photographic shops:
a) Hans Petersen, Bankastræti 4, Reykjavík.
b) Agfa, Skólavörðustígur, Reykjavík.
c) Ljósmyndavöruverslunin, Filmur og Vélar sf, Skólavörðustígur 41, Reykjavík.
d) Ljósmyndavörur hf., Fuji Film, Bankastræti, Reykjavík.

Official Agencies

10. Customs:
Tollstjóraembættið, Tollhúsið, Tryggvagata 19, Reykjavík.
11. Maps:
Landmælingar Íslands (Icelandic Geodetic Survey), Laugavegur 178, Reykjavík.
12. Conservation:
Náttúruverndarráð (Nature Conservation Council), Hverfisgata 26, Reykjavík.
13. Police:
Lögreglan, Hverfisgata 113, Reykjavík.
14. Ministry for Foreign Affairs:
Utanríkisráðuneytið, Hverfisgata 115, Reykjavík.
15. Iceland National Research Council, Laugavegur 13, Reykjavík.

Commercial Services

16. Ministry of Commerce, Arnahvoll 7, Reykjavík.
17. Central Bank:
Seðlabanki Íslands, Austurstræti 11 and Hafnarstræti 10, Reykjavík.
18. Main Banks:
a) Landsbanki Íslands, Austurstræti 11, Reykjavík.
b) Útvegsbanki Íslands, Austurstræti 19, Reykjavík.
c) Búnaðarbanki Íslands, Austurstræti 5, Reykjavík.
19. Iceland Chamber of Commerce, House of Commerce, PO Box 514, Reykjavík.

Addresses in Akureyri
Tourist information and services:
Ferðaskrifstofa Akureyrar, Ráðhústorg 3, Akureyri.
Car hire:
a) Bílaleiga Akureyrar, Tryggvagata 14, Akureyri.
b) Bílaleigan, Bakkahlíð 15, Akureyri.
c) Bílaleigan, Stekkjargerði 14, Akureyri.

Garages:
a) Bílaverkstæði Bílaleigu Akureyrar, Fjölnisgata 2A, Akureyri.
b) Bifreiðaverkstæðið Bláfell sf, Draupnisgata 7A, Akureyri.
c) Bifreiðaverkstæðið Vagninn sf, Furuvellir 7, Akureyri.
d) Bifreiðaverkstæði Gunnars Jóhannssonar, Óseyri 6, Akureyri.

Camping equipment:
a) Sporthúsið hf, Hafnarstræti 94, Akureyri.
b) Sportvöruverslun Brynjólfs Sveinssonar, Skipagata 1, Akureyri.

Bookshops:
a) Bókaverslunin Edda, Hafnarstræti 100, Akureyri.
b) Bókabúðin Huld, Hafnarstræti 97, Akureyri.
c) Bókabúð Jónasar Jóhannssonar, Hafnarstræti 108, Akureyri.

State alcohol shop:
Áfengis og Tóbaksverslun Ríkisins, Hólabraut 16, Akureyri.

Police station:
Lögreglustöðin, Thórunnarstræti, Akureyri.

Reservations on International Flights

Airline	telephone number
Icelandair	91-25100
SAS	91-21199
Eagle Air	91-84477

Reservations on Internal Flights

Settlement	telephone number
Reykjavík	91-26011
Akureyri	96-22000/22005/22008
Bakkafjörður	97-3360
Borgarfjörður	97-2902
Breiðdalsvík	97-5640
Egilsstaðir	97-1210/1208
Grímsey	96-73103
Höfn	97-8250
Húsavík	96-41749
Ísafjörður	94-3000/3400
Kópasker	96-52120
Ólafsfjörður	96-62120
Patreksfjörður	94-1133
Raufarhöfn	96-51169
Sauðárkrókur	95-5630
Siglufjörður	96-71500
Thingeyri	94-8117
Thórshöfn	96-8119
Westman Islands	98-1520/1525

Reservations for Brjánslækur-Stykkishólmur ferry

Telephone: (Stykkishólmur) 93-8120
(Brjánslækur) 94-2020

Useful Addresses outside Iceland

THE FOLLOWING lists give many addresses in a number of countries that can be of use to visitors. The tour operators listed here either specialise in Iceland or have some experience in dealing with the country.

1. Information Offices

a) Iceland Tourist Information Bureau, 73 Grosvenor Street, London W1X 9DD, UK.
b) Iceland Tourist Board, 655 Third Avenue, New York, NY 10017, USA.
c) Verkehrsbüro für Dänemark und Island, Münsterhof 14, 8001 Zürich, Switzerland.

2. Danish Tourist Board Offices

(for information on Greenland and the Faroes)

Australia	60 Market St., PO Box 4531, Melbourne, Victoria 3001.
Austria	Auerspergstrasse 7, A-5020 Salzburg.
Belgium	Rue Ravenstein/Ravensteinstraat 60, B-1000 Brussels.
Canada	PO Box 115, Station 'N', Toronto, Ontario M8V 3S4.
Denmark	H.C. Andersens Boulevard 22, DK -1553 Copenhagen V.
Finland	PO Box 836, SF-00101 Helsinki 10.
France	142 Champs Elysées, F-75008 Paris.
Holland	Piet Heinstraat 3, NL-2518 CB Den Haag.
Italy	Casella Postale 6179, 1-00 195 Roma-Prati.
Japan	Sanno Grand Building, Room 401, 14-2 Nagato-cho 2-chome, Chiyoda-ku, Tokyo, 100 Japan.
Norway	Karl Johansgate 1, N-Oslo 1.
Sweden	Gustav Adolfs Torg 14, Box 1659, S-11186, Stockholm.
Switzerland	Münsterhof 14, CH-8001 Zürich.
UK	169-173 Regent St., London W1R 8PY.
USA	a) 75 Rockefeller Plaza, New York NY 10019. b) PO Box 3240, Los Angeles, California 90028-3240. c) 150 North Michigan Avenue, Suite 2110, Chicago, Illinois 60601.
West Germany	Glackengiesserwall 2, Postfach 10 13 29, D-2000 Hamburg 1.

3. Tour Operators

Austria	a) Airtour Austria, Möllwaldplatz 5, A-1040 Vienna, Austria. b) Reiseburo Hummer, Makartplatz 9, A-5020 Salzburg, Austria.
Belgium	Voyages de Keyser Thort, Rue de la Madeleine 63, B 1000, Brussels, Belgium.
France	a) Kuoni, 3 Boulevard Victor Hugo, 6000 Nice, France. b) Voyages Agrepa, 42 Rue Etienne Marcel, 75002 Paris, France. c) Voyages Bennett, 5 Rue Scribe, 75009 Paris, France. d) Voyages Gallia, 12 Rue Auber, 75009 Paris, France. e) Voyages Kuoni, 33 Boulevard Malesherbes, 75008 Paris, France. f) Voyages UTA, 3 Rue Meyerbeer, 75442 Paris, France.
Holland	a) Arke Reisen, Deurningerstraat 16, PO Box 365, 7500 AJ Enschede, Holland. b) D. Burger and Zoon BV, Willemskade 14, 3016 DK Rotterdam, Holland. c) Holland International, PO Box 58, 2000 AB Haarlem, Holland. d) Reisebureau BBI, Meerstraat 22, Emmen, Holland.
Ireland	Holiday Travel Ltd., 14 Fitzwilliam Street Upper, Dublin 2, Ireland.
Italy	Hotur, International Travel Wholesaler, Via P. de Cannobio 11, 20122 Milan, Italy.
Luxembourg	Keiser Tours, Centre Commercial Louvigny, 34 Rue Philippe 2, Luxembourg.
Spain	Trekking y Aventura, c/d. Ramon de la Cruz 93, Madrid 6, Spain.

Switzerland

a) Danzas Reisen AG, Löwenstrasse 22, Postfach 5076, Switzerland.

b) Hans Imholz Travel Agency, Zentrastrasse 2, 8036 Zürich, Switzerland.

c) Jugi Tours, Postfach 132, Hochhaus 9, Shopping Centre, CH 8958 Spreitenbach, Switzerland.

d) Reiseburo Kuoni AG, Bärenplatz, CH 3001 Bern, Switzerland.

e) Reiseburo Kuoni AG, Neve Hard, Neugasse 231, CH 8037 Zürich, Switzerland.

f) Saga Reisen, Barenstutz, CH 3507 Biglen, Switzerland.

UK

a) Sonicworld UK, 8 The Boulevard, Crawley, West Sussex RH10 1XX, England.

b) Sonicworld UK, 11 Royal Exchange Square, Glasgow G1 3AJ, Scotland.

c) Twickenham Travel, 84 Hampton Road, Twickenham, Middlesex, TW2 5QS, England.

d) Fred Olsen Travel, 11 Conduit Street, London W1R 0LS, England.

e) Dick Phillips, Whitehall House, Nenthead, Alston, Cumbria CA9 3PS, England.

f) Regent Holidays, Regent Street, Shanklin, Isle of Wight.

g) Scantours, 8 Spring Gardens, London SW1A 2BG, England.

h) Donald MacKenzie Travel, 144 St. Vincent Street, Glasgow G2 5LH, Scotland.

i) Arctic Experience Ltd, 29 Nork Way, Banstead, Surrey SM7 1PB, England.

USA

a) Icelandair, Suite 375, 85 West Algonquin Road, Arlington Heights, Chicago, Illinois 60005.

b) Icelandair, Rockefeller Center, 610b Fifth Avenue, New York, NY 10020.

c) Four Winds Travel, 175 Fifth Avenue, New York, NY 10010.

d) Holiday Tours, 40 East 49th Street, New York, NY 10017.

e) Maupintour, 1515 St. Andrews Drive, Lawrence, KS 66044.

f) Questers Travel, 257 Park Avenue South, New York, NY 10010.

g) Travcoa, 875 North Michigan Avenue, Chicago, Il. 60611.

West Germany

a) Airtours International, Kurfürstendamm 65, 1 Berlin 15, West Germany.

b) Airtours International, Rödingsmarkt 31-33, 2 Hamburg 11, West Germany.

c) Airtours International, Prinzregentenstrasse 12, 8 München 22, West Germany.

d) Airtours International, Heilmannstrasse 4, 4 Stuttgart 1, West Germany.

e) Evangelischer Reisedienst, Schützenbühlstrasse 81, 7000 Stuttgart 40, West Germany.

f) Inter Air-Voss Reisen, Triftstrasse 28-30, 6000 Frankfurt/Main 71, West Germany.

g) Reiseagentur Waldemar Fast, Alstertor 21, 2000 Hamburg 1, West Germany.

h) Reiseburo Norden, Ost-West-Strasse 70, 2000 Hamburg 11, West Germany.

i) S.O.T., Titzianstrasse 3, 8200 Rosenheim, West Germany.

j) Wolters Reisen, Bremer Strasse 48, 2805 Stuhr 1, West Germany.

4. Icelandic Embassies and Consulates

The lists below give the addresses of all Icelandic embassies and the towns and cities in which there is a Consulate General (CG), Consulate (C) or a Vice-Consulate (VC). Where there is no Icelandic representative in the country concerned, the name of the embassy that should be contacted is given.

Albania	(Sweden).	Israel	Tel-Aviv (CG).
Argentina	USA (CG).	Italy	Rome (CG), Genoa (CG), Messina
Australia	Melbourne (CG), Sydney (CG).		(CG), Milan (CG), Naples (C),
Austria	Vienna (CG), Salzburg (C).		Turin (C).
Bahamas	Nassau (CG).	Japan	Tokyo (CG).
Bangladesh	Dacca (CG).	Kenya	Nairobi (C).
Belgium	Embassy: Avenue des Lauriers 19,	Lebanon	Beirut (CG).
	1150 Brussels.	Luxembourg	Luxembourg (CG).
	Brussels (CG), Antwerp (C).	Malaysia	Kuala Lumpur (C).
Brazil	Rio de Janeiro (CG), São Paulo	Malta	Valetta (C).
	(CG).	Mexico	Mexico City (CG).
Bulgaria	(USSR).	Mongolia	(USSR).
Canada	Ottowa (CG), Calgary (VC),	New Zealand	Wellington (CG).
	Edmonton (C), St. John's (C),	Nigeria	Lagos (C).
	Montreal (CG), Toronto (C),	Norway	Embassy: Stortingsgate 30, Oslo.
	Vancouver (C), Winnipeg (CG).		Ålesund (C), Bergen (C),
Cape Verde Is.	(France).		Drammen (VC), Hammerfest
Chile	USA (C).		(VC), Haugesund (C),
Cuba	Havana (CG).		Kristiansand (C), Moss (VC),
Cyprus	Nicosia (C).		Sarpsborg (VC), Stavanger (C),
Czechoslovakia	(Norway).		Tromsö (VC), Trondheim (C).
Denmark	Embassy: Dantes Plads 3, 1556	Pakistan	Islamabad (CG), Karachi (C).
	Copenhagen V.	Peru	(US).
	Aalborg (C), Aarhus (C), Esbjerg	Philippines	Manila (C).
	(C), Fredericia (VC),	Poland	(Norway).
	Frederikshavn (VC), Helsingör	Portugal	Lisbon (CG), Oporto (C),
	(C), Hirtshals (VC), Horsens (C),		Portimao (C).
	Nyköbing (VC), Odense (VC),	Romania	(USSR).
	Randers (VC), Svendborg (VC).	Saudi Arabia	(Sweden).
East Germany	(USSR).	Singapore	Singapore (CG).
Ecuador	Quito (CG).	South Africa	Johannesburg (C).
Egypt	Cairo (CG), Port Said (C).	South Korea	Seoul (CG).
Ethiopia	(Geneva, Switzerland).	Spain	Madrid (CG), Barcelona (CG),
Faroes	Tórshavn (C), Klaksvík (VC).		Bilbao (C), Las Palmas (C),
Finland	Helsinki (CG), Hangö (C), Kotka		Málaga (C), Mallorca (VC),
	(C), Mariehamn (C), Åbo (C),		Valencia (C).
	Vasa (VC).	Sri Lanka	Colombo (CG).
France	Embassy: 124 Boulevard	Sweden	Embassy: Kommendörsgatan 35,
	Haussmann, 75008 Paris.		114 58 Stockholm.
	Boulogne (C), Ecully (C),		Göteborg (CG), Helsingborg
	Marseille (C), Metz (C), Nice (C),		(VC), Bankeryd (C), Malmö
	Strasbourg (C).		(CG), Sundsvall (VC).
Greece	Piraeus (CG).	Switzerland	Consulate: 16 Rue du Marché,
Holland	Amsterdam (CG), Harlingen		1204 Geneva.
	(VC), Rotterdam (C).		Berne (C), Zürich (C).
Hong Kong	Hong Kong (C).	Tanzania	(Geneva, Switzerland).
Hungary	(USSR).	Thailand	Bangkok (CG).
India	New Delhi (CG), Bombay (CG).	Tunisia	Tunis (CG).
Indonesia	Jakarta (CG).	Turkey	Ankara (CG), Istanbul (CG).
Ireland	Dublin (CG).	UK	Embassy: 1 Eaton Terrace,

	London SW1.
	Edinburgh (C), Aberdeen (C), Belfast (C), Dover (VC), Felixstowe (C), Fleetwood (C), Glasgow (C), Grimsby (C), Hull (C), Lerwick (C), Manchester (C), Newcastle-upon-Tyne (C).
Uruguay	Montevideo (CG).
USA	Embassy: 2022 Connecticut Avenue, NW Washington DC 2008.
	Atlanta (C), Boca Raton, Florida (CG), Boston (C), Boulder (C), Camp Hill, Pennsylvania (C), Chicago (C), Dallas, Texas (C), Detroit, Michigan (C), Houston (C), Los Angeles (C), Miami, Florida (C), Minneapolis (C), New York (CG), Norfolk (C), Portland (C), San Francisco (C), Seattle (C), Tallahassee (C).
USSR	Embassy: Khlebnyi Pereulok 28, Moscow.
Venezuela	Caracas (CG).
West Germany	Embassy: Kronprinzenstrasse 6, 5300 Bonn 2.
	Bremerhaven (C), Cologne (C), Cuxhaven (C), Düsseldorf (C), Hamburg (C), Hanover (C), Lübeck (C), München (C), Stuttgart (C), Berlin (C).
Yugoslavia	Belgrade (CG).

5. Icelandair

Austria	c/o Tyrolean Airways, Operning 1/R. A-1010, Vienna.
Belgium	Centre International Rogier/Boite 33, B-1000 Brussels.
Denmark	Vester Farimagsgade 1, DK-1606 Copenhagen.
Faroes	Flogfélag Foroya, Aarvegur 6, DK 3800 Tórshavn.
France	9 Boulevard des Capucines, 75002 Paris.
Greece	6 Kriezoutou Street, Athens 134.
Holland	c/o Reisebureau Mueller and Co. B.V., Damrak 90, 1012 Amsterdam.
Italy	Via Ludovisi 36, 00187 Rome. Via Larga 26, 20122 Milan.

Luxembourg	Luxembourg Airport.
Norway	Fridthjof Nansens Plass 9, Oslo 1.
Spain	Rahisa, Marques de Villamejor 3, 1-Derecha, Madrid 6.
Sweden	Humlegardsgatan 6, 4 tr. 114 46 Stockholm.
Switzerland	16 Rue du Mont Blanc, 1211 Geneva.
	Stampfenbachstrasse 117, 8006 Zürich.
UK	73 Grosvenor Street, London W1X 9DD.
	British Airways, 83/85 Buchanan Street, Glasgow G1 3HQ.
USA	Suite 375, 85 West Algonquin Road, Arlington Heights, Chicago, Illinois 60005.
	Rockefeller Center, 610b Fifth Avenue, New York, NY 10020.
	Suite 609, 6th Floor, 910 17th Street, NW Washington DC.
	c/o United Airlines, 1725 K Street, NW Washington DC.
West Germany	Rossmarkt 10, 6000 Frankfurt/Main 1.
	Graf Adolf Strasse 12, Düsseldorf.

6. Scandanavian Airlines System (SAS)

These are too numerous to mention. The SAS Worldwide Timetable lists over 300 offices throughout the world.

7. Eagle Air

Holland	Apollolaan 7, 1077 AA Amsterdam (European Area Office).
Switzerland	Seilergraben 55, 8001 Zürich.
UK	c/o Air Global, Bilton House, 54-58 Uxbridge Road, London W5 2TE.
West Germany	Lyonerstrasse 44, 6000 Frankfurt/Main 71.

8. Smyril Line (ferry)

Head Office	Smyril Line Passenger Dept., PO Box 370, 3800 Tórshavn, Faroes.
Iceland	c/o Úrval Travel, Pósthússtræti 9, Reykjavík.
Denmark	c/o Nordshipping, Coastergade 15, 7730 Hanstholm.

France	c/o Voyages Agrepa, 42 Rue Etienne Marcel, 75002 Paris.	West Germany	c/o J. A. Reinecke GmbH & Co, Hohe Bleichen 11, PO Box 110680, 2000 Hamburg 36.
Luxembourg	c/o Keiser Tours, Centre Commercial Louvigny, 34 Rue Philippe 2, 2340 Luxembourg.		
Norway	c/o Bergenske Reisebyrå, Marken Boks 822, 5001 Bergen.		
UK	c/o P & O Ferries, Orkney & Shetland Service, P & O Ferry Terminal, Aberdeen AB9 8DL.		

9. Specialist help for expeditions

a) Young Explorers' Trust, c/o The Royal Geographic Society, 1 Kensington Gore, London SW7 2AR, UK.

b) Island-Berichte, Hebbelstrasse 26, 6500 Mainz 31, West Germany.

PART THREE
A PICTORIAL VIEW
OF
ICELAND

Reykjavík

Contrasting seasonal views of Reykjavík, Iceland's capital, with (top) Esja in the background and (bottom) Tjörnin, a lake set in the heart of the city. (Left) An illuminated detail from the Flateyjarbók, *a collection of the* Kings' Sagas *made c.1390. (Right) A statue of Leif Eiríksson, dominates the foreground; Hallgrímskirkja, behind, provides Reykjavík with its most distinctive landmark.*

The South-west

The lowlands of the south-west are the most fertile area of Iceland, providing the best farming land on the island. Today sheep and cattle farming predominate, though during warmer periods in the island's history grain was grown. The sheep and cattle population is restricted by the short growing season, limiting winter fodder. Overgrazing was a persistent problem in the past.

(Above) *A typical Icelandic farmhouse.*

(Preceding pages) *Gullfoss on the river Hvítá is perhaps the finest of Iceland's many waterfalls. It gains its nickname 'The Golden Falls' from the rainbows conjured by the sun's rays from the clouds of spray it throws up.*

(Left) *'Strokkur' erupts. Now the most dramatic of all Iceland's geysers, Strokkur can hurl a column of hot water 20-40m up in the air several times an hour.*

(Above) *Hekla is seen with the Thjórsá in the foreground. Iceland's most famous volcano is the product of a 'crater row' (a series of vents along a fissure) which gives it its characteristic ridgelike shape.*

The South
(Preceding pages) *Skógafoss tumbles over old sea cliffs.*

(Above) *Skyscape near Thórsmörk. Dramatic skies are a regular feature of Iceland, mirroring the fantastic contortions found in the landscape.*

(Right) *The startling, jet-black 'snout' of Sólheimajökull provides a fine illustration of a glacier in action. The snout's blackness is caused by the ice melting to reveal the black sand held within the glacier. The 'end moraine' of sand and pebbles which have recently dropped from the glacier can be seen at the foot of the snout.*

(Above) *Skaftafell National Park in southern Iceland is one of the country's most-frequented tourist sites, proving especially popular with hikers and walkers.*

(Right) *This vantage point high over Skaftafellsjökull provides a breathtaking view over the glacier to the sandur and the meltwater streams that lie at its foot.*

(Left) *The waterfall of Svartifoss in Skaftafell National Park gains its charm from the basalt columns that ring its sides. These have provided the inspiration for the design of the National Theatre in Reykjavík.*

Iceland's camping sites must be amongst the most dramatic in the world. Skaftafell (above) is no exception. Behind the campsite the snout of Skaftafellsjökull can be seen. Campsite facilities vary widely around the country depending on the frequency of visitors. Skaftafell is amongst the best-equipped, with a supermarket, cafe and petrol pumps.

119

(Left) *Icebergs drift in the glacial lake of Jökulsárlón, at the foot of Breiðamerkurjökull in southern Iceland. Black icebergs, like the one on the left of this photograph, gain their colour from the dust and stones they carry, which have been ground from the mountainsides as the glacier passes over them. Depending on the crystalline structure of the ice, icebergs may also be a bright, glacial blue, as well as the traditional white.*

(Above) *A spectacular sunset over Vatnajökull, viewed from Höfn.*

(Preceding pages) *The isolation of rural life in Iceland – and the natural beauty that offsets it – are both captured in this study of a lonely cottage near Höfn in south-east Iceland.*

The Eastern Fjords

(Left) *Unloading fish at Djúpivogur. Fishing is Iceland's most important industry, providing a major source of exports. While small boats such as the one shown here are found all around the coast, new technology means that much larger factory ships can freeze and process their catch on board, enabling them to stay at sea longer. Iceland's waters contain fertile fishing grounds, but overfishing, often by foreign boats, threatened stock and led to the imposition of strict fishing limits in the 1970s and the two 'cod wars' with Britain. Main catches are capelin and cod.*

125

(Preceding pages) *Sea mist – often a distinctive feature of the eastern fjord scenery – here lies wrapped about the base of Reyðafjorður's rugged contours.*

(Above) *The racks of drying fish lining the fjord and a kaleidoscopic jumble of fishing nets underline the importance of the fishing industry to settlements such as Seyðisfjorður.*

(Right) *Seyðisfjorður is an important Icelandic settlement, with simple, colourful homes set against a spectacular natural backdrop of mountains that rise up to 1,000m above the fjord. It is not uncommon for avalanches to damage the buildings.*

The North

The area around Mývatn offers perhaps the widest variety of different scenery to be found in Iceland.

   (Left) *The fresh appearance of brightly coloured rocks provides evidence of recent volcanic activity at Bjarnaflag near Mývatn, while in the background clouds of vapour billow from a wellhead. This almost surreal landscape contrasts with the classic volcanic shape of Hverfjall (above), formed by a single eruption c.2,500 years ago. A thick trail of lava fills the foreground; on either side dwarf shrubs thrive in the rich volcanic soil.*

131

(Preceding pages) *Man seems an intruder in a landscape as alien as this view of the volcanically active area behind Víti, near Mývatn, where the extremes of ice and fire coexist in uneasy proximity.*

(Above) *A bubbling mudpool in Námarskarð and* (right) *an active vent in an ashfield at Leirhnjúkur near Mývatn. Scenes such as these make it easy to understand why in mediaeval Europe Iceland was popularly believed to contain the entrance to hell.*

(Left) *Mývatn's sheltered position and plentiful supply of warm water springs support abundant plant life despite its altitude (227m).*

(Above) *These red rocks (called 'Klasar') are lava columns left behind after a lava lake was suddenly drained. They are situated near Höfði on the south-eastern corner of the lake.*

(Overleaf) *This bird's-eye view looks west over lake Mývatn towards Kinnarfjöll. Mývatn is an ornithologist's delight. All the species of ducks found in Iceland breed here: it is estimated that the number of breeding pairs exceeds 15,000.*

(Above) *A farm in the mountains to the south-west of Akureyri, northern Iceland's largest centre of population.*

(Right) *A large and very old town house in Akureyri. Building materials have been in short supply in Iceland since the time of the Settlement. With their architectural options limited, the Icelanders responded with ingenuity, erecting fairly substantial structures using such materials as were available, often driftwood, turf and, later, corrugated iron. In recent years increasing trade with the outside world and the production of new building materials such as concrete have eased the problem, but many houses are still constructed from more traditional materials.*

The North-west

(Left) *This old turf farm at Glaumbær, in northern Iceland, is preserved as a museum depicting Icelandic life in the last century.*

(Above top) *The interior of the museum, showing furniture in one of the better-decorated rooms.*

(Above) *One of the museum's workshops – complete with forge. The wall at the back is made of sods of turf.*

(Left) *Iceland's many internal air routes offer rich opportunities to photographers if the weather is clear (details of the plane trip on which both these photographs were taken are given on p.228). This fine view looks out over Breiðafjörður, towards Snæfellsnes in the distance. The white cone-shaped top of Snæfellsjökull can be seen to the right of the picture.*

(Above) *Iceland's starkly contoured coastline is particularly well-suited to aerial photography. This view of part of the north-western fjords graphically illustrates the glacial erosion which, over the course of thousands of years, gradually created the fjords.*

145

Western Iceland

(Left) *Sheep-shearing at Hellissandur on the Snæfellsnes peninsula. Sheep farming is the single most important activity in Iceland's agricultural industry. There are approximately 800,000 sheep on the island. About half are slaughtered every year; mutton and woollen goods are exported.*

(Above) *The Icelanders have relied on horses for transport for over a thousand years. Those pictured here are direct descendants of the Vikings' horses as no other breed has been introduced since the settlement. Though small, the breed is strong; on many farms horses are now being bred for export. They remain indispensable to the Icelanders, particularly during the autumn when the sheep are rounded up and brought down from the highlands.*

148

Iceland's inhospitable climate and geological youth have discouraged the development of plant life: only one-fifth of its surface has plant cover.

The more primitive types of plants are well represented with c.450 species of lichen (top right) and c.550 species of moss (bottom left) but the more sophisticated plants with stems and flowers such as the bistort (top left) and willow herb (bottom right) suffered during the last 'little ice age'. The flora is essentially Northern European: 97 per cent of Iceland's c.450 vascular plants are also to be found in Norway.

(Above) Flowers throng the shore at Stokkishólmur on the Snæsfellsnes peninsula.

(Overleaf) Kirkufell on Snæfellsnes offers one of the most aesthetically satisfying mountain profiles in Iceland.

149

PART FOUR

THE
TOURING
GUIDE
What to see and how to get there

HOW TO USE PART 4

THE GUIDE cannot attempt to describe everything there is to see in Iceland nor suggest every interesting place at which to stop. However, Part 4 takes the visitor around the most popular routes in the country. Wherever possible interesting detours are pointed out, as are advantageous viewpoints for seeing the surrounding landscape.

Part 4 divides Iceland into 43 sections (plus visits to Greenland and the Faroes), shown on the map at the back of the book.

The two opening sections deal with arrival in Iceland by air and sea respectively. Next (sections 3-16) the visitor is taken on a tour of the ring road (anticlockwise, starting at Reykjavík), which provides the main framework for any visit to the island.

Sections 17-35 detail worthwhile routes off the ring road all round the country. A number of these – such as trips to Thingvellir and Geysir – are of major interest to the visitor.

Sections 36-43 cover tracks into or across the interior. These are for four-wheel drive vehicles only and require careful preparation and planning (see pp.63-64). Lastly, sections 44 and 45 give brief descriptions of the Faroes and Greenland. Visitors who travel to Iceland by ferry may spend some time in the Faroes, whilst a trip to Greenland can easily be made by air from Reykjavík.

The length of each section varies, with the destination chosen because of its particular interest or because it is a convenient stopping place. All the sections that follow the ring road end at a recognised campsite; this is not necessarily the case with other sections. Settlements, campsites and hotels are mentioned en route where appropriate; it may sometimes be preferable to stay at one of these rather than at the section's destination.

A checklist of the facilities available in major towns and settlements is provided on p.255.

Whilst every attempt has been made to ensure the accuracy of information provided in this part of the Guide, some changes in facilities, road conditions, times of opening and so on are inevitable and must be expected.

The Sections

A summary of useful information is given at the start of each section. The following points should be borne in mind when referring to this:

distance: The distance given excludes detours to places of interest. Where detours involve a significant distance, details are given in the main body of the section.

route: The route given excludes detours. Where roads have names as well as numbers, these are given in brackets.

maps: The 1:500 000 map is recommended to all visitors; this should be supplemented where necessary by the 9 general maps (see pp.85-86). It is essential to take the appropriate general map if you intend travelling on one of the four main cross-country routes (Kjölur, Sprengisandur, Askja and Fjallabak), but use of the general maps will add interest to any journey in Iceland. The only other maps referred to are the seven 'special maps' (see p.86) and the new 1:100 000 map 'Húsavík, Mývatn, Jökulsárgljúfur'.

main places to visit: This is a list of most, but not all, of the places described in the section. Some require a detour. All of the places listed can be seen if a day is taken for the section. The system of stars (from nil to four) is intended to give some further guidance as to which places and sites most merit a visit.

road conditions: Conditions on any particular section can vary considerably – even from day to day, so the comments provided here should be

152

read in that light. The word 'reasonable' is used in the context of Icelandic, not mainland European, conditions.

adjacent sections: This includes sections met en route (for instance roads leading off the ring road) as well as the sections that follow on from the section in question.

notes: This gives some additional information to aid route planning; much more detail is given in the main description of the section.

CHOOSING A ROUTE

FEW VISITORS will have the time to travel on all the routes described in Part 4, so this section is intended to help choose a suitable itinerary. Although Part 4 does not cover all of Iceland's roads, it does include most used by visitors and nearly all the tracks considered safe for a lone four-wheel drive vehicle driven by a visitor. The section numbers given below refer to the relevant sections in Part 4.

A star rating system has been employed in Part 4's listing of the most interesting places to visit at the beginning of each section. The rating ranges from nil to four stars. The seven places with the maximum rating are:

Jökulsárlón	glacial lake with icebergs	section 8
Námaskarð	colourful solfatara field	section 12
Almannagjá	large fissure	section 17
Geysir and Strokkur	geysers	section 18
Gullfoss	waterfall	section 18
Dettifoss	waterfall	section 26
Vesturdalur	rock formations	section 27

The grandeur of Iceland's scenery is obviously enhanced by good weather and can be spoiled by rain and low cloud; however, the enjoyment of the seven places listed above may not be affected too severely by poor weather as they are relatively compact natural features. Likewise, many other places listed in Part 4, such as waterfalls, canyons and solfatara fields are still well worth visiting in poor weather.

The fjords of the east and north-western coasts, and the two main cross-country routes, fall into a different category, however. Since it is their outstanding scenery, rather than particular sites, that is their main attraction, bad weather can easily spoil your enjoyment of them. If you are intending to visit these areas for a few days it is advisable to get a weather forecast. In poor weather there is little to see on these routes; in good weather, the scenery is spectacular.

Unless you have a four-wheel drive vehicle, the country's geography dictates that the ring road is the basic route. Its most interesting stretches are:

1. *between Vík and Höfn* (sections 6, 7 and 8) glaciers, icebergs in lakes, glacial sands;

2. *between Djúpivogur and Breiðdalsvík* (section 9) fjords, fishing settlements;

3. *between Egilsstaðir and Mývatn* (sections 11 and 12) wilderness of sand, gravel and lava. Mývatn is probably the most varied and interesting area in the country.

The following are the most worthwhile detours that can be made from the ring road:

South-west — Thingvellir (ancient parliament site, section 17); Almannagjá (huge fissure, section 17); Strokkur (an active geyser, section 18); Gullfoss (waterfall, section 18); Hekla (recently active volcano, sections 19 and 20); Krísuvík (solfatara field, section 21).

South – Westman Islands (site of 1973 eruption, section 24).

North – Dettifoss (waterfall, section 26); Ásbyrgi (horseshoe-shaped canyon, section 26); Vesturdalur (rock formations, section 27).

North-west – fjord scenery. This will take 3-4 days; in good weather it is beautiful but in poor weather there is little to see (sections 29, 30 and 31).

West – Snæfellsnes peninsula (sections 32 and 33) has fine coastal scenery (rock, cliffs, sands); the trip to Húsafell (sections 34 and 35) can be done in one day if the caves are omitted.

If time is limited the following journey is suggested as a basis for visiting the most important places:

1. Reykjavík – Thingvellir – Gullfoss-Sigalda – south coast (sections 17 to 20; 3 days);

2. Hella – Mývatn (sections 5 to 12; 8 days allowing 1 day at both Skaftafell and Mývatn);

3. Mývatn – Grímsstaðir – Ásbyrgi – Húsavík – Akureyri (sections 26, 27, 13; 2 days);

4. Akureyri – Reykjavík (sections 15, 16; 2 days)

This gives a total of 15 days; if you have less than that then the shorter sections can be covered in less than one day.

Choosing a route through the interior
ONLY those with four-wheel drive vehicles should attempt these routes, and even with four-wheel drive you would be safer keeping solely to the tracks described in Part 4. There are six main routes that are popular with visitors (see map at back of book):

  'Kjölur' – Gullfoss to Hveravellir (section 36), Hveravellir to Blöndudalur (section 37)
  'Sprengisandur' – Goðafoss to Nýidalur (section 38), Nýidalur to Sigalda (section 39)
  'Askja' – north of Vatnajökull (section 40)
  'Fjallabak' – Sigalda to Landmannalaugar (section 41), Landmannalaugar to south coast (section 42)
  'Thórsmörk' – north of Eyjafjallajökull (section 43)
  'Kaldidalur' – west of Langjökull (section 35)

Kjölur and Sprengisandur can both offer useful routes across the country over the vast gravelly wastes. The latter is probably more interesting and can be combined with Fjallabak. These three routes all have a good tourist hut after the first section. It is sensible to take two days for each of Sprengisandur and Kjölur. Sprengisandur and Fjallabak together can comfortably be covered in three days. The tracks to Askja and Thórsmörk do not lead anywhere else, so they have to be retraced. 'Sigalda' is no more than a district in which some roads cross (it is desert land); there are no facilities anywhere near it, except for the petrol pumps at the power station.

Kaldidalur is often passable for ordinary vehicles during the summer.

1
KEFLAVÍK TO REYKJAVÍK

Distance:	48 km
Route:	road 41 to just after Hafnarfjörður
	road 40
Map:	general map 3
Road conditions:	highway
Adjacent sections:	21 (Reykjavík to Krísuvík and Hveragerði)
	3 (Reykjavík)
Notes:	This section is mainly for the benefit of those travelling by bus from Keflavík airport (see p.4).

FOR VISITORS who have never previously been to Iceland, the journey from Keflavík to Reykjavík is quite an eye-opener. The route is along the northern coast of the Reykjanes peninsula, a region subject to earthquakes as it is on the Mid-Atlantic fault line. The vast lavafields on the landward side of the road are covered with lichen and moss and slope gently up towards the craters from whence they came. As the highway moves away from the sea there is the large lavafield on Strandarheiði on the right, much of which has subsided due to movements of the earth's surface. Just beyond it is the cone of Keilir (379 m), one of the most recognisable peaks in southern Iceland. While some of the lava is in the form of great jagged blocks, many of the 'domes' of lava near the road have a smoother shape and often have great cracks in them, produced when the lava was cooling.

At Straumsvík the massive red and white towers of the aluminium smelter can be seen. Just beyond it road 42 to Krísuvík branches off to the right, a route that is described in section 21. The road now continues past the important industrial town and port of Hafnarfjörður, behind which is the peninsula of Álftanes, the site of Bessastaðir, the President's home (section 21).

Next the capital's suburbs are entered with a multitude of brightly painted buildings scattered over the hillsides. The scene's brightness is maintained even in the dark days of midwinter, with thousands of coloured bulbs adorning the outside of doors and verandahs at Christmas time. To the north-east the huge mountain of Esja towers over Iceland's most populated area. (Reykjavík is dealt with in detail in section 3).

2
SEYÐISFJÖRÐUR TO EGILSSTAÐIR

Distance:	27 km
Route:	road 93
Map:	general map 8
Main places to visit:	harbour
	monument on road (view)
Road conditions:	rough mountain road
Adjacent sections:	10 (Breiðdalsvík to Egilsstaðir via Búðareyri)
	11 (Egilsstaðir to Mývatn)
	25 (Lögurinn)
Notes:	This section is mainly for those arriving in the country on the ferry 'Norröna', but alternatively can be completed in a few hours after section 10. Good views in fine weather.

THIS ROUTE starts from Seyðisfjörður; for those visitors arriving by the ferry 'Norröna' it will be the first leg of their journey on the island. After Customs the 'feed' road leads straight to the main road where a sign points left to the campsite (100 m) and right to the youth hostel (400 m). The left turn also leads to the settlement and the

road to Egilsstaðir. The campsite (WCs and outside sinks) is on the right, opposite the church. The straightforward route to the youth hostel is to take the signposted turn and then the second turning on the right; alternatively, those on foot can follow the shore to the right after leaving the Customs shed, the single-storey wooden hostel (sitting on a grassy slope) will then be on their left after about 500 m.

Seyðisfjörður is one of the most important settlements in the eastern fjords and is a port that has grown up with the fishing industry. It lies on the eastern side of the curved fjord and has a good harbour and a fish processing factory which deals with the herring catches; along both sides of the fjord are tall wooden racks where thousands of stockfish hang out to dry. It is not typical of settlements found in the eastern fjords, however, having as it does quite a marked Norwegian influence (seen in a number of the buildings). It is the nearest Icelandic port to Norway.

This is a colourful settlement (see p.129), the houses being painted many different colours. Waterfalls cascade down the 1000 metre-high mountainsides that ring the end of the fjord, with the houses sitting (perhaps a little uneasily) under the steep scree slopes. Avalanches, particularly from Bjólfur (to the right of the mountain road), have often caused damage to the buildings.

A walk along the eastern shore is interesting with jetties, the processing plant, oil tanks, workshops and retail shops strung out along this narrow strip of land. Near the campsite there are shops just before the bridge. The bank is between the church and the shore and behind it is a small house with a colourful sea-scene beautifully painted over its front wall. The settlement also has a guesthouse, restaurant, cinema, swimming pool and a museum.

The steep and rough mountain road out of Seyðisfjörður provides an instructive introduction to Icelandic driving conditions. It is narrow and drivers unused to such roads should drive slowly, especially when oncoming vehicles are encountered. There are many fine waterfalls on the left on the Fjarðará and at one of them (during one of the first sections of winding road) there is a car park. Here, by a nearby monument, there is a good view of the settlement and the fjord. There are also some interesting rocks close at hand, showing the effects of both glacial and water erosion.

The lake Heiðarvatn is on a bare and windswept plateau at 585 m (the road's highest altitude is 620 m). The view on the other side of the summit is magnificent, with ranges of hills to the west and north. Below are the settlement of Egilsstaðir, the lake Lögurinn, and to the south-west (at the end of the lake) the glacier Snæfell (1833m). Near the summit is a track (to the left) to a TV relay station at 949 m which should give even better views. A description of Egilsstaðir is given in section 10.

3
REYKJAVÍK

WITH OVER a third of the country's population living in or near Reykjavík, the capital is the centre of nearly everything that happens in Iceland. Although most visitors have come to see the countryside, rather than the capital, it is certainly worth spending some time in the city.

Reykjavík is now a modern European city, a status reached in a remarkably short time as it is only in this century that it has been developed as a centre of population and administration. Indeed, in 1860 its population was only 700, one-seventieth of the island's total. By 1910 its population had increased dramatically to 11,600 and now stands at 86,000. Nowadays Reykjavík is equipped with most of the amenities that a large city is expected to provide without the usual disadvantage of a polluted atmosphere, as there are few factories of any size. In addition, there are hardly any chimneys to be seen as most buildings are heated by natural water, which comes both from near the mountain Esja and from boreholes in the city.

The city centre is relatively small; its heart lies in the area between the harbour and the lake (called Tjörnin). The streets here are narrow: they were not built to accommodate the present volume of traffic. The city has expanded in all directions, with colourful suburbs spread over the hills around the city, while beyond the harbour, warehouses and fuel tanks occupy newly reclaimed land.

Most of the places of interest to the visitor are within a couple of kilometres of Tjörnin with the university to its south-west, the domestic airport to its south, and much of the commercial area to its east. The harbour is to its north. The best views of the city are from Öskjuhlíð hill and the observation platform in the church of Hallgríms-kirkja (see p.165) and for those who want to cram as much sightseeing into as short a time as possible, there are bus trips round the capital (2½ hours).

Getting around the town is fairly straight-forward as its relatively small size and the land-mark of Hallgrímskirkja help you to keep your bearings. Those who are driving round the city will find the following roads most useful (see street plans on pp.158-161):

Hringbraut/Miklabraut;
Fríkirkjuvegur/Lækjargata/Kalkofnsvegur;
Skúlagata/Borgartún/Sundlaugavegur;
Snorrabraut; Kringlumýrarbraut.

Parking can be a problem in the city centre (where there are meters) so it is best to park a little distance out and then walk. Parking places can usually be found to the east of the lake, near Skúlagata or the Roman Catholic Cathedral.

Maps of the city can be obtained from the tourist bureaux and there is also a street plan (scale: 1:15 000). There are numerous buses serving the city and the main city bus station is at Hlemmur. Taxis are also common – there is no special kind of taxicab (as in many other capital cities) so look out for cars with 'taxi' on them or a letter 'L' on a yellow background on the number plate. The sign *'Laus'* means that it is available for hire. Hotels and public buildings often have telephones connected directly to taxi services.

While your tour operator should be able to give you details of current events in the capital, the handiest places for information (and help in emergencies) are the Tourist Bureau office (open June-August, Mon-Fri: 08.00-18.00; Sat-Sun: 08.00-14.00), and the Information Tower in Lækjartorg (as above, except Sat-Sun: 08.00-13.00). A monthly newspaper, *News from Iceland*, also gives information about what is happening in Iceland, and in Reykjavík in particular.

The main shopping areas are Aðalstræti, Austurstræti and Hafnarstræti (these are west of Lækjartorg) and Hverfisgata, Bankastræti/Laugavegur and Skólavörðustígur (these are east of Lækjartorg). There are public conveniences at the west end of Bankastræti, in both the bus stations and at the north-west corner of the lake.

Reykjavík is a city of sculpture and in parks or just on a spare piece of ground statues are often found depicting some aspect of Icelandic life, or one of its favourite sons. A walk round the harbour is also well worthwhile, particularly when the fishing boats are coming in.

Places to visit

The following places are the main buildings (museums, galleries, historical sites etc) that visitors may want to see. They are all shown on the street maps of Reykjavík (see pp.158-161). A number of the most important places have their Icelandic names given as well as their English ones as signposts will carry the Icelandic names. The list divides into six categories:

a) places near Austurvöllur (1-4)
b) places near Lækjartorg (5-11)
c) places near the lake (12-14)
d) museums, galleries, libraries (15-31)
   (Opening times are given, but these times may alter outside the main holiday season.)
e) churches (32-35)
f) miscellaneous (36-38)

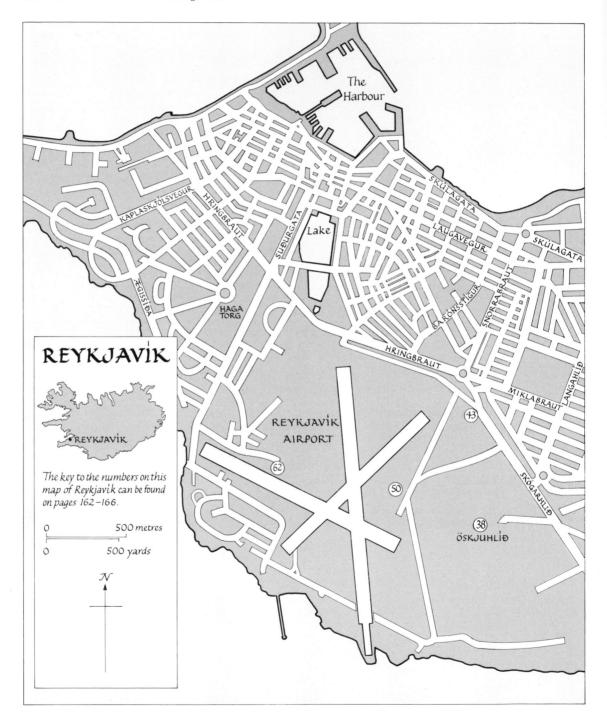

REYKJAVÍK

•REYKJAVÍK

The key to the numbers on this map of Reykjavík can be found on pages 162–166.

0   500 metres

0   500 yards

N

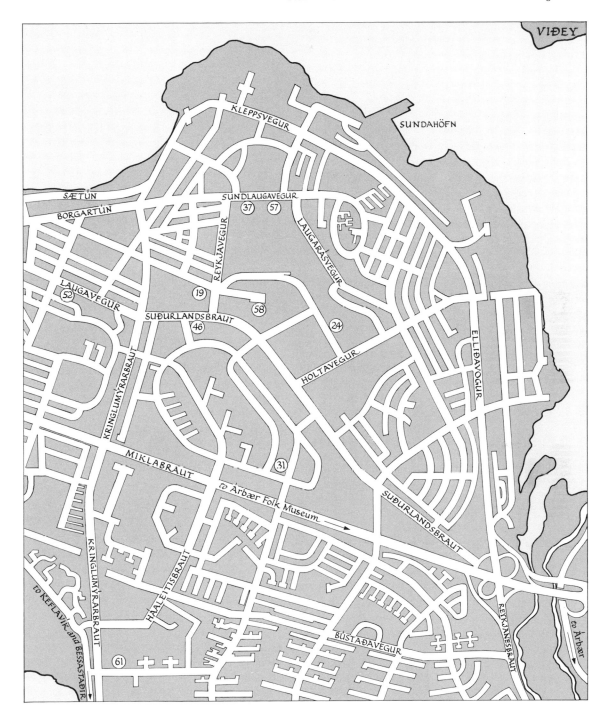

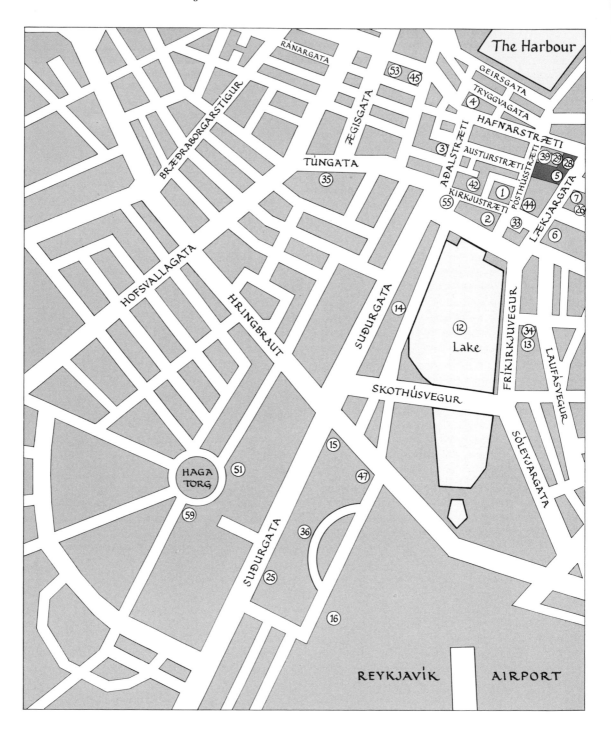

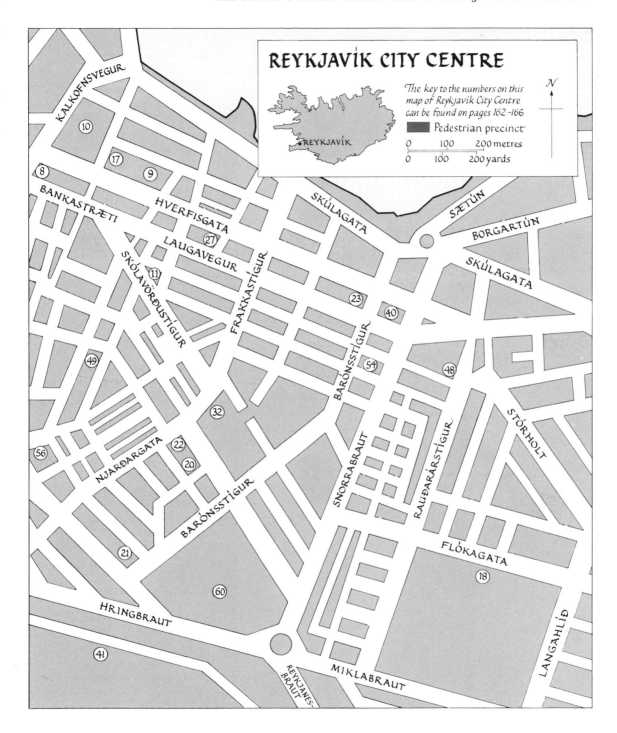

REYKJAVÍK CITY CENTRE

The key to the numbers on this map of Reykjavík City Centre can be found on pages 162-166

Pedestrian precinct

0   100   200 metres
0   100   200 yards

•REYKJAVÍK

N

KALKOFNSVEGUR

BANKASTRÆTI

HVERFISGATA

LAUGAVEGUR

SKÓLAVÖRÐUSTÍGUR

FRAKKASTÍGUR

SKÚLAGATA

SÆTÚN

BORGARTÚN

SKÚLAGATA

BARÓNSSTÍGUR

STÓRHOLT

SNORRABRAUT

RAUÐARÁRSTÍGUR

NJARÐARGATA

BARÓNSSTÍGUR

FLÓKAGATA

LANGAHLÍÐ

HRINGBRAUT

REYKJANES-BRAUT

MIKLABRAUT

1. *Austurvöllur* (Eastfield)
A small square in the heart of the city centre, near the main shopping areas and places of interest. In its centre is a statue by Einar Jónsson of Jon Sigurðsson (1811-1879), one of the most important leaders of the Icelandic people, especially in their fight for national independence (see p. 15). On the statue's plinth is a bronze relief *'Brautryðjandinn'* (*The Pioneer*).

The square is built on the site of Ingólfur Arnarson's homefield. Opposite the statue is the Parliament House, while to the south-east is the Lutheran Cathedral. The Borg Hotel is to the east and the telephone centre to the west.

2. *Althingishúsið* (Parliament House)
This is a dark grey stone building, two storeys high. Its date of erection (1881) is carved in the stonework. It is the best-known of the few stone buildings in the city. The building is not very elaborate compared to other European parliament buildings, but two significant embellishments decorate its facade. The most recognisable is a reminder of the country's previous connection with Denmark – the original stone carving of the Danish crown. More interesting though, especially since the building overlooks Ingólfur Arnarson's homefield, are reliefs showing the spirits that the first settler held in high esteem; a dragon, a vulture, a giant and a bull. It is also decorated with a coat of arms.

Since the Republic was established, the Government has usually been formed by coalitions of various political parties represented in the two-chamber Althing. The Parliament has sixty elected members, with elections held at least every four years. The Presidency is not involved in party politics and a separate Presidential election is held every four years.

3. *Reykjavík's oldest building*
Reykjavík did not really begin to grow until the middle of the eighteenth century. Then buildings like Aðalstræti 10 (number 10 Main Street) were built under the aegis of High Sheriff Skúli Magnússon. This building (it is painted yellow-brown) was one of the original sheds he built, though its appearance gives few clues to its age (a plaque is on the wall, dated 1752).

Just farther south from here and beside the telephone building there is a small park.

4. *Fálkahúsið* (Falcon House)
This building's roof celebrates the famous Icelandic gyrfalcons, once exported all over Europe. The roof has falcons at the ends of its gables and the shape of a Viking ship on the top of a lower roof. The building houses the Icelandic Hand-Crafts Centre.

5. *Lækjartorg* (Brook Square)
This used to be the main traffic centre in the city, now it is a pedestrian precinct and the site of the Tourist Bureau's Information Tower.

6. *Menntaskólinn* (High School)
This white building, which looks over the busy Lækjargata, was built in 1846 and was a meeting place of the Althing before the present-day Parliament House was built.

7. *Bernhöftstorfan* (Bernhoft's Group)
This is a group of small houses overlooking the Information Tower at Lækjartorg. The end one on Bankastræti was built in 1849 by a baker called Bernhöft and has recently been refurbished. It now houses the Lækjarbrekka restaurant which is noted for its sea-food dishes.

8. *Stjórnarráðið* (Government House)
This rather plain but pleasantly proportioned white-painted building houses the offices of the President. It was originally built in 1756 by the Danish government as a prison.

In front of the building are two statues. On the left is Christian IX, King of Denmark, depicted handing over the 1874 Constitution and on the right is Hannes Hafstein who in 1904 became the first Icelandic Minister.

9. *Thjóðleikhusið* (National Theatre)
The columns that decorate this severe building (opened in 1950) are modelled on the basalt pillars that hang from the lip of the Svartifoss waterfall which is at Skaftafell (see p.118).

10. *Arnarhóll* (Eagle's Mound)
Arnarhóll is a grassy mound to the north-east of Lækjartorg upon which there is a very striking statue of Ingólfur Arnarson showing him on the prow of his boat looking out to the bay he later called Reykjavík (see p.10). There is a good view of the harbour area from this hill.

Behind it and to the left are government offices (called Arnarhvoll) and beside them is the Supreme Court.

11. *Hegningarhúsið* (The Old Prison)
This is a utilitarian-looking two-storey building built of the dark rock dolerite in 1872. It is at Skólavörðustígur 9.

12. *Tjörnin* (The Pond)
Its northern end usually bustling with ducks and swans, Tjörnin is situated close to the shopping area. This is home for birds all the year round as parts of the lake are kept ice-free during the winter by natural warm water. There are a number of information boards that show pictures of the birds that live on the lake.

A path runs right round the three sections of the lake and in the small park at the southern end there are a number of statues.

13. *Íshúsið* (The Ice House)
This white building beside Tjörnin is being prepared as a new permanent home for paintings and sculptures that form part of the National Art Gallery's collection. Its pleasant white façade with slender windows set high up in the walls hides a more utilitarian history – it was one of the city's three ice houses. Here, ice from Tjörnin was stored before being used to freeze fish.

14. *Ráðherrabústaðurinn* ('The Minister's House')
Situated at Tjarnargata 32, beside Tjörnin. A corrugated-iron building, this brown and white house has decorated eaves and a balcony. This was the official home of the first Icelandic Minister, Hannes Hafstein; it is used for government receptions.

15. *Thjóðminjasafnið* (National Museum)
This large grey building holds a vast collection of antiquities – both artistic and practical – from Icelandic history. It also holds the National Art Gallery (*Listasafn Íslands*). Open daily in summer: 13.30-16.00; in winter, Tues, Thurs, Sat, Sun: 13.30-1600.

The small park opposite the Museum contains Einar Jónsson's gaunt statue *The Outlaw* showing an outlaw making his way to the lavafields to which he has been banished, carrying his wife's body on his back and his child in his arm.

16. *Norræna húsið* (Nordic Centre)
A white modern building (designed by the Finnish architect Alvar Alto), the Centre was built as a joint enterprise by the Nordic countries whose flags fly outside it. It has exhibitions, films and concerts that reflect aspects of Nordic culture. The library is open Mon-Fri: 09.00-19.00 (Sat: 13.00-19.00, Sun: 14.00-17.00). The cafeteria is open from 09.00-19.00 (Sun: 12.00-18.00) during the summer (closing 1 hour earlier in winter). When exhibitions are on display, they are open daily from 14.00-19.00.

17. *Landsbókasafnið* (National Library)
This fine-looking building was built in 1908 and as well as being the country's most important library it also houses the national archives. Above the entrance is a carving of a falcon (an old Icelandic emblem) and a Danish crown. Open Mon-Fri: 09.00-19.00; during the winter it is also open Sat: 09.00-12.00. The National Theatre is next door.

18. *Kjarvalsstaðir* (Municipal Art Gallery)
This is situated in the Miklatún Park and was named after the Icelandic painter Jóhannes Kjarval (see p.21) (1885-1972) who is probably best known for his landscapes. The gallery shows examples of his work and that of other artists, both Icelandic and foreign. This striking building is open daily 14.00-22.00.

19. *Ásmundur Sveinsson's Studio*
This celebrated sculptor has many of his works on view around the country (for instance *Through the Sound Barrier* outside the Loftleiðir Hotel) and

163

his studio and its garden offer a remarkable display of his eye-catching style. The front part of the studio has small windows set in the concrete hemispherical roof, while the building behind has a mass of huge glass panes. Around the garden are about two dozen statues of metal and stone, some of them of figures, while others are abstracts. The studio is open 14.00-17.00 daily (except Mon) in June, July and August.

20. *Ásmundur Sveinsson's House*
Situated at Freyjugata 41, which is west of Hallgrímskirkja, this was the studio and home of the famous sculptor; art exhibitions are now held here. Open Mon-Fri: 16.00-22.00; Sat-Sun: 14.00-22.00.

21. *Ásgrímssafn*
Located at Bergstaðarstræti 74 this small grey building with red tiles was the home of the artist Ásgrímur Jónsson (1876-1958) and is now a museum of his work. Open June-Aug, Sun-Fri: 13.30-16.00; Sept-May, Sun, Tues, Thurs: 13.30-16.00.

22. *Hnitbjörg*
This stark and unusual-looking concrete building houses the works of the sculptor Einar Jónsson (1874-1954), having previously been his home. It has its own small garden in which there are a number of sculptures. Both house and garden are open daily (except Mon) 13.30-16.00 in summer. During winter they are open on Sun and Wed at the same times. Closed December and January.

23. *Náttúrugripasafnið* (Natural History Museum)
The collection is held in a rather anonymous-looking building (Hverfisgata 116, 3rd floor) directly to the west of the bus station at Hlemmur. The museum has examples of animals (especially birds) and plants that are found in Iceland as well as samples of the main types of rocks found on the island. It is open Sat, Sun, Tues, Thurs: 13.30-16.00.

24. *Grasagarður* (Botanic Gardens)
This is south-east of the large white Exhibition Hall. As well as examples of plants found in Iceland there is a tree-lined park with a number of interesting statues. Open June-Sept, Mon-Fri: 08.00-22.00; Sat-Sun: 10.00-22.00.

25. *Árnagarður* (The Manuscript Institute)
This building now houses the Manuscript Institute and was named after Árni Magnússon (see p.15) who played a leading role in the late seventeenth and early eighteenth centuries in searching out and preserving old and decaying manuscripts of the Sagas and other writings. Árnagarður is situated in the University complex. Open in the summer Tues, Thurs, Sat: 14.00-16.00.

26. *Gallery Langbrók*
The gallery is located at Amtmannsstígur 1, south of Bankastræti. Modern handicrafts such as pottery, sculptures and textiles are on sale here. Open Mon-Fri: 12.00-18.00; if an exhibition is on, also open Sat-Sun: 14.00-18.00.

27. *Living Art Museum*
Located at Vatnsstígur 3-b, off Laugavegur, the Museum houses experimental forms of art. Open Tues-Fri: 16.00-22.00; when special exhibitions are in progress, also open Sat-Sun: 14.00-22.00.

28. *Listmunahúsið*
This art gallery is by Lækjartorg and shows the work of Icelandic artists. Open Tues-Fri: 10.00-18.00; Sat-Sun: 14.00-18.00.

29. *Gallery Lækjartorg*
The gallery shows the work of modern artists. Open daily from 14.00-18.00 (Thurs and Sun: 14.00-22.00).

30. *Árbær*
This collection of old buildings, some of which were brought here from other parts of Iceland, is centred around the farm buildings of Árbær which date from the turn of the century. Iceland's only railway locomotive (used when the harbour was being built) is also on show. Open daily (except Monday) 13.30-18.00, during the summer.

31. *Labour Unions' Gallery*
Situated at Grensásvegur 16, off Miklabraut, this gallery organises touring exhibitions around the country. Open Tues-Fri: 14.00-19.00; Sat-Sun: 14.00-22.00.

32. *Hallgrímskirkja* (Hallgrímur's church)
This is the most striking building in Reykjavik (see p.105), dominating the skyline from every direction. It is starkly simple in design, with pillars of concrete thrusting upwards, emphasising its height. There is an observation platform in the steeple which gives views over the whole city and beyond. In summer the platform is open Tues-Sat: 10.00-12.00 and 14.00-18.00; Sun: 14.00-17.00. In winter it is open on Tues-Fri: 10.00-12.00; Sat: 14.00-17.00; Sun 15.15-17.00.

Just in front of the church there is a statue of Leif Eiríksson, discoverer of Vinland (America) in 1000. This was a present from the United States on the Millenium anniversary of the Althing in 1930.

33. *Dómkirkjan* (Lutheran Cathedral)
A plain, corrugated-iron building of Danish design, this is the main church of the established religion. Usually open daily 09.00-18.30.

34. *(Fríkirkjan)* (Free Church)
This Free Lutheran church is a corrugated-iron structure, like the Cathedral, but has a little more decoration.

35. *Kristskirkja* (Roman Catholic Cathedral)
The Cathedral stands on a hill (Landakotshæð) in its own grounds. It is of neo-Gothic design (built in 1929) and, although modelled on the carved stone examples of mainland Europe, is made of a roughly finished concrete.

Opposite it is the modern Catholic hospital and to the Cathedral's left is a handsome green-tiled Seminary. These three buildings stand out in strong contrast to each other and to the other buildings in the neighbourhood – whether stone villas or more modest homes with corrugated-iron walls. Open Mon, Tues, Thurs and Fri: 09.00-17.00.

36. *Háskóli Íslands* (The University)
This large building was erected in 1940 as the University's permanent home. It stands on a small hill and its situation is made more impressive by the open ground in front of it which it dominates.

In front is Ásmundur Sveinsson's bronze statue of Sæmundur the Learned, showing him about to strike the head of the Devil (the seal) with a book. Sæmundur was an eleventh-century scholar (hence the book) and was the hero of many folk-tales in which he fought the Devil. In the story to which this statue refers, Sæmundur, returning from Paris, was offered a 'lift' to Iceland by the Devil in the guise of a seal, in return for his soul. As the shore was neared, Sæmundur cheated the Devil by striking him with the book; this stunned him, allowing the scholar to swim ashore by himself, thus saving his soul.

37. *Laugardalur* (Sports Centre)
The sports centre houses a huge outdoor swimming pool heated by natural hot water. Beside it are football and athletics stadia and the city's campsite. This area, as the name *'laug'* (hot) suggests, is the source of hot springs. Open Mon-Fri: 07.20-20.30; Sat: 07.20-17.30; Sun: 08.00-14.30.

38. *Öskjuhlíð* (Ash-tree Hill)
This prominent hill to the south-east of the city affords an excellent view both of the city itself and of the surrounding countryside, but has hot-water storage tanks at the summit, which detract from its own appearance.

Other Places of Interest on Maps
39. Main Post office
40. Bus station – Reykjavík buses
41. Coach station – long distance buses
42. Telegraph office (telephones and telegrams)
43. Tourist Bureau office
44. Hotel Borg
45. Hotel City
46. Hotel Esja
47. Hotel Garður
48. Hotel Hof
49. Hotel Holt

50. Hotel Loftleiðir
51. Hotel Saga
52. Guesthouse Brautarholt
53. Guesthouse Ránargata
54. Guesthouse Snorrabraut
55. Salvation Army hostel
56. Youth hostel
57. Campsite
58. Exhibition hall
59. University Assembly and Concert hall
60. State hospital
61. City hospital
62. Reykjavík airport terminal

Theatre, Opera and Concerts	Location
Summer Theatre	Tjarnarbíó at Tjarnargata
City Theatre (Iðnó-leikfélag Reykjavíkur)	Vonarstræti 3
National Theatre (Thjóðleikhúsið)	Hverfisgata 19
Icelandic Symphony Orchestra (Sinfóníuhljómsveitin)	Háskólabíó at Hagatorg
Icelandic Opera (Íslenska Óperan)	Gamla Bíó at Ingólfstræti

NIGHTLIFE IN REYKJAVÍK
Cinemas
The following cinemas often show English-language films with Icelandic subtitles:

Cinema	Location
Austurbæjarbíó	Snorrabraut
Bíóhöllin	Álfabakki 8
Háskólabíó	Hagatorg
Laugarásbíó	Kleppsvegur
Nýja Bíó	Lækjargata
Regnboginn	Hverfisgata
Stjörnubíó	Laugavegur 94
Tónabíó	Skipholt 33

Ósvaldur Knudsen's small cinema at Hellusundi 6A (near the Hotel Holt, to the east of the lake), is also worth visiting. This shows films of eruptions, glaciers, wild life and other aspects of Icelandic life, with English commentary. The films are often advertised as 'The Volcano Show'.

Theatres
Many of Reykjavík's theatres and concert halls are open only during the winter months. The Summer Theatre has a series of 'Light Nights' which are English-language performances of folk singing, Sagas and other forms of performance art.

Discotheques
A number of these have opened in the last few years and one of them (Broadway) is claimed to be the largest in Scandinavia.

Discotheques	Location
Broadway	Álfabakki 8
Glæsibær	Álfheimar 76
Hollywood	Ármúli 5
Klúbburinn	Lækjarteigur 2
Óðal	v/Austurvöllur
Safari	Skúlagata 30
Sigtún	Suðurlandsbraut 26
Thórscafé	Brautarholt 20

Eating out
Icelanders take their eating seriously and food in restaurants and cafés is well prepared in pleasant, clean surroundings. The most common meat dishes are lamb and mutton, and most restaurants offer both Icelandic and international menus. There is an extensive range of fish dishes too, based on varieties of fish that are common in many other European countries; but some dishes feature other varieties (for instance flounder) that may be new to visitors. Eating out is not cheap, but neither is it as expensive as in tourist areas of other capital cities. There are no cheap cafés or public houses in which to eat, but there are a large number of good restaurants which serve a wide variety of dishes, many of which are listed below. Many of the best places to eat are situated between the lake and the harbour or near Laugavegur. Both the bus stations and

the domestic airport have cafeterias. A number of the smaller places may not be open outside the summer season and many restaurants close after Saturday lunch-time until Monday. It is not customary to tip.

Only a few of the restaurants are licensed. Those hotels with a bar are noted in the hotels list and other restaurants with a full licence include: Arnarhóll, Broadway, Leikhúskjallarinn, Naust, Rán, Thórscafé. The following restaurants have a licence for wine: Hjákoknum (Laugavegur 28), Brauðbær, Hornið, Í Kvosinni, Lækjarbrekka, Zorba, Torfan, Hallargarðurinn, Skalkaskjól 2 in Hotel Garður.

The following list contains many of Reykjavík's restaurants, hotel restaurants and cafés. There is a much smaller price differential between a café and an hotel restaurant than is found in other European capital cities.

Restaurants	Location
Arnarhóll	Hverfisgata 8-10
Borg Hotel	Pósthússtræti 11
Drekinn (Chinese)	Laugavegur 22
Gullni Haninn	Laugavegur 178
Hallargarðurinn	Kringlumýrarbraut
Hjákokknum	Laugavegur 28
Holt Hotel	Bergstaðastræti 37
Hornið	Hafnarstræti 15
Hressingarskálinn	Austurstræti 20
Í Kvosinni (dinner only)	Austurstræti 22
Lækjarbrekka	Bankastræti 2
Lauga – Ás	Laugarásvegur 1
Leikhúskjallarinn	Hverfisgata
Loftleiðir Hotel	Reykjavík airport
Mamma Rosa (Italian)	Hlemmtorg
Mensa	Lækjargata 2
Naust	Vesturgata 8
Nlfi (vegetarian)	Laugavegur 20
Potturinn and Pannan	Brautarholt 22
Rán	Skólavörðustigur 16
Sælkerinn	Austurstræti 22
Saga Hotel	Hagatorg 1
Svarta Pannan	Hafnarstræti/ Tryggvagata
Thórscafé (dinner only)	Brautarholt 20
Torfan	Amtmannstigur 1

Self-Service Restaurants	Location
Árberg	Ármúli 21
Askur	Suðurlandsbraut 14
Ásinn	Hverfigata 105
Esja Hotel	Suðurlandsbraut 2
Fjarkinn	Austurstræti 4
Garður Hotel	v/Hringbraut
Glæsibær	Álfheimar 76
Gosbrunnurinn	Laugavegur 116
Hjákokknum	Laugavegur 28
Hallargarðurinn	Kringlumýrarbraut
Hlíðagrill	Stigahlíð 45-47
Höfðakaffi	Vagnhöfði 11
Hotel Hof	Rauðarárstígur 18
Ingólfsbrunnur	Aðalstræti 9
Kaffi-Torg	Hafnarstræti 20
Kaffivagninn	Grandagarður
Kokkhúsið	Lækjargata 8
Loftleiðir Hotel (open 5am)	Reykjavík airport
Múlakaffi	Hallarmúli
Norræna Húsið	v/Hringbraut
Umferðarmiðstöðin	Long distance coach station
Vogakaffi	Súðarvogur 50

ACCOMMODATION IN REYKJAVÍK

The following list gives some details of the main hotels, guest houses and hostels. There is also accommodation available in smaller establishments, mostly private homes, during the summer. Details of these can be obtained through your tour operator.

Of the nine hotels, the most expensive are normally the Loftleiðir, Saga and Esja; then come Hof, Holt, City, Óðinsvé and Borg. The Garður is the cheapest; the Borg is right in the centre of the city; the others are within easy walking distance except for the Esja and the Loftleiðir which are about 2.5-3 km from the centre. The Loftleiðir's main advantage is that it is also the international airport's city terminal; this is to be borne in mind if you have to report there for your bus to the airport. A bus runs from the Loftleiðir to the city every half hour and the Esja is on a busy bus route.

The campsite is in Laugardalur (see p.159),

located next to the swimming pool. The easiest way to reach it from the centre of the town is via Skúlagata, Borgartún and Sundlaugavegur; buses regularly ply this route. There is a warden on duty and the campsite office is a good source of help and information; tours can also be booked from here. Facilities are good (heated washrooms, hot water for washing dishes, flat grass)

but can be hard pressed when large parties (over 100 people) turn up together. The site is more or less flat, but try to keep away from any hollows as the drainage is poor and large puddles can build up in wet weather. The nearest public telephone is in the entrance hall of the swimming pool. To the east of the site a new youth hostel is being built and beyond that there is a group of shops.

Hotels, Guesthouses and Youth Hostels in Reykjavík

Name	Address	Tel. No. (code-91)	No. of Rooms	No. of Beds	Open all Year	Restaurant	Cafeteria	Bar	Conference Facilities
Hotel Borg	Pósthússtræti 11	11440	46	72	yes	yes	no	yes	yes
Hotel City	Ránargata 4a	18650	31	60	yes	yes	yes	no	no
Hotel Esja	Suðurlandsbraut 2	82200	133	264	yes	yes	yes	yes	yes
Hotel Garður	v/Hringbraut	15918	44	90	no	no	yes	no	yes
Hotel Hof	Rauðarárstígur 18	28866	31	62	yes	no	yes	no	yes
Hotel Holt	Bergstaðastraeti 37	25700	52	—	yes	yes	no	yes	yes
Hotel Loftleiðir	Reykjavík Airport	22322	218	434	yes	yes	yes	yes	yes
Hotel Óðinsvé	Óðinstorg	25224	20	36	—	—	—	—	—
Hotel Saga	v/Hagatorg	29900	106	181	yes	yes	no	yes	yes
Guesthouse	Flókagata 1	21155	9	—	yes	no	no	no	no
Guesthouse	Flókagata 5	19828	13	—	yes	no	no	no	no
Guesthouse	Brautarholt 22	20986	24	48	no	no	no	no	no
Guesthouse Vikingur	Ránargata 12	19367	10	29	no	no	no	no	no
Guesthouse	Snorrabraut 52	16522	18	42	yes	no	no	no	no
Salvation Army hostel	Kirkjustræti 2	13203	24	72	yes	no	yes	no	no
Youth hostel	Laufásvegur 41	24950	—	70	no	no	no	no	no

Useful Information

1. *Banks:* National Bank (Landsbanki Íslands) head office: Austurstræti 11
Fisheries Bank (Utvegsbanki Íslands) head office: Austurstræti 19
2. *Chemists:* Ingólfs Apótek, Hafnarstræti 5 (tel 29300); Laugavegs Apótek, Laugavegur 16 (tel 24045); at least one of these major chemists will be open any time of the week, day or night.
3. *Emergency:* fire brigade: tel 11100
                ambulance: tel 11100
                police: tel 11166
            (doctor on call: tel 81200/*nights: 21230*)
4. *Golf:* Golfklúbbur Reykjavíkur at Grafarholt;

Golfklúbbur Ness at Suðurnes; Golfklúbburinn Keilir at Hafnarfjörður.
5. *Hospital:* The City Hospital (tel 81212) is at Sléttuvegur, south-east of Öskjuhlíð.
6. *Left Luggage:* at the BSI (long-distance) coach terminal.
7. *Lost Property Office:* at the Police Station at Hverfisgata 113.
8. *Offices:* Usually open Mon-Fri: 09.00-17.00. Lunch is usually taken 12.00-13.00.
9. *Post Office:* The Main Post Office is on the corner of Austurstræti and Pósthússtræti. Open Mon-Fri: 09.00-17.00; Sat: 09.00-12.00. The Post Office in

the BSI terminal is open Mon-Sat: 14.00-19.30.

10. *Shops:* The main shopping hours are Mon-Fri: 09.00-18.00 (some close at 20.00 or 22.00 on Fri); kiosks are often open until 23.30 each day. Many shops are closed on Sat in summer.

11. *Swimming Pools:* Sundlaugarnar at Laugardalur (outdoor, by campsite); Sundhöllin at Barónsstigur (indoor); Sundlaug Vesturbæjar at Hofsvallagata (outdoor).

12. *Telegraph Office:* Kirkjustræti/Thorvaldsensstræti. Open Mon-Sat: 09.00-19.00; Sun: 11.00-18.00.

13. *Telex:* At the Telegraph Office and some hotels.

4
REYKJAVÍK TO HELLA

Distance:	93 km
Route:	ring road (1) east
Maps:	general maps 3 and 6
	1:15 000 map of Reykjavík
Main places to visit:	Elliðavatn (lake) ★
	Hveragerði (hot springs, glasshouses) ★ ★
	Selfoss (town)
	Urriðafoss (waterfall) ★
	Ægissíða (caves)
Road Conditions:	highway
Adjacent sections:	21 (Reykjavík to Krísuvík and Hveragerði)
	22 (Selfoss to Geysir)
	20 (Sigalda to the south coast)
	5 (Hella to Vík)
Notes:	This is a short journey (half a day) giving an easy start to the trip round the island. Good farming land.

AS THE main road makes its way out of the capital it passes many of the new pastel-colour apartment buildings that are springing up all around the growing city. To the right, road 410 leads to Elliðavatn where there are summerhouses (still in view of the suburbs) and pleasant walks by the trees round the shore. The important salmon fishing river of Elliðár flows from the lake's northern shore and through Reykjavík's suburbs on its way to the sea. To the south of the lake is the Hjallar fault and to the north are the pseudocraters at Rauðhólar. There are about one hundred of these red and black craters, many of which have been destroyed for building materials, leaving behind gaunt, distorted shapes by the roadside.

To the right is a vast complex of mountains, much of it part of the Bláfjöll (685 m), with smaller hills and craters to its south-east. The Bláfjöll area gives good skiing during the winter as does Hveradalir, just a few kilometres farther on.

On the left is the exposed moorland of Mosfellsheiði and then Hengill (803 m) which has a number of geothermal sources on its southern foothills. There is a very fine view just over the summit of the mountain road from a viewpoint/car park that appears quite suddenly on the right. From here you can see the flat and fertile agricultural plain that stretches to the sea some fifteen kilometres south of the ring road. The Westman Islands lie just off the coast to the east.

The road now descends to the plain and enters Hveragerði ('garden of hot springs').

The settlement's numerous glasshouses are heated by natural warm water tapped from the hills just above it and tomatoes, cucumbers, gherkins, bananas and flowers are grown here; in a large florist's shop in the settlement's main road there are tropical plants happily growing just 250 km south of the Arctic Circle. Hveragerði has been built up as one of the country's most important horticultural centres and it houses the National Horticultural College. There are two petrol stations, a bank, swimming pool, supermarket and an hotel. The most interesting place to visit is the northern bank of the river that runs behind the town; just beyond the main part of the housing area there is a bridge that leads to a number of bubbling hot springs. The bare hillside has many small vents with wisps of steam coming from them and farther up there is a large grey concrete tank and a collection of steel pipes that distribute the hot water to the glasshouses and the homes. About a kilometre upstream there is another bridge and beyond that there are two massive white concrete wellheads that throw out clouds of vapour with a thundering sound.

The road continues through the rich farming district, with Ingólfsfjall (551 m) and its fine scree slopes to the north.

Just before Selfoss, the centre of the surrounding dairy farming area, there is a turning to the left (road 35) to Thingvellir, Geysir and Gullfoss (section 22). Next, the Ölfusá is crossed by a suspension bridge.

Selfoss is a neat and prosperous town which boasts many trees and shrubs in its gardens and in the small park. It has a good shopping centre, including a large supermarket (on the left as the town is entered): this should be borne in mind as the next large town is Höfn, some 419 km further on. The bus station is by the supermarket; the swimming pool and the campsite are to the right of the main road after the shops and there is a dairy at the far end of the town. There are also a hospital, two hotels, a museum and art gallery.

Just before the road crosses the mighty Thjórsá, a turning to the right (road 302) goes down to the farm of Urriðafoss, about 1 km away. From here there is a short walk to the waterfall of the same name. The river is very wide and the grey mass of water thunders as it goes over the V-shaped notch in the river bed. Just below the falls, 'dead ice' (ice which has not been recently formed) may be found even though there is no snow lying elsewhere in the district. Here the dead ice is probably left over from winter. (Elsewhere in Iceland dead ice can be found which may be 100 years old, perhaps having ash on top of it.) The Thjórsá is the country's longest river (230 km long), coming all the way from the Hofsjökull glacier. Urriðafoss is its last waterfall before the sea.

The turning north to Hekla (road 26 – section 20) is at Tunga (where there is a petrol station) and there is a view of the Westman Islands as the settlement of Hella is approached. Hella is situated in a grassy area, bounded by an expanse of black sand and gravel though which the Ytri-Rangá flows, the river that drains the western side of Hekla. The settlement has two supermarkets, a petrol station, restaurant, hotel, and a bank. The campsite can be a little difficult to find: after the shops on the main road a dusty track goes seawards and then curves right towards a race-track. The site is down this track, on the east bank of the river; it is reasonably flat and very well equipped with showers, WCs and hot water. From Hella, Hekla is seen in profile, along the direction of the volcano's main fissure.

At the farm of Ægissíða, on the western bank of the Ytri-Rangá and opposite the campsite, there are some man-made caves, one of which has a circular hole in the roof. These may have been made by the Irish hermits who lived in this area prior to the arrival of the settlers.

If the eastern bank of the river is followed back northwards, road 264 leads to some disused farms in Hekla's lavafields. Not all the farms are disused, however. At Gunnarsholt there is an experimental farm, where research is carried out into cultivation of the deserts. Farther on is Næfurholt, the farm with the unenviable distinction of being closer to Hekla than any other. It has twice been destroyed by the volcano and twice rebuilt.

5
HELLA TO VÍK

Distance:	99 km
Route:	ring road (1)
Map:	general map 6
Main places to visit:	Seljalandsfoss (waterfall) ★ ★
	Skógafoss (waterfall) ★ ★
	Sólheimajökull (walk to glacier) ★ ★
	Dyrhólaey (viewpoint) ★ ★ ★
Road Conditions:	highway until just after Hvolsvöllur, thereafter intermittently
Adjacent sections:	23 (Hvolsvöllur to Markarfljót via Fljótsdalur)
	43 (Thórsmörk)
	6 (Vík to Skaftafell)
Notes:	Good views of the glacier at the start of the journey. Section 23 can be taken as a detour between Hvolsvöllur and the Markarfljót.

THE ROAD to Hvolsvöllur goes through an area of black sand, gravel and ashes, with farmland stretching southwards to the sea. The settlement owes its importance to the co-operative headquarters there and it has an hotel, bank, petrol station, supermarket and a campsite. Section 23 starts at road 261 to the left. The good highway surface unfortunately ends after the settlement, so drivers coming directly from Reykjavík will soon have their first experience of the real Icelandic road conditions: take care until you get used to them!

The land on each side of the road is now much poorer with less plant cover and the few farms that exist are perched on higher ground. The glacier Eyjafjallajökull beckons, with the isolated hill of Stóra-Dímon (78 m) standing guard over the district round Thórsmörk. The most interesting sight here is the mounds of gravel that have been built up to stop the glacial waters from flooding such sparse meadowland as there is. The whole district from Hvolsvöllur to the hills below Eyjafjallajökull has long been at the mercy of the ever-changing watercourses that are fed mainly by the glaciers. In the area around Thórsmörk the glacial rivers join up and form the Markar-

fljót, said in old tales to be the home of a monster that grew out of a large skate thrown away by a farmer. This wide and well-braided river system used to divide into four distributaries: Markarfljót, Álar, Affall and the Thverá (the Thverá was joined to the Markarfljót during a *jökulhlaup* caused by an eruption of Eyjafjallajökull).

The land bounded by these rivers used to be marshy and continually flooded, so the barriers were built to ensure that the Markarfljót didn't flood the Thverá again and the latter now only collects water from Fljótshlið, the district sheltering under the hills to the north. A long bridge crosses the frighteningly strong current of the Markarfljót. The latter carries a lot of sand and gravel down to the sea where it is building a large area of sandur beyond the wet meadows. Just after the bridge is crossed is the track (road 249) to Thórsmörk – this is described in section 43.

The road runs below Eyjafjallajökull glacier (1666 m), which used to be joined to the larger Mýrdalsjökull to its east, but the gradual warming-up of the climate has shrunk the ice cap. The glacier has erupted twice since the Settlement, in 1612 and 1821. As the road goes south there is a most attractive waterfall, Seljalandsfoss (60 m).

Not much water comes over the lip of the cliff (actually an old sea cliff); it is the wispy and wind-blown character of the fall that gives it its charm. It is possible to walk behind it but the path is wet and rather slippery. To the left there are a couple of smaller falls and to the right is an interesting rock formation, including layers of basalt pillars. On the narrow ledges on these cliffs are numerous gulls' nests, the birds wheeling about in the air currents funnelled against the rock face. There is plenty of flat grass here for camping, but no facilities.

The very narrow coastal strip has a number of farms sheltering under the tall cliffs, the most prominent cliffs being under Steinafjall (810 m); this strip is narrowest at the almost totally enclosed lagoon of Holtsós. Another waterfall, Skógafoss (62 m, see p.114), is some 10 km farther on; it is much broader and has a greater flow of water than Seljalandsfoss. There is a campsite with a primitive toilet at this waterfall and the nearby settlement of Skógar has an Edda Hotel, a swimming pool and a museum. West of the waterfall a track runs up to a tourist hut at Fimmvörðuháls; this is the site of craters high up in the hills between the two main glaciers.

Skógasandur is a wasteland, a black mass of sand and gravel with a number of large boulders strewn across its surface; it was partly created by a *jökulhlaup*, possibly in the tenth century. The eastern section (Sólheimasandur) lies below Sólheimajökull, a valley glacier from Mýrdalsjökull that reaches down to only 150 m above sea level. The glacier's snout can be reached by a track going along the eastern bank of its river, Jökulsá, whose strong smell of solfataric hydrogen sulphide has resulted in the alternative name of Fúlilækur ('Stink River'). The track goes on for about 2 km; then there is a pleasant and straightforward walk (about 3 km) over grass and moss towards the eastern section of the glacier. If you keep the glacial streams to your left and begin to climb when you are opposite the rock that divides the glacier into two, there is a good view of the black and deeply crevassed snout. The glacial streams and the snout can then be reached from below the cliffs after descending a slope with a lot of loose rock on it.

At Skeiðflötur a turning to Dyrhólaey (road 218) goes off to the right and leads across a narrow causeway of sharp stones. This road is closed and admittance restricted during the nesting season (May and June). Once across, the track then splits into two. The left-hand track climbs above the lagoon of Dyrhólaós and leads to a beautiful view eastwards over to the stacks (rock columns) and the black sands below Reynisfjall. The other track leads to the Dyrhólaey lighthouse and gives a wide view stretching from the Westman Islands in the west over to Eyjafjallajökull and Mýrdalsjökull to the north. Below this promontory are magnificent black sands and the crashing surf of the Atlantic. The far side of the cliff looks down to the mainland's most southerly tip and one of the country's best-known views − a natural arch through which small boats can (with great care!) sail. The cliffs are very dangerous (110 m high) and caution is needed. The track that leads up to the lighthouse is steep and has a number of tight bends. The surface is also loose so if it is wet then the journey up could be tricky. If in doubt, walk.

The ring road then continues over the interesting, sometimes steep route to Vík, which until the 1920s was used by small ships; but since then the sea has retreated some 200 m, leaving the settlement without a harbour. There is a garage, hospital, hotel, some shops, a petrol station and a bank. The campsite is found by turning left just as the main road starts to curve in the same direction. The site has grassy terraces and is quite exposed; it has a couple of WCs and sheltered sinks with cold water. There is an arctic tern breeding ground opposite the site; these audacious birds constantly wheel about in the air and dive on anyone who seems to be approaching their territory. Overlooking the settlement is Reynisfjall, which has a navigation mast on its summit. From Vík, a road leads to the top where there are many sea-birds, including puffins and fulmars.

6
VÍK TO SKAFTAFELL

Distance:	151 km
Route:	ring road (1)
Maps:	general maps 6 and 9
	1:100 000 map of Öræfajökull
Main places to visit:	Kirkjubæjarklaustur (pseudocraters) ★ ★
	Skeiðarárjökull (walk to glacier) ★ ★ ★
Road Conditions:	poor, and the journey over Mýrdalssandur can be very rough.
Adjacent sections:	42 (Landmannalaugar to south coast)
	7 (Skaftafell)
Notes:	Hard driving over glacial sands. Good views of the glaciers but watch out for skuas.

THE FIRST part of the journey is dominated by Mýrdalsjökull, which has been responsible for creating much of the surrounding landscape. Mýrdalsjökull is the country's fourth biggest glacier and two great domes of ice about 200-400 m thick rise above the mountain, giving it a maximum height of 1480 m. The ice makes its way down by valley glaciers, some of which can be seen on its eastern side. While the glacier has been building the black wasteland of Mýrdalssandur by the steady grinding down of the hillsides, the main force that created the sandur was the sub-glacial volcano of Katla. This is one of Iceland's most active volcanoes and has erupted some sixteen times since the Settlement, the last occasion being in 1918. The eruptions cause *jökulhlaups* which follow the Kötlujökull (Hofðabrekkujökull) glacier; the quantity of water involved is quite massive – five times the rate of flow of the mouth of the Amazon! The flood may only last for a day but can cause terrible damage. During the 1918 eruption, ice to a depth of 200-300 m was swept past the rock of Hafursey which is just below Kötlujökull.

The sands are usually flat or gently sloping, with a few boulders and clumps of vegetation scattered about. The isolated and massive palagonite rocks of Hjörleifshöfði (221 m) and Hafursey (582 m) stand towering above this black expanse, with rather meagre-looking tracks leading over to them. The (usually rough) road is covered with gravel. In dry weather it is very dusty and deep ruts may develop which can sometimes lead a light vehicle off the road. Cold and very strong winds sweep down the open sands from the ice. Sheep graze on either side of the road, somehow finding enough grass to feed on, though conditions for them improve just before the bridge over the Skálm where there are numerous grassy mounds of gravel. After the bridge there is the Skálmarbæjarhraun lavafield and a little later on there is a curious collection of small cairns erected by passing travellers. The bridge over the Hólmsá comes up very quickly (at a bend) and from here on there is a pleasant area of grass and shrubs, with a campsite at Hrífunes (sharp turn right a little after the petrol station), which has running water and a WC.

Once the next big river (the Kúðafljót) is crossed, road 208 goes left up to the track that leads to Eldgjá, Landmannalaugar and, farther on, to Sprengisandur. (This is described in section 42.) Beyond the river is the broad valley of the river Skaftá, which comes down from the western side of Vatnajökull. Two huge streams of lava have flowed down this valley: from Eldgjá (about 700AD) and from Laki in 1783. This lava can be clearly seen under the cliffs of Skálarheiði

173

and it has split the river into two courses (one to the Kúðafljót, the other below the hills and then to Kirkjubæjarklaustur).

The crater row of Lakagígar is reached by a track, found by taking road 206 just after the lavafield of Nýja-Eldhraun is crossed. This lava came from Laki and together with Eldhraun, covers much of the lava from Eldgjá. Laki was the site of the most disastrous eruption the country has seen when, in 1783, a 25-km long crater row was formed with more than 100 craters, now mostly between 30 m and 70 m high. The eruption was preceded by earthquakes which lasted a week, the eruption beginning on 8 June 1783 and ending eight months later in February 1784. During the initial stages, lava flowed at a rate of about 5,000 cubic metres per second and filled the Skaftá valley to a depth of 200 m, causing a bluish dust haze to hang across the whole country during the summer. Its high sulphur content together with the poisonous gases killed half the country's cattle and three-quarters of the sheep and horses by completely destroying their grazing lands. This disaster brought about a famine that led to the deaths of about one-quarter of Iceland's 49,000 population, forcing the Danish government to consider the complete evacuation of the country.

The approach to Kirkjubæjarklaustur is heralded by what look like dunes, but are in fact Iceland's biggest collection of pseudocraters, made of black and red ash and now grassed over. The shelter provided by these craters (perhaps 3 m to 10 m high) offers good campsites, but there are no facilities. In this area of 50 sq km (called Landbrotshólar) there are over 1,000 pseudocraters, the lava coming from the eastern side of the lavafield produced by Eldgjá. Just before the settlement a turning to the right (road 204) leads to Landbrot; this route goes between the craters and the river Skaftá, passing a few small lakes on the way. Kirkjubæjarklaustur is a small but important settlement in this region, with a garage, petrol station, two hotels, a bank and a swimming pool. Irish priests lived here before the Settlement and in 1186 a convent was built at Kirkjuhólar just outside the settlement; its remains can still be seen.

Beyond Kirkjubæjarklaustur lies Brunahraun lavafield, which is covered in green and yellow mosses; this lava also came down from Laki in 1783, after following the Hverfisfljót's valley. There are many fine hills on the landward side; Kálfafell in particular shows good layering of volcanic rock including pillars of basalt. Núpsvotn, the last river before the great glacial outwash of Skeiðarársandur, takes water from a variety of places, including the glacial lake of Grænalon which overflows on occasions, causing huge floods in the river.

The Skeiðarársandur provided the last obstacle to the completion of the ring road, before the glacial river Skeiðará was finally bridged in 1974. The sandur is fed by the largest valley glacier in Europe, Skeiðarárjökull, and covers some 1,000 sq km. The road and its numerous bridges are monuments to man's attempts to control the glacial rivers; during summer the volume of water flowing over the sands may be 200-400 cubic metres per second (compared to the river Thames's summer flow of perhaps 40 cubic metres per second); in the winter it is very small, but spring thaws can raise the rivers' levels substantially. Apart from the volume of water the bridges must also cope with the quickly changing pattern of the river beds.

Beneath the Vatnajökull ice cap is the Grímsvötn caldera (a caldera is an old volcano which has collapsed in on itself), some 40 sq km in area and lying below the ridge of Svíahnúkar, where there is a lot of solfataric activity. The heat from this melts the ice and a deep lake, covered by a 200 m thick layer of ice, gathers in Grímsvötn. Every few years the ice is lifted up by the water and a massive flood flows under the ice of Skeiðarárjökull, causing a *jökulhlaup*. This may produce a flow of over 50,000 cubic metres per second with perhaps 10,000 cubic metres per second of that through the Skeiðará. The sudden flood breaks up the moraines and the area of sandur under water increases dramatically.

During the *jökulhlaup* of 1934 the Skeiðará was a massive 9 km wide at the glacier's snout and huge icebergs up to 20 m high were carried along by the rush of water. Where these ended up and eventually melted they left depressions ('kettle holes') in the sand and a number of these can be found during a walk towards the snout.

There are a number of tracks leading to the glacier's massive snout; great care must be taken if driving in a two-wheel drive vehicle as these tracks often have boulders on them. The sheer mass of the ice at the snout is overwhelming. Depending on the direction you walk, you will come across gently sloping areas of ice or crevasses or lakes. The walk up to the snout can be a hazardous undertaking, however, as the sandur is the breeding ground for some 3,000 pairs of skuas. These birds can be menacing towards humans if they think that their young are in danger. If you are attacked, safety can best be found by sheltering next to one of the telegraph poles on the sands or perhaps by holding a stick above you, as this will discourage the skuas from getting too close.

Just before the Skeiðará is crossed, and on the landward side of the road, there is a single pillar of rock, rent by fractures caused by frost shattering. It is fenced off to stop people picking at the crumbling surface and destroying this lone survivor in the wasteland. Towards the eastern side of the sands are huge gravel embankments, manmade and built to prevent the farming land from being inundated with water; over a long period of time the Skeiðará has been moving steadily eastwards. The view towards Skaftafellsjökull and the hills around it is breathtaking. Behind the dark grey of the sand and beside the white of the glacier is the lush green moorland of Skaftafellsheiði, a beautiful setting for the Skaftafell National Park.

7
SKAFTAFELL

Maps:	general map 9
	1:25 000 map of Skaftafell
Main places to visit:	Skaftafellsjökull (glacier) ★ ★ ★
	Svartifoss (waterfall) ★ ★
	Skorarbrýr ridge (long walk) ★ ★ ★
	Svínafellsjökull (glacier) ★ ★
Adjacent section:	8 (Skaftafell to Höfn)
Notes:	It is worth spending at least a day here if time permits.

IN 1968 Skaftafell was established as Iceland's second national park (the first one was created in 1928 at Thingvellir). All or parts of three glaciers (Skaftafellsjökull, Skeiðarárjökull and Morsárjökull) and their rivers lie within the park. Skaftafell campsite is one of the country's finest, with a toilet block, showers, supermarket, cafe and petrol pumps; a leaflet, the 1:25 000 map of the area and a lot of helpful advice can be obtained from the warden. From the campsite (see p.116) there are a number of good walks (well marked out) above and around Skaftafellsheiði which provide spectacular views. The weather in Skaftafell can be particularly fine.

Skaftafellsjökull
One of the most popular short walks from the campsite is to the snout of Skaftafellsjökull.

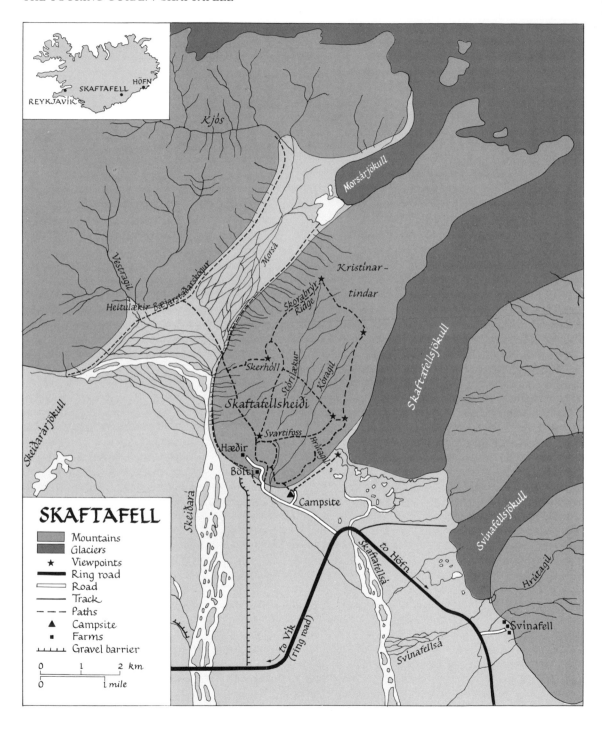

REYKJAVÍK
SKAFTAFELL
HÖFN

Kjós

Morsárjökull

Vestragil

Morsá

Heitulækir Bæjarstaðarskógur

Kristinar-
tindar

Skorabryr
Ridge

Skerhóll

Storilækur

Kóragil

Skaftafellsheiði

Skaftafellsjökull

Skeiðarárjökull

Svartifoss

Hrútagil

Hæðir

Bölti

Campsite

Svínafellsjökull

SKAFTAFELL

Mountains
Glaciers
★ Viewpoints
Ring road
Road
Track
--- Paths
▲ Campsite
■ Farms
⊥⊥⊥ Gravel barrier

0   1   2 km
0   1 mile

Skeiðará

to Höfn

Skaftafellsá

to Vík
(ring road)

Svínafellsá

Hrútagil

Svínafell

The eastern side of the park is dominated by the great mass of snow and ice on Hrútsfjall; behind it, ice from Öræfajökull feeds the eastern section of Skaftafellsjökull, while its western section flows from Vatnajökull. The rocky spur that divides these two sections (Súlukambur) is being worn away and provides grit and rocks for the black medial moraine that lies towards the eastern side of the glacier.

The path skirts the ragged and shattered face of Loshellrar, its scree slopes of sharp boulders and stones contrasting with the smooth stones of the moraines just to the right of the path. Along the walls of this steep cliff glacial striae can be seen – marks on the solid rock surface that have been produced by the scraping past of the ice and the rocks held within it.

The glacier's snout is easily approached though it should be remembered that while it might be sunny and warm by the tents, it will be cold by the ice; no matter whether there is a wind or not, there is a layer of very cold air between the snout and the moraines. The meltwater at the side of the ice can be crossed and the snout reached. While most of the upper part of the glacier is quite white, the snout is jet black; it is difficult to remember that this is ice. In front of the snout are the sand and gravel that are being dumped by the glacier. The first part of this end moraine may be safe to walk on, but going on the ice needs crampons and an ice axe. Behind the snout there are great crevasses, with long and steep ridges of ice between them. If care is taken these ridges can be walked along, but a couple of hundred metres up, the steepness and scale of the ridges makes progress much more difficult. Since the glacier has retreated from the valley wall it is possible to scramble over the rocks by the side of the ice, though care must be taken in case scree tumbles down the slopes. The high moraines just below the river give a good view of the snout, the crevasses and the meltwater streams.

Svartifoss

This waterfall (see p.118) is easily reached. It is a pleasant walk from the campsite but care should be taken on the path as it goes near the edge of some cliffs. There is a rich variation of plants on the hillside as the district is quite sheltered and has only a few sheep (there are two farms in the park). The cover given by the vegetation provides shelter for a number of birds, including grouse, red wing, meadow pippit and snipe.

The path runs below Svartifoss, an unusual waterfall whose charm lies in the basalt columns that ring the amphitheatre which the stream has opened up. A great number of these actually hang from the lip as the bottom part of them has dropped off. This unusual configuration has been the inspiration for part of the design of the National Theatre in Reykjavík.

Once on the moorland, there is a good view of Skeiðarárjökull and of its zig-zag medial moraines and the steep cliffs far away on its western limit. The huge complex of streams running from it is much easier to see from this height, as are the massive man-made gravel barriers that have been built to the east of the Skeiðará to protect the farmlands from being flooded.

Skorarbrýr ridge

For those who want a whole day's walk over the moorland, there is a path across Skaftafellsheiði to see Morsárjökull. After Svartifoss has been reached, the path skirts Skerhóll (526 m) and climbs the Skorarbrýr ridge (about 700 m), from which there are fine views of Morsárjökull. This glacier tumbles over an ice-fall to reach the valley below and the loud cracking sound this produces can sometimes be heard. There is a medial moraine running from the exposed rock in the ice-fall, and in the lower part of the glacier the regular black curves called ogives are very clear to see. These ogives are convex bands of dirty ice; their shape is produced by the ice's greater flow in the middle of the glacier rather than at the edges and the distance between successive bands is an indication of how far the glacier has moved in a year. Great care must be taken on the ridge as the cliffs are very steep.

The path now turns south-east and back below the peaks of Kristínartindar that dominate the moorland and then on to the cliffs above Skafta-fellsjökull. From here there are spectacular views of the whole expanse of the glacier – from the smooth, white ice-cap to the jet black snout. Throughout its length in the valley, the crevasses that criss-cross it can be seen quite clearly, though it is difficult to judge their size from so high above the ice. The bare walls of the other side of the valley rise steeply above the glacier and, to the south, the tip of Svínafellsjökull's snout can be seen.

The surface of this cliff-top path is frost shattered and very loose and farther on, going down through the vegetated area, the path passes close to the edge in some places.

Further information on suitable walks from the campsite can be obtained from the warden.

Svínafellsjökull
Although not within the park, Svínafellsjökull is very close to it and is worth a visit. The glacier's western edge is easily approached by a rocky track that starts just after the ring road crosses Skaftafellsá. There are large boulders by the track as it passes under the pinnacles of Illuklettur and care should be taken if you are travelling in a two-wheel drive vehicle. This glacier used to be joined to Skaftafellsjökull until the 1940s, but since then they have receded from one another to such an extent that now they are over a kilometre apart. However, Svínafellsjökull has begun to grow again; this accounts for the snout riding up over some of its old moraines. The ice nearest the car park can be walked on as it is covered by a thick layer of gravel. Beside the ice are tall moraines which afford good views up the glacier towards the mountains on Öræfajökull and also to the eastern side of Skaftafellsjökull and its medial moraine.

8
SKAFTAFELL TO HÖFN

Distance:	137 km
Route:	ring road (1)
	road 99 to Höfn
Maps:	general map 9
	1:100 000 map of Öræfajökull
Main places to visit:	Kvíárjökull (glacier) ★ ★ ★
	Fjallsárlón (icebergs in glacial lake) ★ ★ ★
	Jökulsárlón (icebergs in glacial lake) ★ ★ ★ ★
Road Conditions:	loose surface over glacial sands
Adjacent section:	9 (Höfn to Breiðdalsvík)
Notes:	Jökulsárlón is particularly beautiful, but watch out for skuas on the sandur.

THE AREA between Skaftafell and Breiða-merkurjökull (just a few kilometres east of Öræfa-jökull) was the most isolated place in Iceland until a few years ago; Breiðamerkursandur was bridged in 1967 and Skeiðarársandur in 1974. Iceland's first settler, Ingólfur Arnarson, landed in this area in 874, but subsequently moved to Reykjavík. Originally, the area round the ice-cap was called Litla Hérad ('little settlement') but was destroyed by the massive pumice eruption from Öræfajökull in 1362, which covered Skafta-fell to a depth of 30 cm. An old Icelandic story of the eruption tells of the shepherd called Hallur who heard two mighty crashes coming from the mountain at milking time. After the second one he ran off to a cave, leaving the bemused milkmaids behind. He was the only person in the district to survive; when the third crash came the glacier exploded and forty farms were covered in the mud flow that created Skeiðarársandur. After resettlement at the beginning of the fifteenth century, it was renamed Öræfi ('wasteland').

Öræfajökull's slopes, which are very steep, support many valley glaciers, a few of which come near the road. At its summit is a caldera which is ringed by a number of ice-free peaks; one of these, Hvannadalshnúkur (2119 m), is the highest peak in Iceland. The volcano has erupted twice since the Settlement, in 1362 and 1727. A few farms are found in the district, many of them fairly close to each other and sheltering under the hills. At Hof there is a turf church and the excavated ruins of the old farm of Gröf, a victim of the 1362 eruption. The sands around Öræfi are fairly bare but nonetheless support some sheep, while the hillsides have enough grass and shelter to ensure that there is sufficient farming land to keep the settlement viable. Near the tip of Öræfi there is an airstrip at Fagurhólsmýri which was built in 1938; until then, the local people had had to rely on the surefooted Icelandic ponies for contact with the outside world.

Lying a few kilometres offshore is the rocky outpost of Ingólfshöfði (76 m), named after Ingólfur Arnarson. This was the place where he spent his first winter in Iceland. It was a fishing centre in the seventeenth century until it was silted up by the Skeiðará; today a steep bank of sand rests behind the rock and a long sandbank trails north-east to the mainland. With care, and in the right tidal and weather conditions, a four-wheel drive vehicle can approach the rock, the large sand dune giving access to the cliff top. No track is shown on the 1:100 000 map of the area and local advice should be sought before attempting this journey. On the rock there is a lighthouse and a monument to Ingólfur Arnarson that was erected in 1974, the eleven-hundredth anniversary of his landing.

On a visit to the eastern side of the ice-cap you may experience a sudden change in the weather, such is the effect of the glacier on local conditions. There are only a few farms along this stretch of road as the unstable glacial sands just under the hillsides provide poor foundations for construction. A number of glaciers reach down to near the road and three of them, Kvíárjökull, Fjallsjökull and Breiðamerkurjökull, offer beautiful views and interesting walks, since they all have glacial lakes, icebergs and many moraines. An added interest is that this district has changed more than almost any other in Iceland during the last fifty years (excepting those experiencing eruptions). Skuas provide a potential hazard, however (see p.175).

There is an excellent view of the glacier Kvíárjökull from its long and high (213 m) moraine Kvíármýrarkambur, which is on its south-western flank. A track just before the bridge continues for less than 1 km; from here the moraine is easily reached. From the ridge the whole of the glacier can be seen with its eroded valley walls on either side; below are the lake, icebergs and smaller moraines. To the west there is a good view of the surrounding sands and the lagoons along the shore. A path goes across the smaller and more sheltered moraines; these give a pleasant walk over their mossy and grassy tops and the edge of the glacier can be reached. Just a few hundred metres after the river Kvíá is crossed by the ring road there is a campsite on the left.

As the road moves away from the hills, it starts to cross the 25 km-wide sands of Breiðamerkursandur, with its remarkable landscape of tall moraines that is gradually and constantly changing. The surrounding scenery is extremely stark: black mountains and sand, white snow and blue sea – and a sudden patch of brilliant green grass at Kvísker, the farm from which the first ascent of Öræfajökull was made, in 1794. Towards the end of last century the three glaciers of Hrútárjökull, Fjallsjökull and Breiðamerkurjökull were joined at their snouts, forming a massive sheet of ice at the foot of the surrounding mountains. Since then they have retreated and the first of the two beautiful glacial lakes in the area, Fjallsárlón, lies at the bottom of the second glacier, Fjallsjökull.

Fjallsjökull towers above its glacial lake and the view of it, especially from the eastern side of the lake, is spectacular. Fjallsárlón can be reached by a track just a few hundred metres after the Hrútá is crossed or from either side of the bridge over the Fjallsá. On the western side, it is only a short walk to the edge of the snout and it is possible to walk onto the ice. The lagoon is dotted with icebergs (many of them black with moraine) that are slowly melting and making their way across the calm water. Only when they are very small can they move through the channel out to the sea. From the top of the moraines the neighbouring glaciers of Hrútárjökull and Breiðamerkurjökull can also be seen.

Breiðamerkurjökull is a more gently sloping glacier and is the most interesting of the three in this section. While two surges last century (1869 and 1875) brought it almost to the sea, this century it has retreated by about 2.5 km and now a large depression between the ice and the tallest moraines is filled by the lake Jökulsárlón. New lakes are being created as the glacier's shape continues to alter. One of the striking aspects of this glacier is the medial moraines: a jet-black ridge of material stretches down from the peaks Skálabjörg and Austurbjörg, some 17 km and 23 km respectively from the snout. At their greatest altitude these moraines are approximately 100 m wide and up to 60 m high. Farther down they lose height but regain it near the snout where the moraine becomes a black band almost 2 km wide. On the west side of the glacier, other medial moraines appear a few kilometres from the snout. Jökulsárlón is much bigger than Fjallsárlón and has many more icebergs (see p.120); some black (perhaps striped), others white, clear, or a cold blue colour. The blue colour is produced as the ice reflects the blue part of the sun's rays, the red end of the spectrum being more readily absorbed. The intensity of the blue may depend on the history of the ice and the

consequent size of the crystals of ice frozen inside it. While the smaller icebergs' movement can be observed, the largest ones (some are 100 m long and 20 m proud of the water) may well be grounded and unable to move.

The lake is only 6 m above sea level and it extends some distance underneath the glacier, allowing the glacier's bottom surface to dip below sea level. Icebergs break off when the buoyancy provided by the water begins to crack the ice. The river that flows from the lake to the sea, Jökulsá, has continually changed its course during this century and like the Skeiðará was a great obstacle to travel until it was finally bridged in 1967. Its mouth is only a short walk away and is populated by many seabirds; seals may be sighted there.

The strange landscape of mound after mound of gravel across the sandur ends abruptly at the rocky outcrop at the river Fellsá and the terraced mountain of Steinafjall (789 m). Here the landforms become more stable. There are numerous farms dotted around, although there are no large and continuous expanses of farming land. The road now moves away from the glaciers, though it passes within a few kilometres of Skálafellsjökull. There are long sandbars along the coast, allowing no place for a harbour. These sandbars are usually built up from rock islands with the glacial streams bringing down the sand which is then piled up by the prevailing winds. The sand ridges are continually changing their shape, some channels closing while others are opening up and behind them areas of sandur may be built up as the flow through the channels is restricted. As the sandbars become higher, they raise the water level behind them, making the pasture land marshy; in springtime the sandbars may be breached to allow grass to grow.

The entrance to the broad fjord Hornafjörður is marked by Viðborðsfjall (537 m) and its long scree slopes; the long bridge over the river is guarded by gravel embankments, protecting it from Hoffellsjökull's meltwater. Höfn ('harbour') is approached by a road made from the red gravel of the nearby slopes and a good road surface completes the journey past an information board and into the town. This is the most important centre in the south-east and it is the first large town since Selfoss on the difficult south coast route. It acts as a communications centre and has an important role in serving the surrounding districts. There are good shopping facilities and the other services expected of a settlement of its importance, including cinema, swimming pool, youth hostel, hotel, museum and golf course. There is a campsite just at the entrance to the town, on rising ground to the left, with 2 WCs and sinks under cover. On the hill beside it is a viewdial (showing positions of the major mountains and glaciers) which gives marvellous views of sunsets over the glaciers and of the pastel scree slopes of the hills to the north-east. Below the viewdial and amongst the numerous small islands in Skarðsfjörður many ducks, geese and seabirds can be found. There are also large numbers of arctic terns near the harbour.

Snowcat trips over the Vatnajökull glacier are organised by Jöklaferðir hf. (tel. 97-8558).

9
HÖFN TO BREIÐDALSVÍK

Distance:	181 km
Route:	road 99
	ring road 1
	road 96
Maps:	general maps 9 and 8
Main places to visit:	Djúpivogur (small fishing settlement)
	Teigarhorn (rocks and birds)
	Breiðdalsvík (walk on to hills)
Road Conditions:	may be difficult round headlands, especially if there is sea mist.
Adjacent section:	10 (Breiðdalsvík to Egilsstaðir via Búðareyri)
Notes:	Very fine fjord scenery after Djúpivogur. This route detours off the ring road, heading for Egilsstaðir via Búðareyri on road 96, to take advantage of the scenery.

THE ROAD out of Höfn leads along the base of Skarðstindur's slopes and up the very steep hill to the mountain pass of Almannaskarð at whose top there are fine views over Hornafjörður to the glaciers. From now on there are only occasional glimpses of glaciers, but there are a number of glacial and clear rivers to be crossed, as well as a number of gravel beds. Stretching far along the coast there is a long series of sandbanks.

On the western bank of the wide glacial river Jökulsá í Lóni there is a campsite (at Thóris-dalur), while on its eastern bank there are some picturesque coloured hills.

Once the north-western part of Lónsfjörður has been passed, the road branches; the right (coastal) road should be taken. This new part of the ring road is not marked on the general map; the road that is shown on the most recent (1976) map is now signposted *'Lokað'* ('closed'). The new section of road begins after the lighthouse and gives an exciting journey passing in two places under steep scree slopes. At this point the road passes high above the pebble beach and careful driving is needed if the sea mist comes in (there is a rescue hut en route). The stretch round Krossanes is particularly beautiful with brown, grey and green scree slopes and pebble beaches; the slopes were originally sea cliffs, the scree falling to the level of the old beach. This change is due to the land having risen above its previous level as the load of the glaciers has lifted. In some places the cliffs provide nesting places for gulls.

Once the new section of road and the bay of Álftafjörður have been passed there is the somewhat bare scenery of Hamarsfjörður. The start of the fjords with their fishing communities is marked by the sighting of racks of drying fish just before Djúpivogur. This is a bustling little fishing village whose history goes back four hundred years. It has a garage, petrol station, hotel, bank and shop. The harbour (which has a processing plant) is busy, mainly with small boats. There is a campsite on a hill on the left side of the road into the settlement. It overlooks the harbour and is a little difficult to find. The only facility is a WC.

Just off the coast is the island of Papey, whose name comes from the early Irish monks known as Papar (possibly from the Irish 'Papa' [Pope]).

Behind Djúpivogur stretches the long and beautiful fjord Berufjörður with many bare and charmingly sculptured hills, such as Stöng (942 m) on its northern shore. Its most notable sight is Búlandstindur (1068 m), one of the finest mountains in eastern Iceland. Its basalt terraces have a pronounced slope, a result of the land rising after its great burden of ice melted at the end of the last ice age, 11,000 years ago. Below its slopes is the farm of Teigarhorn where examples of the mineral zeolite are found (these are large crystals that grow in cavities in the basalt). Permission to enter the area must be obtained from the farmer, but entry may not be permitted. There are many sea birds around Teigarhorn, both by the fjord's shore and higher up on the cliffs. On the northern shore there is a good farming area around Berunes, where there is a youth hostel.

The region of the eastern fjords ('Austfirdir') is one of the geologically oldest parts of Iceland, with no solfatara fields or other examples of continuing volcanic activity. The region is dominated by grand basalt mountains (some topped by quite flat plateaux) whose sides have been scraped by glacial action. This scouring produced deep troughs far out to sea, leaving trenches beyond the mouths of the fjords which can be traced for up to 200 km in some cases. But Lónsfjörður, Álftafjörður and Hamarsfjörður, with their sandbars built upon rocks that were not scraped away by glaciers, cannot really be classed as true fjords. Breiðdalsvík, a little farther to the north, also falls into this category. After glaciers had broken up the mountains and left them with steep sides, frost caused the formation of the scree slopes which often run so close to the shore that only a small strip of land remains upon which it is possible to build. In those fjords where there was reasonably level land available, small settlements were slowly built up, usually on the northern side of the fjord in order to get as much sunlight as possible (Seyðisfjörður is an exception to this).

The road surface round the fjords is varied. In the settlements it is good but by the headlands (which are very exposed) the potholes, rubble on the road, and the precipitous drop to the sea may make the journey rather daunting. In the smaller settlements, which may only have a small harbour, the fishing boats bring in their catches which are then transported to processing plants in the larger ports. Some of the bigger settlements such as Kirkjuból (often called Stöðvarfjörður), Seyðisfjörður and Búðareyri have harbours deep enough to take freighters, so heavy goods come from Reykjavík by ship rather than by truck along the coastal road.

Breiðdalsvík is much shorter and broader, with richer soil than the other fjords already mentioned. Its gravel patches and wet meadows are shielded from the sea by a gently curved sand spit, and the flatter profile of this fjord enables it to support many more farms than the other fjords in the district.

The route continues round the coast on road 96. This road now passes the Edda Hotel at Staðaborg and makes its way to the settlement of Breiðdalsvík. This is a relatively new settlement, with its first house built just before the turn of the century. During the last forty years it has grown substantially and it has an hotel, petrol station, garage, shop and a bank. Its main industry is fishing and it has a processing plant. Breiðdalsvík's campsite is a little rough, but not rocky, with a WC and running water; after the settlement's garage turn left: the site is immediately behind the Hotel Bláfell.

There is a pleasant walk along the hills above the settlement: from the junction with the ring road walk up towards the waterfall and bear right at the end of the fencing. This takes you above the lower section of terraces and gives a good view of Ósfjall (716 m) opposite, the other hills in the fjord, the sandspit and the settlement. The route has to be retraced in order to avoid the cliff faces.

10
BREIÐDALSVÍK TO EGILSSTAÐIR VIA BÚÐAREYRI

Distance:	126 km
Route:	road 96 to Búðareyri
	road 92
Map:	general map 8
Road Conditions:	headlands may be rather rough
Adjacent sections:	11 (Egilsstaðir to Mývatn)
	2 (Seyðisfjörður to Egilsstaðir)
	25 (Lögurinn)
Notes:	A fairly short journey with general fjord scenery rather than specific places of interest.

DRIVERS WILL not get much opportunity to admire the tall basalt pillars of Súlur (664 m) which can be seen while the headland of Kambanes is rounded, since the road is narrow, twisting and a bit rough, and has a long drop on the seaward side. Stöðvarfjörður is sufficient reward in itself, however, as it is fertile and ringed by numerous grassy hills. There is a campsite on flat land just before the bridge over the Stöðvará. Kirkjuból (often called Stöðvarfjörður), the fjord's fishing settlement, is a little smaller than Breiðdalsvík. The road past the next headland is good and Faskruðsfjörður's northern shore has interesting red-coloured hills which are partially grassed over. While most of these hills have pointed summit ridges, Suðurfjall (918 m) at the fjord's western end has a plateau on top. There are numerous small hills on the southern shore that give a good view of their higher neighbours as well as over the water to the settlement of Búðir. The headland at Hafnarnes, like the one at Kambanes, is rough and exposed, although the road is a little wider.

The road then winds along the shore of the very long and curving Reyðarfjörður. The finest hill here is Hólmatindur (985 m) which splits the head of the fjord into two arms. At its western end, the fjord has rich soil and consequently supports a number of farms.

While the mountain road (92, west) leads to Egilsstaðir, the road that follows the northern shore (92, east) leads to Búðareyri (often called Reyðarfjörður). This road then continues round the fjord to Eskifjörður, before striking north-east to Norðfjörður, whose main town, Neskaupstaður, is the biggest settlement in the eastern fjords. The mountain section after Eskifjörður includes a 626 m-long tunnel and crosses the Oddsskarð Pass (632 m and the highest pass in the country) between hills about 1000 m high.

The mineral Iceland spar is found at Helgu-staðir, east of Eskifjörður, where it was mined from the seventeenth until the present century. The road to Neskaupstaður has to be retraced as it does not lead farther round the coast. All three settlements (Búðareyri, Eskifjörður and Nes-kaupstaður) have hotels and camping sites.

The mountain road to Egilsstaðir (92) has an initial climb, followed by a fine journey through the pass of Fagridalur, with grass on the more gentle slopes and numerous waterfalls in the clefts in the mountainsides. Soon afterwards there is a view of the lake of Lögurinn and the mountains to its north. The approach to Egils-staðir is, unusually for Iceland, richly wooded with birch.

Egilsstaðir gained importance as a base for the cooperative movement and has grown quite quickly to become an important communications centre, especially for buses and aircraft. Conse-quently, there are 2 hotels, garages, a dentist, chemist, swimming pool, cinema and hospital. To the west and on a small rise just before the lake are the handsome buildings of the Egils-staðir farm, around which the settlement grew. An important area for visitors is by the junction between the ring road and the road (to the right) to Seyðisfjörður. The tourist bureau and the campsite (WCs and hot and cold water under cover) are both situated here, as are attendant shops and facilities.

Egilsstaðir is a good centre from which to explore the many interesting places in the district. It is situated by the Lagarfljót, the outflow of Lögurinn (the trip round the lake is described in section 25). Behind the town there is a steep and spectacular pass to Seyðisfjörður which is the landing place of the Norröna ferry; this journey is described in greater detail in section 2.

11
EGILSSTAÐIR TO MÝVATN

Distance:	175 km
Route:	ring road (1)
Maps:	general maps 8 and 7
	1:100 000 map of Húsavík, Mývatn, Jökulsárgljúfur
Main places to visit:	Jökulsá á Brú (glacial river) ★ ★
	Geitasandur (desert) ★ ★
	hill after Geitasandur (view-point) ★ ★
	Jökulsá á Fjöllum (glacial river) ★ ★
	Hrossaborg (crater, view) ★ ★
	Búrfellshraun (lavafield) ★ ★
Road Conditions:	may be rough with possibility of sand or snow storms
Adjacent sections:	26 (Grímsstaðir to Ásbyrgi)
	40 (Askja)
	12 (Mývatn)
Notes:	A long journey with no settlements en route. In good weather this is an enthralling spectacle of various types of wilderness. Probably the most exciting journey on the ring road.

THE RING road leads past Egilsstaðir's airfield, over a long narrow wooden bridge crossing the green-coloured Lagarfljót, and climbs for a short time through cultivated land. (The river's green colour is due to the large number of fine rock particles held in suspension in the water; the water's colour thus changes as these particles settle in stiller water). After passing the small fishing lake of Urriðavatn you ascend into the hills through moorland. As the road winds its way downwards towards the bridge over Jökulsá á Brú, there is a view of the river's path to the bay of Héraðsflói (to the north-east).

The river is 150 km long and carries meltwater and sand from the Brúarjökull glacier (part of Vatnajökull); the bridge is certainly worth a stop since the river has carved a deep canyon here. The water is a deep grey colour as it is so heavily laden with particles of ground-down rock.

The road now follows the northern bank of the river inland, with the cultivated area limited to a thin strip on either side of the river; on the opposite bank the farms appear hemmed in and dwarfed by the huge mounds of grey gravel that have been brought down by the glacier. While usually well above the river, the road does go down to within a few metres of the water as it flows relatively quietly through a gravel bed. At this point (at Hofteigur) there is no solid rock in the vicinity, just pile upon pile of moraine, much of it grassed over and providing grazing land. The last section before the river Gilsá has cliffs and waterfalls to the right and far more large boulders than elsewhere by the river. There is a petrol station by one of the farms.

The long and steep road after the Gilsá leads to a boggy moorland and then to a windswept and rather barren wasteland. (Road 923 to Brú heads south in the direction of Snæfell; this route is met just after the Gilsá.) Over much of the rest of the journey the landscape is bare and often without shelter, the winds sweeping up duststorms or snowstorms with little warning. The area is one of ash and cinders, products of the many volcanoes (now vanished) that once erupted near here; there are also patches of mossy and boggy land. The road often has a line of cairns running parallel to it, marking the path that was used before the road was built and to each side there are tracks leading off into the bare hills. Few vehicles are met on this stretch of road as there is little long-distance traffic in Iceland and a small population in this region. On the first downhill section after the Gilsá there is a view of the summit of Herðubreið (1682 m) to the south-west. A track to Brú leads past the fishing lake of Ánavatn and a little later on the road passes another lake, Sænautavatn.

After the zig-zag mountain road the route goes through smooth-sided hills and then over the area of Geitasandur, rows of cairns marking a previous path. This is a desert of pumice and ash with only scant plant life and a walk is certainly worthwhile here to see how tenuous a hold plant life has in such a hostile (but sheltered) environment. From the top of the next hill it is possible to look south-westwards into the desert area of Grjót with a number of hills visible, including the long ridge of Herðubreiðartögl and the cone of Vaðalda beyond that. Unfortunately Herðubreið is hidden unless the next hill is climbed, but there is a good view of it from lower ground just a little farther on.

As the road begins its turn to the north there is an oasis at a height of 469 m; this is the site of the highest occupied farm in the country, Möðrudalur. Since it is just a few kilometres after the track leading south to Kverkfjöll and Brúarjökull, this is a sensible place to enquire about the possible hazards that might be encountered there. To the south, west and north of the farm is the sand and gravel desert called Grjót ('rock'). This wasteland seems almost unending, with only occasional peaks rising above the undulating surface; to the north there is a line of red palagonite hills. While the main desert area of Grjót is to the left, this whole section of the journey is extremely sandy. Indeed there may be sandstorms in this dry and exposed district and the hollowed-out sides of sand dunes demonstrate how the wind is able to break up the fragile landforms.

185

Farther on, there is another green oasis at Grímsstaðir, the southern tip of the sheep-farming district of Hólsfjöll. There are petrol pumps here.

While the ring road now turns westwards, the road up to Dettifoss, Ásbyrgi and the coast heads north (this route is described in section 26). A little farther on there is a suspension bridge over Jökulsá á Fjöllum; the moraine beside it gives a good view over the surrounding desert areas. Herðubreið stands out clearly as it rises above the surrounding level land and to the west is the wasteland of Mývatnsöræfi, which is littered with black rock, gravel and ash. Jökulsá á Fjöllum, northern Iceland's biggest river, comes from Dyngjujökull, one of the huge glaciers at the northern edge of Vatnajökull. This great river has only been bridged twice in its entire length: the other bridge is at the coast. It tumbles over many waterfalls (including Dettifoss) on its way to the sea, where it has built up a large sandur.

A little farther on there is a signpost on the left to the track to Herðubreið and Askja with the notice 'only four-wheel drive cars'; this route is described in section 40. However, it is possible to take an ordinary car a short distance along the track to the nearest point of interest, the crater of Hrossaborg (426 m). This volcano was produced by an explosive eruption and has had much of its outer wall removed by a glacier, opening up an entrance to its flat, circular crater. There is a path up to the crater rim (50 m high) from which you can look out towards the desert.

Back on the ring road, the route next passes through sand dunes overlying quite level ropey lava, the previous route through this open area is again marked by cairns on the right. Also on the right is the original line of telegraph poles (erected in 1906) that revolutionised Iceland's communications with the rest of the world. The undulating nature of the surface is broken abruptly at times by great heaps of the lava of Búrfellshraun, a mass of clinkery block lava, whose dull grey or black colour is now brightened by a thick carpet of yellow, orange and green mosses and lichens. Here, huge blocks of lava have solidified into grotesque shapes, the cracks and voids between the sharp-edged rocks providing shelter for the plants. On the left (after the track on the right to Dettifoss) there is a group of three hills, part of the Kræðuborgir crater row, the source of much of Búrfellshraun. Behind the lavafield rises Búrfell (953 m), formed as a subglacial volcano, with a crater on its summit plateau.

Towards the western end of Búrfellshraun tall white columns of evil-smelling vapours rise from the solfatara field of Námaskarð. This marks the boundary between the old lavafields and the new, volcanically active area around the volcano Krafla. Beyond Námaskarð is one of the most beautiful areas in the whole of Iceland, Mývatn. (The rest of the route from Búrfellshraun to Mývatn is included in the next section).

12
MÝVATN

MÝVATN ('midge lake') is one of the most interesting places in Iceland, as it has a remarkable variety of scenery – mountains, lavafields (including very recent ones) solfatara fields, desert and moraines. It also boasts a large population of birds, especially ducks, during the summer. With an area of 38 sq km, it is the third largest lake in Iceland and was formed some 3,800 years ago by the damming effect of a lava flow. After Möðrudalur it is the second highest (277m) inhabited part of Iceland and as well as farming, the local people now have some industry based on utilising the geothermal energy.

Although its altitude means that snowstorms can occur in summer, Mývatn has a dry climate as it is situated within Vatnajökull's 'rain shadow'. A plentiful supply of natural warm water means that the plant life is luxuriant for a district at such a latitude. Since the lake's greatest depth is only four metres, a lot of sunlight penetrates the clear water to the lakebed, resulting in abundant plant life. During winter the lake does not freeze on the eastern side thanks to the incoming warm water, but has ice on other parts for about 190 days a year. The geothermal heat comes from local active sources and there have been recent eruptions (1984) that have produced lava. Any warnings about possible eruptions must therefore be taken seriously – for those who wish to make a quick exit, the airstrip is on a large flat terrace above the campsite!

While the midges are important as a source of food for other animals, their numbers are legion (sometimes there are enough dead bodies on the road to make the surface slippery) and they may swarm about four times a year. Although the midges do not bite, they are a real nuisance and due to sheer weight of numbers may become unbearable. If this is the case then a 'net' that fits over the head and has an elasticated neck can be bought at the tourist bureau.

The midges' numbers are usually greatest in still weather, especially near the shore or by the Laxá. When they die the mass of their bodies is sufficient to act as a valuable fertiliser for the plant life.

The most common fish is the arctic char, with trout and stickleback also to be found in the lake.

All the species of duck found in Iceland (except the eider) breed here, most notably Barrow's goldeneye (this is their only breeding place in Europe), the tufted duck (the most common species here) and the harlequin (found on the river Laxá).

On average there are about 15,000 pairs of birds on the lake, each pair producing 8 eggs. About one-third of the eggs never hatch, and many ducklings fall prey to ravens, skuas and gulls; nevertheless 30,000 ducklings may survive each year. Egg collecting has been for a long time an important activity for the local people and as late as 1941, 40,000 eggs were collected in one season. Many other birds gather on or around the lake, including whooper swans, greylags, phalaropes, black-headed gulls and terns.

The settlement of Reykjahlíð

THE two hotels are the Reynihlíð (at the north-western end of the settlement) and the Reykjahlíð (in the centre of the settlement) and they offer the following services:

Reynihlíð: accommodation, restaurant, petrol, bicycle rental, car rental, roadside shop/cafe, bus tours.

Reykjahlíð: accommodation, restaurant, petrol.

In the centre of the settlement is the supermarket and opposite it is the Eldá Tourist Bureau (bus tours, books, maps, fishing permits, boat hire, and general tourist information). Behind the supermarket is the post office (with tall masts on top) where the (automatic) telephone exchange is located.

The campsite is behind the Reynihlíð hotel and has washrooms with WCs and cold water (there is also hot and cold water from taps outside). This can be extremely busy in summer, especially when tour buses arrive.

On the road from the site to the settlement, the road off to the left goes to the swimming pool and to the 'bank', which occupies the school house a couple of times a week. The garage is found by taking the ring road about 1km towards the diatomite factory; it is on the left in a group of large sheds.

The guide to the lakeside given below follows its shoreline in a clockwise direction from Reykjahlíð round to the north-western shore. The diatomite factory, Námaskarð, Krafla and Víti are found by going east of Reykjahlíð along the main road.

Campsite

The campsite is built on a collection of moraines left by a glacier c.10,000 years ago. Between the site and the lake there is an interesting example of ropey lava formed by the eruption of 1724-1729 ('The Mývatn fires'). This lava flowed down to the lakeside from Leirhnjúkur which is north-east of Hlíðarfjall, the red rhyolitic cone about 4km north-east of the site. The local church, which is between the campsite and the hotel, is built on rising ground and beside it are the remains of the previous church building which was surrounded by the lava flow but not damaged. The lavafield is in the form of great lava domes, or 'tumuli' which cracked under the strain of their own weight as they cooled. Moss has begun to gain a foothold on the rock, especially in the cracks. Behind the airstrip this lava flow can be followed to the north-east, the relatively smooth convex surface of the lava being easy to walk on; towards Hlíðarfjall is the lava fall Eldá, where the slope of the lava is much steeper.

Stóragjá

South-east of the main junction with the ring

road is the deep fissure of Stóragjá, the path to its east marked by a thick safety rope. There are steps leading down to the bottom where there are warm pools in which to bathe. Farther along its length, the path meets the pipe carrying diatoms from the lake to the factory (see below). This can be traced towards the lake where the pumping station is. The floats on the water lead out to where the pipe's submerged opening sucks up the diatoms. The small inlet near the pumping station is fed by warm water from the nearby fissures.

Grjótagjá

This large fissure is reached by a track through a lavafield (negotiable by two-wheel drive vehicles). The fissure is much larger than Stóragjá and is a huge zig-zag crack through the top of large domes of ropey lava. While the clear water pools found here used to be popular with bathers, recent underground lava flows have heated the water to such a degree that it is now too hot (the nearby notice says 60°C) for safety. The track continues through the lavafield and ends up at the diatomite factory.

Hverfjall

Farther down the lakeside road is the ash cone of Hverfjall (452m), perhaps one of the most attractive hills in the country due to its almost perfectly symmetrical shape. The cone, formed by a single eruption (possibly lasting only one day) some 2,500 years ago, is 163m above ground level with a crater 1km across and 140m deep. The track to Hverfjall is a pleasant walk through dwarf birch and blocks of lava. Just before the hill is reached there are long and wide cracks in the ground. The path up the hill is steep but straightforward and is well worth the effort, as it offers fine views. Numerous gullies decorate the hill's slopes which are strewn with ashes and boulders. Inside the crater is another small cone, marking the position of the vent.

South-east of the rim's highest point is the other large crater of Lúdent and between these two craters and stretching south are the crater rows of Lúdentsborgir and Threngslaborgir. To the south-west is Dimmuborgir (see below). Due west is the volcano of Vindbelgjarfjall and at its foot are two large pseudocraters at the farm of Vindbelgur; other pseudocraters can be seen on Mikley (to the south-west) and on a number of other islands nearby. The major mountains are (from the north-east and going clockwise): Krafla, Jörundur, Búrfell, Bláfjall, and Sellandafjall.

Lúdent

The path to Lúdent (482m) is through an interesting array of ash cones, dwarf shrubs and ground-hugging plants in an ash field. There are some large cracks in a section of lava plates and at a couple of points, equipment has been set up to measure their (changing?) separation. The crater row of Lúdentsborgir is passed on the right, with Threngslaborgir further south. These rows produced a huge flow of lava 2,000 years ago that followed the course of the Laxá all the way to the sea. The approach to the crater is very colourful with red ash, green grass and jet black cinders on its slopes. The path (and, alas, the tyre tracks) goes up to the rim. The 6,000 year-old crater is 113m deep and is about the same diameter as Hverfjall, but its ash is much more coarse and brittle. The northern side has shrubs growing on it and is abutted by Dagmálahóll. The view is again quite outstanding with the nearby mountains of Búrfell, Hvannfell, Stórihnjúkur and Bláfjall being the most prominent. The two crater rows are much easier to see from this altitude.

Dimmuborgir

About halfway along the eastern shore, a narrow, winding and sandy track leads to the park known as Dimmuborgir ('The Black Castles'). About 2,000 years ago a lake of molten lava suddenly dropped its level, leaving behind strangely shaped black lava blocks that tower above the paths; the rock formations are at various levels and on some of the walls 'tide marks' left by molten lava are clearly discernible. The depression, 1km in diameter and 20m deep, is now covered in dwarf birch. It is very easy to get lost

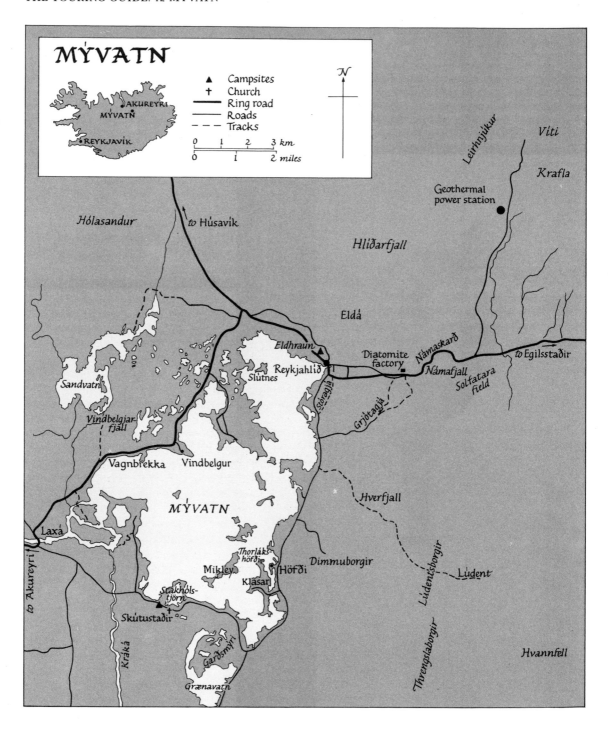

here, even though the park is quite small, as the weird rock shapes are difficult to recognise when trying to retrace your steps. Take a compass.

Höfði

The park on the Höfði promontory near the south-east corner of Mývatn offers a good view of the lake itself and of its birdlife. A richly vegetated rocky outcrop, it overlooks some curious red rocks in a little inlet. These rocks (called 'Klasar') are lava columns remaining after a lava lake has been suddenly drained. There are also good views over to the nearby grassy islands and their pseudocraters, and well-secluded places from which to watch birds catching insects on the lake's surface.

Thorlákshöfði

This peninsula (which has pseudocraters on it) offers an interesting walk, giving a different view of Klasar. The bird life is very good as there are a few sheltered ponds. There is also a closer view of Mikley and its pseudocraters.

Southern shore

Just after the road off to the lake of Grænavatn there is a group of pseudocraters on the right and a good view of the lake from the group's highest point. To the south there is a flat and boggy area (Garðsmýri) which has many nesting ponds for the birds. By the settlement at Skútustaðir (which has an hotel, camping site, cafe, shop, swimming pool and petrol station) is the lake's best-known group of pseudocraters, Skútustaða-gígar. These are in the form of a ring and give a pleasant walk round the small sheltered lake of Stakhólstjörn.

Laxá

This is the lake's only outflow and is a popular fishing river, its valley marking the route taken by the old lava flows that produced the lake. It is a fast-flowing river with many small islands sporting a lush vegetation.

North-western shore

Lying under the slopes of Vindbelgjarfjall, this is the main bird nesting area. The restricted zone, where no-one is allowed off the roads, runs from near the Vagnbrekka farm (before Vindbelg-jarfjall) until just before the Húsavík road is met. Usually the restrictions apply only from May 15-July 20, however notice boards at each end of the zone give details about any changes in these dates (the campsite also has this information). The main breeding grounds are in swampy pools, with swans and ducks gliding peacefully through the reeds looking after the young. They are surprisingly tame, as is much of the birdlife in Iceland, even though for centuries Icelandic farmers have taken eggs from nests. The main path up Vindbelgjarfjall (529m) starts before Vagnbrekka and goes up its western slopes.

The country's two biggest pseudocraters are found just by the farm of Vindbelgur which is on the right of the road. From this side of the lake there are good views (to the south-east) of the table mountains Búrfell (953m), Bláfjall (1222m) and Sellandafjall (988m). These three mountains, all formed as subglacial volcanoes, rise high above the surrounding lavafields.

Diatomite factory

This was built in 1967 to exploit the lake bed's enormous reserves of diatomite, the very porous skeletal remains of the minute plants known as diatoms. The diatomite is dried (using geothermal energy) and used in Europe's chemical industries as a filtering material. Pipes carry the diatomite from the lake's eastern side to settling ponds behind the factory.

Although the factory billows huge clouds of vapour into the air, the visitor's attention is soon focused not on this, but on the many wisps and streams of vapour coming from holes or cracks in the ground near the road. East of the buildings and on both sides of the road is the active geothermal area of Bjarnarflag and walking here can be dangerous. New fissures have recently appeared and more vents have begun to alter the colour of the ground so care should be taken and the light-coloured clays are unsafe to walk on. On the southern side of the road is a factory that uses geothermal energy to make building blocks out of volcanic ash.

Námaskarð

A visit to this area of sulphur pits, ponds of bubbling mud and jets of superheated steam is something never to be forgotten and provides spectacular photographic material. The eastern flank of Námafjall is an array of colour – brown, red, yellow, orange and white – as a result of centuries of solfataric activity (during the Middle Ages sulphur was mined here). The vents give out little water as this is an active high-temperature area with jets of steam, hydrogen sulphide and other gases being given off, giving the whole place a strong sulphurous smell.

There are numerous mud pools, some with very viscous mud slurping away noisily as the vapours bubble up to the surface. A few of these pools are very large, perhaps 3m in diameter, some with spatter cones nearly a metre high. A warning sign reminds visitors that the area is potentially dangerous and that while the brown clay areas are safe to walk on, the lighter or coloured patches can give way, resulting in severe burns.

While most visitors just see the lower part of the field, there are more vents and mud pits up on the ridge. A viewdial is on the summit and there is a marvellous view all around.

Krafla

To the north of Námaskarð a road (marked as a bridle path on the 1:250 000 map) leads towards the volcano Krafla (818m). This goes to the Krafla geothermal power station which was built in 1975. Bright silver-coloured pipes buried into Krafla's red mountainside gather steam for the station's generators and a huge inverted U-shaped pipe crosses the road. The power station, the only one of its kind in Iceland, stands starkly modern and functional against the bare background. Lying around the site of the station are small pieces of black ash that are still shiny; these are from the eruption at Leirhnjúkur in 1981. Small patches of yellow and white (and warm!) ground near the main buildings are also symptomatic of recent geological changes.

The road continues under the large pipe then up a steep slope to a ridge that offers a good view of Krafla's western slopes, and the power station; farther south is Námaskarð, the lavafields and Blájall. To the left is a car park and the active area of Leirhnjúkur. Plumes of vapour rise from the yellowish hillside, and from the black areas just behind and to the right a few ash cones lazily give out vapour. There were two eruptions here in 1981 and one in 1984.

Víti

Further up the hill, a track leads to Víti. This crater was the site of the start of the five-year-long eruption from 1724-29, and after its formation, the crater was filled with a lake of mud that boiled for 100 years. Today Víti is peaceful, a deep crater with steep brown clay sides and banks of snow by the edge of its blue-green lake which is over 30m deep. This is by far the biggest crater here (320m in diameter at the rim) but there are others in the clay hillsides nearby. Behind Víti is another solfatara field whose character is rather different from Námaskarð's as the streams of hot vapour melt the huge blocks of winter snow that still lie in this sheltered spot (see pp.132-133).

13
MÝVATN TO AKUREYRI

Distance:	100 km
Route:	ring road (1)
Maps:	general maps 7 and 4
Main place to visit:	Goðafoss (waterfall) ★★
Road Conditions:	reasonable
Adjacent sections:	38 (Goðafoss to Nýidalur)
	14 (Akureyri)
Notes:	A short journey with a steep mountain road near the end. Plans have been made to change the route of the ring road so as to avoid the zig-zag mountain road. The new route will be farther north through Fnjöskadalur; it will officially be opened in 1985.

AFTER CROSSING the Laxá, the road follows this island-studded river for a while before climbing into the moors. From here on, and especially after the road skirts Lake Másvatn, the countryside is fertile, with farms well stocked with cows and sheep. The settlement of Laugar (road 846) is not marked on the 1:250 000 (1979) map, but it is a pleasantly situated community which has a summer hotel, pool, campsite, shop and garage. The long climb that follows over the Fljótsheiði moorland gives a good view at the top over the rolling landscape, both back to the mountains around Mývatn and forward to the river Skjálfandafljót with its waterfall, Goðafoss.

Although only 10 m high, Goðafoss ('Falls of the gods') carries a huge volume of water and is most impressive, its name celebrating the throwing of Thorgeir's pagan gods into the falls in the year 1000 (Thorgeir was president of the Althing that decided in favour of Christianity). There are two car parks by the waterfall; the western one is more popular, but the eastern path (found after the small bridge over the stream) gives a view from under as well as above the falls and it also enables you to see the curved basalt pillars on the western bank.

Skjálfandafljót is a long glacial river that flows through the valley of Bárðardalur, flowing

178 km from north-west Vatnajökull to the sea. About 8,000 years ago an eruption in Trölladyngja (north of Vatnajökull) produced lava that followed the course of the valley and this can be seen around Fosshóll. The farm (and hence the area) near Goðafoss is called Fosshóll and there is a good roadside shop/supermarket and petrol station here. For those going south across the interior track of Sprengisandur this is the most convenient place to stock up with fuel and food and to find out what conditions on the track are like. This route starts on the western bank of Skjálfandafljót and is described in section 38. It is possible for normal cars to follow the river up the Bárðardalur valley to the last farm (Mýri). From here, there is a 8-km walk to see the Aldeyjarfoss waterfall and the spectacular view from just above it; this is all described in section 38.

After the Trölladyngja lava has been crossed there is a series of very large moraines and then the greener scenery round the lake Ljósavatn (home of Thorgeir), where there is an Edda hotel.

After crossing the river Fnjóska and its valley, the road then follows a mountain route, climbing over Vaðlaheiði, with fine views of the eastern valleys. This road often gets blocked during winter so the longer route to the north is used after a lot of snow. Around the summit of this

193

ear-popping road there are a number of small lay-bys, giving wide views over Eyjafjörður. Most impressive are the mountains to the west with their common summit plateau (Flár). Beyond these hills and also to the south of them there are high peaks, a few of them with small glaciers. At the northern end of the fjord the island of Hrísey can be seen.

The road down to Akureyri is not as steep as the climb and it crosses the three arms of the Eyjafjarðará as it flows through wet meadows. Eyjafjörður is a very sheltered fjord with fairly low rainfall. The river does not flow from a glacier and so the meadows by its banks are not affected by ever-changing water courses. These factors have allowed the district to develop as one of the richest dairy farming centres in Iceland, with many modern farms on the hillsides.

14
AKUREYRI

WITH A population of over fourteen thousand people, this is northern Iceland's capital and a centre for commerce, transport, education and culture. It is an attractive place too: one of the most striking aspects of this northern town is its tree-lined streets.

When Akureyri was given its municipal charter in 1862 it only had 286 inhabitants, but its favourable position and the development of the cooperative movement ensured its steady growth and it is now the country's third largest centre after Reykjavík and Kópavogur (the capital's neighbour). Today it is an industrial town with shipbuilding, engineering, printing, confectionery and clothing factories as well as processing plants for the fishing industry.

The town centre has been built next to a spit of land, made of sand and gravel brought down by the glacial river Glerá; part of the town is on the spit itself and has many of the commercial and industrial premises. The ring road runs through Akureyri but with the new traffic system and pedestrian precinct in Hafnarstræti, the centre is now less crammed with vehicles, though still very busy. The centre of the town is at the Ráðhústorg Square.

Although there are a number of interesting things to see in Akureyri, it is mainly a centre from which to tour – details of trips that are available are given in Part 2 (see pp.54-56). Locally, there are good walks up to and beyond the Ski Hotel (500 m). Súlur (1144 m) to the south-west is a popular hill for climbing, while farther to the west and north there are some fine hills and peaks that offer challenges to skilled walkers and climbers. A local touring club, (Ferðafélag Akureyrar at Skipagata 12), organises outings to these and other areas for walkers. In the winter, Akureyri offers good skiing, weather permitting.

Key to street plan of Akureyri
The following places are all shown, numbered as below, on the street map of Akureyri.

1. *Kirkjan* (Lutheran church)
   This dominates the town, not only due to its position but also thanks to its twin concrete spires. Open daily during the summer: 09.30-11.00 and 14.00-15.30.
2. *Minjasafnið* (Municipal Museum)
   This is a modern building with a vast collection of everyday objects from days gone by. Open daily during the summer, 13.30-17.00.
3. *Lystigarður Akureyrar* (Botanic Gardens)
   This garden has a comprehensive collection of Icelandic plants, set within a park. Open daily in summer 09.00-22.00.
4. *Matthíasarhús* (Matthías Jochumsson's Memorial House)

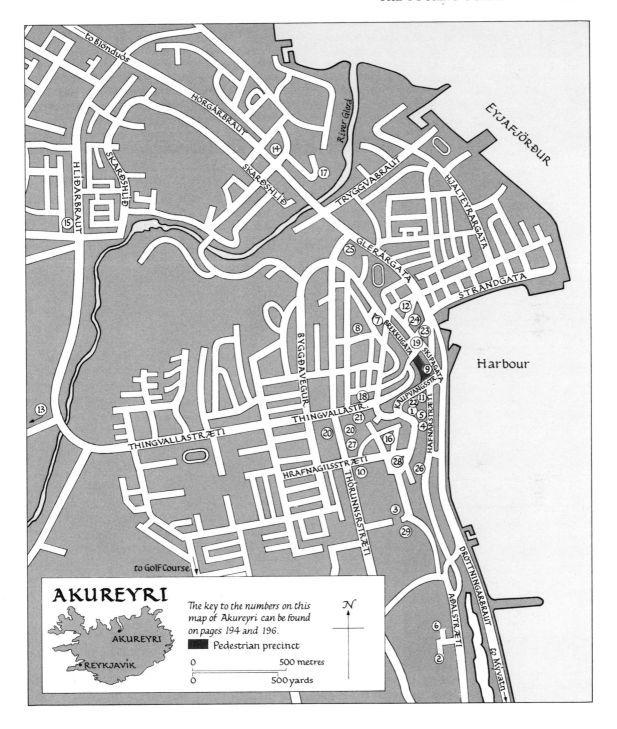

to Blöndúos

HÖRGÁRBRAUT

River Glerá

EYJAFJÖRÐUR

SKARÐSHLÍÐ

14

17

HLÍÐARBRAUT

SKARÐSHLÍÐ

TRYGGVABRAUT

HJALTEYRARGATA

15

GLERÁRGATA

25

STRANDGATA

12

24

7

8

BREKKUGATA

23

19

Harbour

BYGGÐAVEGUR

SKIPAGATA

9

18

KAUPVANGSSTR.

22

11

1

THINGVALLASTR.

21

5

13

20

20

4

THINGVALLASTRÆTI

27

16

HAFNARSTRÆTI

28

26

HRAFNAGILSSTRÆTI

10

THÓRUNNSRSTRÆTI

3

29

to Golf Course

DROTTNINGARBRAUT

6

AÐALSTRÆTI

2

to Mývatn

AKUREYRI

The key to the numbers on this
map of Akureyri can be found
on pages 194 and 196.

N

■ Pedestrian precinct

AKUREYRI

REYKJAVÍK

| 0 | | 500 metres |
| 0 | | 500 yards |

This is the house that belonged to the poet Matthías Jochumsson (1835-1920); it still contains his works, furniture and personal belongings. As well as being a poet and dramatist, Jochumsson was the author of the words of the Icelandic National Anthem and also translated into Icelandic some of the works of Shakespeare and Byron. The house is reached from the path half-way up the steps to Kirkjan and is open daily in summer, 14.00-16.00.

5. *Náttúrugripasafnið* (Museum of Natural History) Contains collections of rocks, sea creatures, plants and birds from all over Iceland. Open daily (except Sat) in summer: 11.00-14.00; in winter, Sun only: 13.00-15.00.

6. *Nonnahús*
This was the home of Jón Sveinsson (1857-1944), known as 'Nonni', who spent much of his life outside Iceland and wrote many children's books (*The Nonni Stories*) based on his own childhood which was spent in and around Akureyri. It is one of the oldest houses in Akureyri and contains original furnishings as well as many examples of the writer's work. Open daily in summer, 14.00-16.30.

7. *Amtsbókasafnið* (Municipal Library)
Contains a copy of all material published in Icelandic. Open Mon-Fri: 13.00-19.00; also Sat 10.00-15.00 in winter.

8. *Davíðshús* (David Stefánsson's Memorial House) The poet's former house is at Bjarkarstígur 6. He was one of the country's first and best-known modern poets and lived from 1895-1964. Open daily in summer: 16.00-18.00.

23. Taxis
24. Bus station
25. Viewdial
26. Theatre
27. Gymnasium
28. Statue of *The Outlaw* (identical to that in Reykjavík)
29. Hospital

Restaurants	Location
Hotel Akureyri	Hafnarstræti 98
Hotel Edda	Hrafnagilsstræti
Hotel K.E.A.	Hafnarstræti 89
Hotel Varðborg	Geislagata 7
Bautinn	Hafnarstræti 92
Sulnaberg	Hafnarstræti 87
Smiðjan	Kaupvangsstræti 3
Sjallinn	Geislagata 14

Discoteque

H-100	Hafnarstræti 100

Information
The information office, in Hafnarstraeti, is open daily.

Other Useful Places
 9. Hotel Akureyri
10. Hotel Edda
11. Hotel KEA
12. Hotel Varðborg
13. Winter Ski Hotel
14. Youth hostel
15. Guesthouse Árgerði
16. Guesthouse Brauðstofan
17. Guesthouse Dalakofinn
18. Guesthouse Eining
19. Rádhústorg Square
20. Campsite (one part on either side of the road)
21. Swimming pool
22. Public toilets (under steps to church)

Accommodation

The following list gives details of the main establishments. Information on private homes should be obtained from your tour operator.

Name	Address	Tel No. (code-96)	No. of rooms	Times of opening	Sleeping Bag Acc.
Hotels, Guesthouses and Youth Hostels in Akureyri					
Hotel Akureyri	Hafnarstræti 98	22525	19	all year	no
Hotel Edda	Hrafnagilsstræti	24055	68	summer	no
Hotel K.E.A.	Hafnarstræti 89	22200	28	all year	no
Hotel Varðborg	Geislagata 7	22600	26	all year	no
Guesthouse Dalakofinn	Lyngholt 20	23035	—	all year	yes
Guesthouse Eining	Thingvallastræti 14	24315	—	summer	yes
Youth Hostel	Stórholt 1	23658	(60 beds)	all year	yes
Ski Hotel	Hliðarfjall	22930	—	Jan-Apr	—
Guesthouse Brauðstofan	Skólastigur 5	23648	4	all year	yes
Guesthouse Argerði	Tungusiða 2	24849	—	—	—

Campsite

The campsite (about two hundred metres behind Kirkjan) is grassy and on sloping ground. An overflow site operates during the summer period; this is just over the road and is probably a little quieter. The main part of the site is busy and has heated washrooms. A warden is on duty and the office has a public telephone. The swimming pool is next door.

A visit to Grímsey

Those who want to cross the Arctic Circle, can most easily do so by visiting the island of Grímsey (which is cut in two by the Circle). It is a small island with important bird colonies and can be reached by air and sea from Akureyri, either by scheduled service or on special trips. The 'tourist' air trip does not allow much time on the island so the visitor may prefer to take scheduled flights and stay overnight.

When the weather is good there is a fine view over Eyjafjörður and the surrounding hills as the plane flies due north from Akureyri. On nearing the island there is a view of the sea-cliffs and a natural arch jutting out into the sea.

The airfield is just beyond the settlement. At the far end of the runway, those who manage to brave the terns can get to the pole marking the Arctic Circle; on it, arrows point to various faraway cities (Paris: 2335 km; London: 1972 km; Rome: 3436 km; New York: 4448 km). If you want proof of your journey it is possible to get a certificate to mark your crossing of the Circle.

This is a journey for good weather since there is little to see or do if the cloud is down.

15
AKUREYRI TO BORGARNES

Distance:	319 km
Route:	ring road (1)
Maps:	general maps 4 and 2
Main places to visit:	Kotagil (canyon) ★★
	Glaumbær (museum) ★★
	Grábrók (crater) ★
	Hreðavatn (lake)
Road Conditions:	rough in parts, in others of highway standard
Adjacent sections:	37 (Hveravellir to Blöndudalur)
	28 (Dalsmynni to Bjarkalundur)
	34 (Borgarfjörður to Reykholt and Húsafell)
	35 (Húsafell to Kaldidalur and Borgarfjörður)
	33 (Búðir to Borgarnes)
	16 (Borgarnes to Reykjavík)
Notes:	This is a long journey which does not offer much to visitors compared to other sections. However there is some good scenery, especially in the mountains at the beginning.

THE HIGHWAY out of Akureyri goes through good farming land which is continually being extended by the draining and ploughing of moorland. On turning south-west, the road passes through magnificent scenery with fine mountains (1000 m and with sheer cliffs) lining both sides. There are some views of glaciers, including Bægisárjökull (seen from the north, at Bægisá) and many of the hills will have snow on them. The pinnacled ridges above the farm of Hraun on the right are of particular beauty. There is a steep climb through the Öxnadalsheiði pass (535 m) which has a rescue hut beyond its summit. A few kilometres after the road crosses the river Norðurá it passes the fine canyon of Kotagil which is deep, twisting and has many layers of rock exposed by water erosion. The rock faces and the pinnacles that can be seen from below are even more impressive when viewed from above, and on the far side of the bridge over the Kotá there is a faint path beside a gully that takes you to a vantage point above the canyon.

After Silfrastaðir, the valley becomes much broader and the river Héraðsvötn (which the road follows for quite some time) divides into a system of braided streams through gravel brought down from the Hofsjökull glacier. This is horse country and many sturdy Icelandic ponies can be seen here on the numerous farms. While the ring road turns westwards, the road that follows the river (76) leads to Skagafjörður and then up to Siglufjörður, an important fishing town on the north coast. Branching off from it, road 767 leads to Hólar, which was the home of the northern bishops from 1106 to 1798; Jón Arason lived here from 1524 to 1550.

Back on the ring road, Varmahlíð, a pleasant settlement which is well placed as a centre for exploring the surrounding countryside, is situated on the western side of Héraðsvötn. There is a campsite (this is on the left just before the settlement), hotel, garage, shop and a swimming pool.

While the ring road now goes left, a right turn

(road 75) can be taken towards Sauðárkrókur to the museum at Glaumbær (7 km), said to be on the site of the home of Thorfinn Karlsefni after he returned from trying to establish an Icelandic colony in America (see p.12). This is an old turf farm, dating from the eighteenth/nineteenth centuries, that was once a nunnery. The bedrooms, workshops, kitchen and other rooms to go through give an insight into what everyday life must have been like last century (see pp.142-143). Both the interior and exterior walls are of neatly laid and well-maintained turf sods, with small windows set into the sloping turfed roof.

The climb out of Varmahlíð leads past a view-dial on the left and then crosses moorland, the only real point of interest being the view at the beginning of the downward section. Just as the river Blanda is reached, road 731 (left) leads to the Kjölur track which is described in section 37. After following the Blanda through its gravel beds, the trading centre of Blönduós is reached; there is an information board as the settlement is entered. Blönduós has an hotel, swimming pool, hospital, dentist, museum, shops and an airfield. Beside the petrol station there is a garage; the campsite is just across the road.

The Stóra-Giljá campsite (about 13 km farther on) is extremely difficult to find. It is after road 724 to the Edda Hotel and is on the left and opposite a small roadside shop. The sign, which unfortunately faces the opposite direction, is just before a collapsed bridge. The only facilities are provided by nature: grass and the running water from the river Giljá.

After the road turns west again and crosses Hnausakvísl there is a large collection of heaps of soil and rock which came from a big landslide from Vatnsdalsfjall, the large hill to the east. As the road climbs a little, there is a view of the lagoon of Hóp which is nearly cut in two by a long curved sandbar. The long haul over the moorland continues with some neat farms and a few lakes by the roadside. Miðfjörður is just skirted by its southern shore but there is a better look at Hrútafjörður (with an Edda hotel just as the road nears the shore). The region's major mountain,

Tröllakirkja (1001 m) now begins to dominate the landscape. This used to have two glaciers on its eastern side until the 1930s, but these have now receded. Both sides of the fjord and its main rivers are lined with vast piles of moraine, the farms sitting on the flatter ones. At Staður at the head of the fjord there is a roadside cafe and a campsite. During the long climb that follows there is an excellent view of Tröllakirkja and its lower neighbour, Snjófjöll, but attention is soon focused on the smooth outline of the Langjökull glacier to the south-east. At the top of the exposed mountain pass there is a large shelter. As the road comes back down to farming land there is a good view of the mountain Baula (934 m) on the right. Farther on is the farm of Dalsmynni and road 60 branches off to the right to the north-western fjords (described in section 28); then to the right is the magnificent face of Hraunsnefsöxl.

Since the journey has been through very old mountains, it is quite a surprise to come across the 3,800 year-old ash cone of Grábrók and its surrounding lavafield of Grábrókarhraun which is extensively covered with bright mosses. There are numerous paths up the side of the cone which have been made to preserve the rest of the outside walls. The paths are steep to begin with but give a good view of the surrounding countryside, the mountains and lake Hreðavatn to the south-west. There is a smaller cone and another crater inside the main one; there is also another crater (Raudbrók) behind Grábrók.

Also behind Grábrók there is a campsite, which is reached by the rather rough track immediately after the crater. There is no direct track between the campsite and the lake but after the roadside cafe and the hotel on the main road, a good track leads to dozens of wooden summer homes round the lake. This is a pleasant situation, sheltered and with a rich shrub vegetation round the shore. The lake is fished for trout.

As the road turns south-west, the hills of Skarðsheiði come into view on the left, with Hafnarfjall to their right. As Borgarnes is approached, the farms look more prosperous, with many horses in the fields. Borgarnes is heralded by its golf course on the left and the long string of new buildings along the approach road. This is an expanding town, with shops, factories and services that cater for a large population in the surrounding countryside. It therefore provides a number of facilities including a hospital, hotel, pool, museum, bank, and garages.

The campsite is at the beginning of the settle-ment, immediately after the main road has gone off to the left over the new bridge. The site is well grassed and has WCs and cold water in two washrooms. A rocky outcrop above the site gives good views to the hills opposite. The harbour is reached by going through the settlement and over a bridge.

16
BORGARNES TO REYKJAVÍK

Distance:	117 km
Route:	ring road (1)
Maps:	general maps 2 and 3
Main places to visit:	Hvalfjörður (whale factory) ★
	Glymur (waterfall)
Road Conditions:	highway nearly all the way
Adjacent sections:	17 (Reykjavík to Thingvellir and Thingvallavatn)
	3 (Reykjavík)
Notes:	A short journey that is completed quickly.

THE NEW bridge over Borgarfjörður saves a detour along the fjord and makes the last section of the ring road quite short. The road goes under the long scree slopes of Hafnarfjall (884 m) and over on the northern shore is the boggy farmland of Mýrar, beyond which is the Snæfellsnes peninsula. To the south the prominent sharp peak of Keilir (379 m) on Reykjanes peninsula can be seen, some 60 km away. The rich farming area of Grunnafjörður is interesting, with text-book post-glacial valleys and gravel beds around it. The bay is almost completely closed by a sand-spit and on its western shore, the two salmon rivers of Leirá and Laxá tumble into the sheltered water. To the south the busy town of Akranes can be seen (the tall chimney belongs to the cement factory). This is an important town with a population of over 5,000 people. While it originally gained its importance as a fishing port, it is now also an industrial centre and has the

shops and services to match. It is connected to Reykjavík by a regular ferry service.

As the road passes some small lakes and then crosses into Hvalfjörður ('whale fjord'), the pointed hills in the foreground are the group called Botnssúlur (1095 m). The fjord is particularly beautiful, especially the hill of Múlafjall (391 m) at the head, but the view is somewhat spoiled by the ferro-silicon plant on the northern shore and the ugly collection of oil tanks by Múlafjall. Before the hill a whale factory, the only one in Iceland, is passed. Bus excursions come from Reykjavík to see the factory and it may be possible to watch the cutting up of the whales from an observation platform above the open factory floor (this is up steps just before the factory gate is reached). The scale of the operation is massive, with knives 1.5 metres long used to cut up the whales and strong winches needed to haul the great chunks of flesh. After it has been sliced up into smaller sections there are still remnants lying about, including a backbone perhaps 15 m long and huge curved jawbones.

Before Múlafjall is rounded, there is a track up to the left past the oil tanks which goes on for about 1 km. From here Glymur can be seen, a series of waterfalls collectively 1 km long and 195 m high and thus the highest falls in Iceland; unfortunately here too oil tanks detract from the valley's beauty. The southern shore of the fjord has tall basalt hills above it, a small waterfall over the river Brynjudalsá and, farther on, the good salmon river called Laxá which flows into Laxárvogur. Once the green pastureland of Kjalarnes is reached there is a wide panorama of Reykjavík (rather farther away than it seems). Behind the city is the jumble of peaks of Reykjanes peninsula, with the hills around

Bláfjöll to the left.

The road rounds the massive Esja, with its steep scree slopes, sheer cliffs and a summit plateau at 909 m. Between Esja and Reykjavík is the wide fjord of Kollafjörður which has a number of islands, the largest of which is Viðey. This has a long history and was the site of a monastery (built in 1226). It also boasts the country's oldest stone house, built in the middle of the eighteenth century, by Skúli Magnússon (see p.15). As the ring road heads due south, road 36 heads east to Thingvellir and Thingvallavatn, a route described in section 17. The good farmland soon gives way to the ever-expanding suburbs of the city and for part of the route the concrete-covered pipe that carries natural hot water to the capital runs alongside the road. Reykjavík itself is described in section 3.

17
REYKJAVÍK TO THINGVELLIR AND THINGVALLAVATN

Distance:	Reykjavík to Thingvellir 52 km
	round Thingvallavatn 60 km
Route:	ring road (1) north
	road 36 east to Thingvellir
	road 36, 360, 36 round Thingvallavatn
Maps:	general map 3
	1:25 000 map of Thingvellir
Main places to visit:	Almannagjá (fissure) ★ ★ ★ ★
	Thingvellir (parliament site) ★ ★ ★
	Spöngin (rock island) ★ ★
	Nesjavellir (solfatara field) ★ ★
Road Conditions:	highway until after Mosfell; the rest of road 36 is
	reasonable. Road 360 (west and south of lake) can be
	slippery.
Adjacent sections:	16 (Borgarnes to Reykjavík)
	18 (Thingvellir to Gullfoss)
Notes:	The site of the Althing until the nineteenth century,
	Thingvellir remains the spiritual centre of Iceland. A
	most important place for visitors to see.

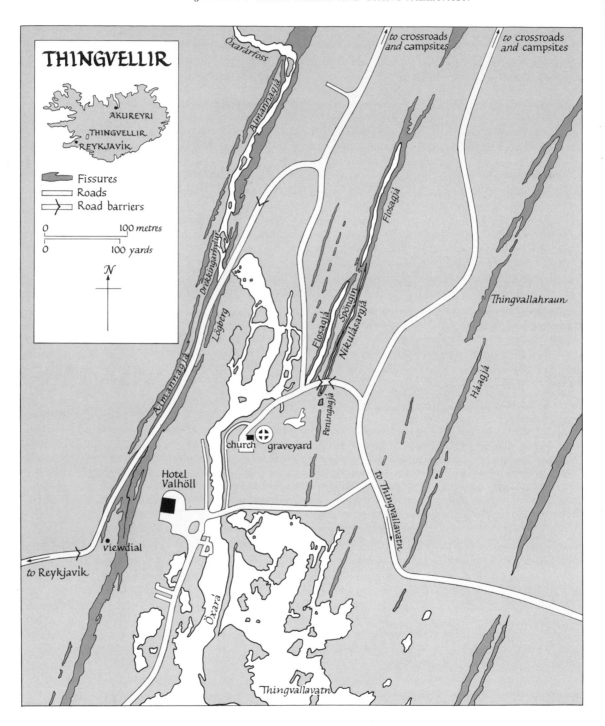

THINGVELLIR

AKUREYRI
THINGVELLIR
REYKJAVÍK

Fissures
Roads
Road barriers

0   100 metres
0   100 yards

N

Öxarárfoss

to crossroads
and campsites

to crossroads
and campsites

Almannagjá

Flosagjá

Flosagjá

Spöngin

Nikulásargjá

Peningagjá

Thingvallahraun

Háagjá

Drekkingarhylur

Lögberg

Almannagjá

church   graveyard

Hotel
Valhöll

viewdial

to Reykjavík

Öxará

to Thingvallavatn

Thingvallavatn

THE EASIEST route to Thingvellir from Reykjavík is to head north along the ring road and then east along road 36, past Mosfell (285 m). There are geothermal energy sources in the valley and there are a number of naturally heated glasshouses at Reykjahlíð, one of the sources of Reykjavík's hot water. Just after it and on the left is the farm of Laxnes, which is a pony-trekking centre. Next the road climbs through rather boggy land; on the left (opposite Leirvogsvatn) is the skiing area around Skálafell (771 m) (with a mast on top). By the southern side of the road lies the vast open expanse of Mosfellsheiði, a gently sloping and mossy lavafield that was produced by Borgarhólar (410 m), to the south. As Thingvallavatn is approached there is a fine view of the lake and its islands of Sandey and Nesjaey. Next the road goes past a lavafield, some of whose huge plates of rock have been rent by fissures.

Now continue along the main road until you reach the crossroads by the campsite's cafeteria. A right turn brings you onto the road that runs parallel to the biggest fissures and towards the major one, Almannagjá ('gorge of all men'). If you keep on the road running parallel to it, there is a convenient place before the waterfall to start exploring this remarkable fissure; a carpark is placed near a stand 'of conifers. The walk up to the lip of the first gorge (Stekkjargjá) is over plates of 9,000 year-old lava, once level but now at an extremely steep angle, such has been the movement of the land.

The only river to flow into Thingvallavatn, the Öxará, falls into this fissure over the Öxarárfoss; it then follows the start of Almannagjá until it meets the lake. From near the waterfall there is a good view of a great line of fissures about 7 km long and elsewhere in the park there are many others – all of them lying in the same southwest/north-east direction, parallel to the mid-Atlantic fault. A path runs along the main line of fissures for much of its length, allowing a close look at the cliffs that have been torn apart from each other; they are made up of dozens of layers of grey basalt, some of which are as much as a metre thick.

This is probably Iceland's best example of the effect of continental drift; Almannagjá is 50 m wide in places and its walls some 30 m high. There is another major fissure (Hrafnagjá) at the north-eastern corner of the lake and the lavafield (Thingvallahraun) between these two fissures has sunk about 70 m (in 1789 it subsided by nearly a metre). This is a result of the two fissures slowly moving apart, at an average rate of 8 mm a year since the eruption that formed the lavafield. This subsidence is the reason why the two sides of the main fissure are not the same height.

The Öxará blocks the way through the fissure but wooden steps allow the top of the gorge to be regained; a route must be taken along the sloping lava. About halfway between the waterfall and the nearest flagpole there is a good viewpoint which gives a commanding view of the fissure system, including some of the smaller ones on the other side of the road. Just after the bridge over the Öxará the deep pool 'Drekkingarhylur' can be seen in which witches and adulteresses used to be drowned in the Middle Ages. There are other small waterfalls above and below the bridge.

The path passes behind a flagpole which marks the site of the Althing (there is a gap in the fissure's wall that gives easy access). Below the flag is a plaque inscribed 'Lögberg' ('The law rock'). This was the site of the ancient parliament that was established at Thingvellir in 930. Annual gatherings were held until last century and a few remains of old huts can be seen below the flagpole. It was from the Lögberg that the Law-speaker recited the laws from memory and conducted the proceedings of the parliament and the courts. The spot was chosen for its natural beauty and possibly also for the acoustical effect of the gorge. Probably as a way of enhancing the setting, the Öxará's channel was altered so that it tumbled over the cliff into the gorge. It had previously entered the lake much farther to the south, at the farm of Skálabrekka.

The path now passes along the floor of the fissure; on the towering cliff on the right dozens of lava layers can be seen. As the fissure peters out, a viewpoint (on a clifftop), with a viewdial, gives a wide panorama over the other fissures, the lake and the surrounding district. This is the best place from which to see Thingvallavatn, which was formed by land subsidence and is the largest lake in Iceland – 83 sq km in area and 125 m deep. It is fed by subterranean rivers from Langjökull as well as taking run-off water from the surrounding hills. In its centre is the island of Sandey, an old volcano with two craters.

The path is now retraced and there are wooden steps that lead to the back of the Valhöll summer hotel; from there a bridge over the Öxará leads to a church. This stands on the site of Úlfljót's temple; he was the Law-speaker at the Parliament that adopted Christianity in 1000.

Behind the church is Iceland's equivalent of a national cemetery. It is typical of the country that the only two graves in this raised platform are not of politicians or soldiers, but of poets: Einar Benediksson and Jónas Hallgrímsson.

Just north-east of the cemetery there is a small bridge by a complex of long and deep fissures, many with crystal-clear water that has seeped through the porous lava. To the bridge's right is the fissure Peningagjá; to its left the fissure Nikulásargjá. A long promontory (Spöngin) has been left between Nikulasárgjá and the wide fissure of Flosagjá, whose end was passed before the bridge. A walk along Spöngin is interesting but care must be taken as the thick mosses can hide crevices in the rocks.

A road goes right round the lake, the north-western section of which is the main road (36). After this, the road (360) becomes much narrower and can be rather muddy after rain, with a couple of steep hills which can be slippery. There are a number of farms and dozens of summer houses set above the lakeside in pleasant surroundings, with the tall cliff of Jórukleif running close to the road at the south-western corner of the lake.

Shortly after this cliff and the Nesjahraun lavafield, there is a track off to the right to the farm of Nesjavellir near which there are huge billowing clouds of vapour that can be seen from Thingvellir. The best place to park is before the gate on the track to the active area. The first group of buildings have some large wellheads with their associated pipework but the biggest source is above, up a small hill. This wellhead thunders and makes the ground tremble, shattering the tranquillity of the surrounding countryside. Nearby there are pools of hot, blue water with little jets dancing up, keeping the surface in constant motion. Farther on, especially to the right, there are streams and pools worth exploring with blue, yellow, cream, brown and maroon rocks and clays set against the surrounding green vegetation. Numerous hot springs are dotted around, some with a rich growth of dark green algae in them.

A little after the fine conifers at Hagavík there is a view of one of the hydro-electric power stations south of the lake of Úlfljótsvatn. This is at the waterfall Ljósifoss and the road crosses the river Sog at the (lower) power station at Írafoss. The route by the eastern shore (now road 36 again) goes past this small but popular fishing lake and then past a third power station, at Steingrímsstöð. Just before the hill of Miðfell there is a long-established 'village' of summer homes of various designs and once the hill is rounded there is a good view of Almannagjá and the system of faults to the north-west. As the road nears the lakeside a junction is reached, with road 36 continuing to the right, while the lakeside route is on the left. After this junction, road 36 meets the turning (road 365, right) to Laugarvatn on its way to the crossroads with the cafeteria mentioned earlier. The lakeside road goes past the other major fissure (Hrafnagjá) which has a great jumble of rocks lying in it; this route then continues either to the hotel or the crossroads.

The main camping areas are between the cafeteria at the crossroads and the hotel, the sites being grassy and flat; there are also a few small areas for camping along the north-eastern shore. The camping areas have some primitive toilets and running water at sinks while the cafeteria has good washrooms with WCs and hot water, but no petrol. The area is very popular at weekends as it has many pleasant walks through vegetated lava-fields. The 1:25 000 map is on sale at the cafeteria and a number of paths near Thingvellir are marked for those who wish to spend some time exploring the area. Petrol can be obtained at the hotel.

18
THINGVELLIR TO GULLFOSS

Distance:	62 km
Route:	road 36 east
	road 365 to Laugarvatn
	road 37 to just before Geysir
	road 35
Maps:	general maps 3 and 6
Main places to visit:	Laugarvatnsvellir (caves) ★
	Laugarvatn (lake) ★ ★
	Geysir and Strokkur (geysers) ★ ★ ★ ★
	Gullfoss (waterfall) ★ ★ ★ ★
Road Conditions:	the road between Thingvallavatn and Laugarvatn can be rough as can the final stages of the section.
Adjacent sections:	22 (Selfoss to Geysir)
	19 (Gullfoss to Sigalda)
	36 (Gullfoss to Hveravellir)
Notes:	Strokkur and Gullfoss should not be missed by anyone.

AFTER going round part of the Thingvalla-vatn's north-eastern shore, road 365 is fairly steep and rough as it climbs up towards good views of the lake and the hills behind it. A little after the downward journey begins there is a sign (left) to the Laugarvatnsvellir caves; the track to these is easy and ends at a car park from which there is a path up to the left. The soft black palagonite rock has been hollowed out, making two caves that were lived in by a family until 1922. The caves are quite small (only about 10m long) and not at all well protected from the elements.

Just a little farther on there is a viewpoint before the road dips down to Laugarvatn. In the distance is Hekla (to the south-east) and beyond is the glacier Eyjafjallajökull. Immediately below is the warm lake of Laugarvatn and behind it, Apavatn and the very rich agricultural land of south-east Iceland.

As the settlement of Laugarvatn is entered, one of the Edda Hotels (the Húsmæðraskóli or HSL) is on the right; the other Edda Hotel (the Mennta-skóli or ML) is nearer the centre of the settle-ment. A little beyond the first hotel and on the right is a road leading to the 'Gufubað' (sauna) by the shore. To the sauna's left are glasshouses and a place where rowing boats can be hired, whilst a walk along the shore to the right comes to a big walled pool of hot water that heaves noisily. This provides warm water to nearby buildings.

The lake is only 2.5m deep and is fed by springs, some of them as hot as 95°C, so the water is warm enough for pleasant swimming even when the air temperature is low and hot steam baths and mud baths for relieving rheumatism are popular. The lake's warmth has been appreciated by Icelanders for centuries – after the Althing's decision in 1000 to accept Christianity (see p.11), those who found the water of the river Öxará (at Thingvellir) too cold came to Laugarvatn for their baptism. Farther down the main road there is a garage, a supermarket and a petrol station. Next, on the left, there is a well-equipped campsite.

The road continues past a number of modern summer homes and the pony-trekking centre at the farm of Miðdalur, from which there are tours to places of interest in the district. From now on much of the farmland is crossed by deep drainage ditches, evidence of the farmers' struggle to make the most of this marginal land. North of here sandstorms may occur as the winds sweep down from the highlands. Once the junction with road 35 is reached, the park containing Geysir and Strokkur (the two most famous geysers in Iceland) can be seen, marked by the plumes of water vapour rising into the air. Although Strokkur is still 5km away, you may see it erupting, leaving behind a cloud that takes a few seconds to evaporate and disappear from view.

The small park has a good roadside cafe, petrol station and a campsite – with further facilities in the 'Hotel Geysir', which also has a swimming pool. The geyser 'Strokkur' ('the churn') is the main attraction in the park. The hot water comes up through a tube 2m in diameter and fills a pool about 10m in diameter. Outside that is the wall of an older and larger pool, made up of silicates deposited by the water. As you watch from about 15m away, the water level keeps rising and falling, tempting spectators to guess just when it will erupt. Sometimes it teases by spurting only a couple of metres, but usually it sends a tall and narrow column of water 20-40m up (see p.110). The water then falls back, some of it running away through a breached wall, and the process starts all over again. The interval between eruptions during the course of a day is fairly constant but from week to week this time may vary from just a few minutes to 20 minutes or more.

Geysir ('the gusher'), after which all geysers are named, is now a still, blue pool of water about 10m in diameter, with a massive cone of silicates built up around it. The area round it is roped off as visitors' feet have damaged the delicate layers of rock built up by countless eruptions. Geysers are usually deep cylindrical holes full of hot water heated by steam rising from the hot rocks below and when the water becomes very hot then an eruption may begin. On occasions, dormant geysers have been encouraged to erupt either by blocking the top (reducing the heat loss) or by adding soap to the water (reducing its surface tension), and unfortunately throwing things into Geysir to encourage it to spout might have been the reason for it ceasing to erupt early this century.

In recent years Geysir has been artificially encouraged to erupt every Saturday during the summer season. When Geysir erupted regularly, it used to throw columns of hot water up 70 metres, each eruption lasting for minutes, compared to the single spout of Strokkur. However, at the end of last century, Strokkur could erupt for over two hours at a time.

There are numerous other pools bubbling away in the park, many with water so clear that you can see the narrow tube up which the hot water comes. Some of the pools have coloured mud in them and others have small jets of water barely breaking the surface. There are some still pools too, and two near Geysir are very beautiful; one being clear, the other an exquisitely delicate shade of blue. Higher up in the park and above the pools is a path to a viewdial. Bláfell (1204m) to the north-east and Hekla (1491m) to the south-east are the most prominent hills.

As you leave the park and continue along road 35, the terrain becomes rather more barren. There are a few sightings of the canyon below Gullfoss before the waterfall is reached, but its main advertisement is the huge cloud of spray it throws up, especially from the lower of the two falls. The river Hvítá (which carries meltwater from Langjökull) has created what is considered to be the country's finest waterfall and when the sun shines, the rainbows that are produced show why it is called 'the golden falls' (see pp.108-109). After the car park, the path goes down past a plaque dedicated to Sigríður Tómasdóttir who campaigned for the return of the falls to Icelandic ownership after it had been foreign-owned.

The path continues to a sheltered ledge just below the upper fall and within a few metres of the torrent – the water rushing past at just above head height and frighteningly close. Going higher up the hillside, there is a view of the rapids above the falls and the impressive canyon farther downstream.

The campsite is before the car park (WCs and sinks in two washrooms) and at the junction with the track up to Kjölur (described in section 36); behind the washroom is another fine view of the canyon (70m high), this time from above it. Its sides are sheer and it contains the remains of landslides upon which healthy clumps of trees are growing. The most popular place for camping is on the broad grassy ledge below the toilet block. Apart from the shelter (from the wind, not from the spray) it also looks directly down the canyon as well as up to the falls; its main disadvantage is the stream of visitors who walk past the tents to get to the edge of the canyon. On the opposite cliff the layers of basalt and palagonite can be distinguished and there are basalt pillars in a number of places.

19
GULLFOSS TO SIGALDA

Distance:	99 km (to start of road 26)
Route:	road 35 west
	road 30 south to Thjórsá
	road 32 to junction with road 26
Map:	general map 6
Main places to visit:	large moraine by Hvítá (view) ★
	Gaukshöfði (view) ★
	Hjálparfoss (waterfall) ★
	Stöng (excavated farmhouse) ★ ★
	Thjóðveldisbærinn (reconstructed farmhouse) ★ ★
	Sámsstaðamúli (view) ★ ★
Road Conditions:	reasonable, except for river before Stöng
Adjacent sections:	20 (Sigalda to south coast)
	39 (Nýidalur to Sigalda)
	41 (Sigalda to Landmannalaugar)
Notes:	The route beside Thjórsá gives views towards Hekla and the wastelands around this famous volcano.

AFTER HEADING back towards Geysir on road 35 and then turning south (onto road 30) at the farm of Kjóastaðir, the route goes through a rather stony farming district with many flat-topped moraine terraces, especially on the right. At the bridge over the Hvítá the river has cut a new canyon through the soft rock; the river's previous bed is crossed first and is littered with round grey boulders. A large moraine stands above the river's eastern bank and, once this is rounded, a walk to the moraine's summit gives a very good view, especially to the north: Bláfell stands high above the beginning of Gullfoss's gorge and to the left is the massive glacier of Langjökull, flanked by the huge jagged hills (Jarlhettur) that guard its slopes. Below, the farmland stretches away into the distance, with ranges of hills to the west and south-west.

Farther along the road there is a waterfall on the left, beside a farm appropriately called 'Foss'. As the land opens out, the hills first seen from the moraine are sighted. This is very picturesque farmland, concentrated round small settlements like Flúðir where there is a motel, summer hotel, pool, shop and garage. The campsite (which has no facilities) is in a small park surrounded by trees, on the right just before the football pitch. As well as cows and horses on Flúðir's farms, there are a number of glasshouses heated by warm water springs.

With a small range of hills to the left with farms sheltering under their slopes, the route crosses the Stóra-Laxá river and then heads east along road 32 to meet the mighty Thjórsá. This is Iceland's greatest river and it carries a vast amount of water and sand from the Hofsjökull glacier. The river, however, soon disappears from view. By the time it reappears the hulking shape of Búrfell (669 m) can be seen in front, but it is Hekla (1491 m) to the east that completely dominates the scene. Hekla is described in section 20. The highest hill on the left of the road is Hagafjall (472 m). As the road climbs past it, a prominent rock (Gaukshöfði) that juts up on the right is an excellent viewpoint. This looks over to the river, the volcano and its lavafields. Just upstream the river is fairly wide and has built up extensive sand and gravel banks. The Thjórsárdalur campsite is about 3 km after this viewpoint; this is at the Skriðufell farm but unfortunately there is no camping sign to help lost travellers. Follow the sign (left) to the farm, then keep to the right; this site is popular with caravanners but tents and vehicles can be accommodated in the

field which is reached after skirting the caravans. There are a couple of primitive toilets and a cold water tap and sink. The area is wooded and is pleasant for walking.

Next the scenery undergoes dramatic changes with black lavafields and black and brown ash in abundance, the result of Hekla's convulsions. To the right a track leads to the waterfall of Hjálparfoss where the river Fossá tumbles over the two arms of the fall; below, the pool is decorated with walls of twisted basalt columns. From the slope above the falls the Búrfell power station is seen, the mountain standing directly behind it. The track to the waterfall can be retraced or the one on the right (to the north) can be followed back to the road. The land now becomes increasingly barren with the huge carpet of black ash giving little protection to plants, but at one point on the right there are experimental plots, laid out to help find out how best to replant this desolate district. Just before the Fossá is crossed there is a notice board (an unusual occurrence in Iceland, except outside some towns) with a first-class map, showing the layout of the hills, the roads and the rivers.

After the bridge there is a track (left) to the farmhouse at Stöng; the track has one steep hill at the beginning and may (in wet weather) have some streams flowing over the otherwise smooth ash surface. The surface is much better than the 1:250 000 map would suggest and the only real problem for two-wheel drive vehicles is the rocky river just below the farmhouse; however, it is not necessary to take the vehicle across since the track must be retraced to regain the main road. The scenery is particularly interesting with a section of brilliantly coloured vegetation, countless hillocks of black ash, green and bright red plants and some light-brown rhyolite hills to the west, making this a very colourful journey.

Stöng and fifteen other farms in the valley were destroyed in the Hekla eruption of 1104; Stöng was unearthed in 1939, having been preserved by the ash for over eight hundred years. The building is very large, perhaps 50 m by 20 m with compartments off the main chamber. The old lava walls remain, topped by earth and thick sods; stones mark the position of fireplaces in the floor. The reconstruction is protected by a modern wall with windows in the corrugated iron roof. Banks of ash (a good insulating material) lie against the outside wall. The small sheltered valley in which the farmhouse lies is extremely well vegetated with a thick growth of small plants and shrubs. Just before the river is reached a track leads east that eventually comes out at the main road. Below the farmhouse another track runs below the mountain of Stangarfjall in the direction of Háifoss which, at 122 m, is the second-highest waterfall in the country.

The main road now goes left up the side of Skeljafell while the road to the right leads to the power station buildings; if this latter road is followed, the first left turn leads to Thjóðveldis-bærinn, a reconstructed mediaeval farmhouse. On top of stone foundations there is a neat wall of turf layers and then a turf roof. The farmhouse also has an ornate wooden door (possibly locked), two chimneys and two compartments joined on at the rear.

As the main road reaches up to Sámsstaðamúli there is a short track to the right leading to a stupendous viewpoint, looking down on the landscape destroyed by Hekla. The black fields of ash are spread out, reaching down to the farming communities near the coast. In good weather there is a remarkable view over this devastated landscape.

A short distance behind the viewpoint is Lake Bjarnalón, which gathers waters from the Thjórsá, acting as a reservoir for the power station. Because the Thjórsá comes from a glacier, the sand and gravel it brings down must be removed from the reservoir and a dredger can often be seen at work on the lake. As the road heads north-east by the river, there are two bridges with power-station equipment on them but the road continues past more ash and lava until the Thjórsá is crossed by a long bridge, well protected by large gravel embankments. The route then meets road 26 after a few kilometres. Continuing on 32 leads to Landmannalaugar (section 41) and Sprengisandur (section 39) while a turn to the south-west on road 26 leads past Hekla (section 20).

20
SIGALDA TO THE SOUTH COAST

Distance:	65 km
Route:	road 26
Map:	general map 6
Main places to visit:	Fossabrekkur (waterfall) ★
	Tröllkonuhlaup (waterfall)
Road Conditions:	reasonable
Adjacent section:	4 (Reykjavík to Hella)
Notes:	This is a short section which will take those coming from Gullfoss (section 19) or Nýidalur (section 39) back to the south coast. The road runs to the west of Hekla and gives a very good view of the volcano and its many lavafields.

THE ROAD south from Sigalda travels below Hekla's foothills, permitting a closer look at some of the effects that the volcano has had on the surrounding landscape. Hekla, in common with many other Icelandic volcanoes, does not erupt from a central crater (which would produce a conically shaped mountain), but through a fissure. The present fissure ('Heklugjá') is about six kilometres long and has produced the south-west/north-east ridge. When an eruption occurs, the fissure opens up and a number of craters usually appear, throwing out lava, ash and gases. Apart from Katla and Grímsvötn, Hekla has erupted more often than any other volcano in Iceland and because of its proximity to populated areas it has been the subject of more research than any other volcano in the country.

The first eruption of Hekla to be recorded was that seen by the Irish monk St Brendan (see p.8) and up to the seventeenth century it was thought to be an entrance to hell, so powerful were its powers of destruction. Well before that, about 2,800 years ago, an eruption produced an enormous mass of airborne material that fell over an area of 260,000 sq km, (80,000 sq km of that on Iceland). In the eruption of 1104 Hekla destroyed a great number of farms (including Stöng, see p.208) and a farm 50 km distant from the eruption was inundated by a fall of 20 cm of

ash. Only two centuries later, in 1300, a twelve-month-long eruption destroyed grasslands by the north coast, causing a famine the next winter. More recently (1947), a lava bomb 50 cm in diameter was thrown a distance of 32 km; that eruption added some 50 m to the height of the mountain. *Jökulhlaups* have sometimes been caused by Hekla's eruptions, causing great damage as small glaciers and snowfields have been melted and, augmented by ground water, have resulted in a slurry sweeping down the hillsides. These flows can be quite warm (40°C), the heat coming from lava bombs, whose temperature may be as high as 1,000°C. The most recent eruption, in 1980, produced a light brown ash that can be seen to the west and north-west of the volcano.

Although climbing the mountain has always been seen as a challenge to Icelanders and visitors alike, many climbing clubs now avoid Hekla as it can erupt with little or no warning – so visitors should not attempt an ascent unless accompanied by Icelandic experts. Hekla was first climbed in 1750; the usual route to the summit is from the north-west.

Depending on the condition of the hot magma, Hekla ejects a number of different types of volcanic material. Along the roadside there is a stretch of fine ash, littered with 'lava bombs' that have been thrown out. Parts of the mountain are dark or black in colour, others are a lighter grey or red-brown. A number of streams carry water down the mountainside and help sustain the scant green vegetation that exists.

Opposite Hekla is Búrfell (669 m), the site of a huge power station; when the road is nearly opposite Búrfell's summit, a track to the left goes to the waterfall of Fossabrekkur. Down this track, a right-hand fork leads to the ash banks of the Ytri-Rangá where there is a small oasis. This river drains the volcano's western slopes and the many small lavafields that lie below Hekla's ridge; here it has formed a small waterfall over some of the exposed lava. By the fall are terraces of ash that support plant life and on the eastern bank there is a canyon where some of the different layers of ash and lava that have been produced by the volcano lie revealed. Returning to road 26, 1 km farther on, the Thjórsá has cut the wide waterfall of Tröllkonuhlaup under Búrfell; the name recalls the Trolls who are said to have lived ·in the mountain and to have used the rocks in the falls as stepping stones. Yet another waterfall (Thjófafoss) is south-west of Búrfell and is reached by a signposted track farther on.

Since Hekla has destroyed so much vegetation it comes as a surprise to see the large birch plantation around the farm of Galtalækur. There is a campsite, the entrance being at the farm. A little farther on there is another campsite and the youth hostel at Leirubakki. The tremendous variation in landforms continues with rich flat fields, rocky lava, sand dunes and wet meadows. Some of the farms have turfed buildings, providing a beautiful contrast to the barren lands around Hekla. The road winds through this pleasant farming district, passing the small settlement of Laugaland which is on the right. This has a source of geothermal heat and a swimming pool. The 1980 edition of general map 6 has the road veering south-east before this settlement is reached. This is incorrect according to the route seen and taken by the author: road 26 keeps a south-westerly direction and meets the ring road at Tunga where there is a petrol station. The correct route is shown on the 1983 edition of the 1:500 000 map as well as on the 1973 edition of the 1:250 000 map. This is a good example of why care is needed in following some details on the maps.

21
REYKJAVÍK TO KRÍSUVÍK AND HVERAGERÐI

Distance:	92 km
Route:	road 40 to just before Hafnarfjörður
	road 41 to just before Straumsvík
	road 42
	road 38
Map:	general map 3
Main places to visit:	Bessastaðir (President's home) ★ ★
	Sveifluháls (walk along ridge) ★ ★
	Kleifarvatn (lake) ★ ★ ★
	Krísuvík (solfatara field) ★ ★ ★
	Raufarhólshellir (lava tube) ★ ★
Road Conditions:	highway until road 42 starts, then probably a bit rough. The road along the south coast is tricky (and very slow) as it goes over bare rock.
Adjacent sections:	1 (Keflavík to Reykjavík)
	4 (Reykjavík to Hella)
Notes:	This is a fine one-day trip from Reykjavík or an alternative route to section 4. For those not going to Heimaey or Húsafell, this trip offers the chance to explore a lava tube.

HEADING SOUTH out of Reykjavík, the two most noticeable man-made sights are the tall concrete hoops of the Kópavogur church and the massive red and white towers of the aluminium smelter at Straumsvík. The route goes past the suburbs of Kópavogur and Garðabær, then detours right (road 415) to Bessastaðir.

The house at Bessastaðir is just over two hundred years old. Ever since Iceland became a sovereign state, the country's President has lived there. Both the President's home and the church (which has fine stained-glass windows) are neat and well-proportioned white buildings with red tiled roofs. Although they are not very high up, the surrounding low land gives them good views over to Reykjavík.

After passing the town of Hafnarfjörður the route turns left (road 42) just before the smelter and goes through the Kapelluhraun lavafield, passing a great number of racks for drying fish. A winding section of road through coloured hills

leads to the bare, inhospitable, but intriguing lake of Kleifarvatn. This is a reasonably large lake, 10 sq km in area and 97 m deep. One unusual aspect about it is that it has no surface outlet; every few years it mysteriously changes its level by about 5 m.

Just above the lake's western shore is Sveifluháls, a long and steep volcanic ridge made of brown palagonite tuff. (This rock is made from much looser volcanic material, such as ash, that has been compressed and cemented together.) It is certainly worth walking along part of the 7 km-long ridge. The most interesting part is best approached when the lake is first sighted as there is a small track on the right that gives an easy start to the walk. There are a number of peaks along the middle section of the ridge which give wide views of the surrounding area and in the distance Reykjavík and Keflavík can be seen, as can even Snæfellsnes on very clear days. Stretching away from the northern corner of the lake is

Langahlið (621 m), which has a summit plateau on which there is a lavafield. To the north-east and in line with Sveifluháls there are a number of other hills, notably Helgafell (340 m) with Húsafell (278 m) behind it, both surrounded by lavafields. To the west there is more lava, with the cone of Keilir (379 m) and just nearer, Trölladyngja (393 m). Sveifluháls erupted during the fourteenth century; after the lava flow the area between it and Trölladyngja subsided. As might be expected, all the rows of craters, ridges and depressions lie in the same south-west/north-east direction parallel to the North Atlantic Ridge. Great care needs to be taken when coming off the ridge as small lumps of rock lying on the bare surface make the slope dangerously slippery; there are also steep cliffs and a number of canyons in some places that have to be avoided.

To those visitors accustomed to greener scenery, this landscape is almost like a science fiction film set with its bare, twisted and contorted rock shapes formed out of the upheavals of earthquakes and eruptions. Along the shore there are various promontories from which the lake can be viewed. The cliffs often show definite bands of tuff, sometimes black, brown or red – and very bare. A popular place for stopping (especially for fishing) is a stony beach on the southern shore to which there is a track. There is a toilet hut here and some flat grassy areas suitable for camping. Just a little farther along the road there is another track to a popular picnic spot at the south-eastern corner of the lake.

At the end of the lake, wisps of vapour on the right mark the approach to the Krísuvík geo-thermal area. Backed by cliffs, this relatively small but active field has mounds of brown clay with hot springs trickling inbetween. Everywhere there are small pools with tiny fountains of hot water jumping up, releasing pent-up energy received from the hot rocks below. At the beginning of the walk through the pools there is a thundering jet of superheated steam, safely funnelled upwards in still weather, but in windy conditions going through its cloud is like walking through warm rain. There is a mass of colour, with the blue/grey of the volcanic mud dominating a background of yellow, white, red and green. Dotted around are numerous small holes in the ground that once were vents, their mouths now encrusted with a lace-like pattern of silica that has been built up over a long time.

Only a few metres south-west, but where few bother to look, is an old stream with banks of dark red clay produced by previous solfataric activity. Following this stream leads to another active area, with gurgling mud pits. A cold stream passes through this field, slowly becoming warmer as a few small jets of hot water come up through its muddy bed. Across the road from here there is a massive pond of bubbling blue/grey mud some 10 m across. From beside this pond other wisps of vapour can be seen higher up on the hillside. The district round Krísuvík has been an important solfatara field for some time, becoming even more active after earthquakes, which are relatively common in this district. Sulphur mining was carried out near here during the eighteenth and nineteenth centuries.

A little farther on and on the left is the large explosion crater Grænavatn, now filled with green water; directly opposite but hidden from the road by its stony rim, is another water-filled crater, Gestsstaðavatn. After the road to Grindavík is passed on the right, there is a grassy area which leads down to some of the peninsula's best bird cliffs, Krísuvíkurberg. As the road turns to the east it has a crater on each side; Geitahlíð (386 m) is on the left, while on the right is the smaller Eldborg. Beyond Eldborg there are some rocks of a beautiful dark red colour as well as a fine view along the coastline. The road now goes over bare (but fairly smooth) rock at times, allowing passengers plenty of opportunity to walk alongside the vehicle and admire the old sea cliffs on the left since the vehicle must travel at a tortuously slow speed. While the road surface here is particularly bad, it is in no way dangerous so long as a sensible speed is maintained. Around the good fishing lake of Hlíðarvatn the road improves and then begins a long climb through moorland which eventually gives a superb view of the southern coast. Almost straight ahead is the level plateau at the top of Ingólfsfjall with the town of Selfoss on its right, below the cliffs. In front of the town lies the lagoon into which the Ölfusá flows before entering the sea. Much farther away to the east the Westman Islands can be seen, with the rocky promontory of Dyrhólaey (the mainland's most southerly point) to their left. Below the viewpoint is the port of Thorlákshöfn from which the ferry sails to the Westman Islands.

The junction with road 39 (a highway) gives a quick route back to Reykjavík. One very interesting place to visit along that road is the kilometre-long cave of Raufarhólshellir. About 2 km after the turning there is a cairn on the right. Nearby is the collapsed roof of a lava tunnel, along which molten lava once flowed. Entry is not by the large hole in the roof, but by a smaller and easier entrance near the cairn. The first part of the cave does not require a torch for exploration and has numerous solid 'drips' of lava left behind by the molten rock. Elsewhere the walls and ceiling are jagged; the many rocks that have fallen off them litter the floor and make walking very slow. Winter snow lies in the cave for much of the year.

Road 39 meets the ring road opposite Hengill; this part of the journey is described in section 4.

Continuing along the coastal road, the farmland is good and supports many well-maintained farms that either nestle under Skálafell's cliffs or lie farther east in the wet meadows. A concrete-covered pipe carrying natural hot water runs alongside the road from Hveragerði, which is entered after the ring road is met. This settlement is described in section 4.

22
SELFOSS TO GEYSIR

Distance:	56 km to junction with road 37
Route:	ring road (1) west
	road 35
Maps:	general maps 3 and 6
Main places to visit:	Kerið (explosion crater) ★ ★
	Skálholt (church) ★ ★
Road Conditions:	possibly very badly potholed
Adjacent section:	18 (Thingvellir to Gullfoss)
Notes:	this short journey is an alternative route to Geysir and Gullfoss.

TWO kilometres west of Selfoss, the ring road meets road 35. This heads north, with the steep boulder-strewn slopes of Ingólfsfjall (551m) on the left and the broad river Ölfusá on the right. As the road runs close to the river there are some fine turfed farm buildings on the left at Tannastaðir and after crossing the river Sog numerous summer cottages can be seen amongst the trees in the old lavafields.

During the climb into red ash hills that follows there is a short, unsignposted track to the right to the explosion crater of Kerið. This is c. 6,000 years old and about 200m in diameter. It is 50m deep with sides of red ash and lava. A pool of green water lies at its base. A path goes round the rim and its highest point gives a good view of the district as well as looking down to other craters. These belong to the Tjarnarhólar group, which was partly responsible for the lavafields in this region. Farther along this road and to the left is another group of red cones called Seyðishólar, which produced much of the surrounding lava.

The route now goes through farming land and after the Brúará is crossed there is a road (31, right) to Skálholt. Skálholt has been the site of a church for many centuries; the present handsome building is constructed of concrete with a grey tiled roof and stained-glass windows. It was at Skálholt, in 1550, that Bishop Jón Arason was illegally beheaded with two of his sons (see p.14); shortly before the church is reached there is a memorial on the left (dated 7 November 1550) marking the spot where the execution took place. There is a summer hotel beside the church.

Back on the main road, 5km further on, the settlement of Aratunga is reached, where there are a number of glasshouses and a swimming pool (Aratunga is the site of a good source of geothermal energy). Further on there are numerous farms many of which have extensive systems of drainage ditches.

The small park around Geysir is seen just before the junction with road 37. The route after this junction is described in section 18.

23
HVOLSVÖLLUR TO MARKARFLJÓT VIA FLJÓTSDALUR

Distance:	35 km including retracing route to Fljótsdalur
Route:	road 261 to Fljótsdalur
	road 250 to Markarfljót
Map:	general map 6
Road Conditions:	reasonable at first, getting rougher once the gravel starts.
Adjacent sections:	5 (Hella to Vík)
	43 (Thórsmörk)
Notes:	This short journey is an alternative to the ring road between Hvolsvöllur and the Markarfljót (section 5). It gives access to some good walking routes as well as views of the glaciers.

WITH WET gravelly meadows on the right and richer farming land on the slopes to the left, the road heads east along the valley of Fljótsdalur towards the glaciers Eyjafjallajökull and Mýrdalsjökull. The district is well cultivated and supports many trees, especially near the forestry centre at Tumastaðir. The twin peaks of Thrihyrningur stand high above the valley, but it is the ice and snow of the two glaciers that dominate the pleasant scenery. These peaceful surroundings soon give way to a harsher scene: as the lone rock of Stóra-Dímon is passed on the right, the road moves nearer to the cliffs on the left, down which tumble a number of small waterfalls. At the farm of Múlakot there is a stand of trees and a waterfall, while at the farm of Eyvindarmúli the cliff is decorated with columnar basalt.

After the farm of Háamúli the first rivers and the long gravel embankments are met and even more waterfalls decorate the cliffs. The road surface now deteriorates and ends at the farmhouse and youth hostel at Fljótsdalur, which is a hill-walking centre. A track continues north after the hostel but another track, heading farther east, may be closed. Looking towards Eyjafjallajökull, the two valley glaciers of Gígjökull (called Fall-jökull on the general map) and Steinsholtsjökull can clearly be seen reaching down into the valley.

After retracing the route to road 250, the journey continues across gravel beds that until recently were crossed by countless glacial streams. These are now controlled, although a few tiny streams may have to be forded. Just before Stóra-Dímon (78 m) is rounded there is a fine view up the valley to Thórsmörk.

24
WESTMAN ISLANDS

Map:	general map 6
	1:50 000 map of Westman Islands
Main places to visit:	harbour ★ ★
	aquarium ★ ★
	Eldfell (the new volcano) ★ ★ ★
	east coast (new lava) ★ ★
	lava tube ★
	boat trip ★ ★
Road Conditions:	reasonable
Adjacent sections:	21 (Reykjavík to Krísuvík and Hveragerði – for ferry).
Notes:	Well worth a visit, but wait for good weather if going by air.

THE Westman Islands lie just off the country's southern coast. The only inhabited one, Heimaey, is the home of the country's largest and most important fishing fleet. The island is connected to the mainland by daily sailings of the large vehicle ferry 'Herjólfur' from Thorlákshöfn and a few flights each day from Reykjavík. Apart from the beautiful scenery on and around Heimaey the effects (and remains) of the 1973 eruption (see p.25), are fascinating to explore. Since weather conditions on Heimaey often mean cancellations of flights (and perhaps an unexpected stay on the island), the flight should not be made near the end of your holiday unless the weather is very good. Because of the interest in the island caused by the 1973 eruption, many leaflets have been produced and these should be available from your tour operator or in Reykjavík. A well-produced pamphlet called *The Westman Islands Weekly* also provides useful information.

Heimaey's population is about 5,000 and it has a very good range of shops and services, including hotels, cinema, museum, aquarium, campsite, garage, swimming pool, hospital, golf course and numerous shops. Bus and boat tours are available. All round there are reminders of the terrible onslaught of the lava but now, more than a decade after the eruption, the town has been rebuilt. Behind the town are the two volcanoes: the old Helgafell (226 m) and, beside it, the recently created and larger Eldfell, with the new lavafield of Kirkjubæjarhraun between it and the harbour. Around the edge of the lava are the crushed remains of houses (and the old swimming pool by the sea wall) that were destroyed just before the lava stopped its final advance; more than 300 homes that were completely lost lie under the lava. One artistic reminder of the eruption is the wall mural near the Guesthouse Heimir that depicts the dramatic scene, with the

216

town's inhabitants being evacuated by a flotilla of fishing boats. There are other murals showing different aspects of Heimaey's life on other walls (for instance on a building on Bárustígur there is a scene of fishermen in old rowing boats).

The harbour is well protected, with the huge rock-face of Heimaklettur joined to the flatter land by an embankment. On the eastern side of the harbour the tall edge of the lavafield towers over the old sea wall, ironically affording increased protection to the harbour. Fish processing factories and sheds line the dockside; due to the importance of the local fishing, this is a busy place and well worth visiting. To the west of the harbour there is a tall cliff with ropes hanging from it and here children aged three and upwards are coached in swinging and climbing the ropes. The sport stems from the old tradition on the island of catching puffins on cliff faces.

Round to the north-west of the island is the campsite in Herjólfsdalur (this is signposted from the ferry terminal). The site is grassy, lies under cliffs and has a washroom with WCs and hot and cold water. Every year, during the first weekend in August, this is the centre of a well-attended, three-day national festival; the setting (in an old crater) is where the island's first settler, Herjólfur, is believed to have lived.

As befits an island so dependent on the sea for its livelihood, the town boasts an interesting aquarium. This has a collection of sea-creatures (such as cod, halibut, catfish, sea anenomes, large crabs, coral and so on) that are found off the shores of the islands. There is also an extensive collection of stuffed fish (including sharks) and birds (eagles, owls, puffins, guillemots, falcons). The museum is normally open daily in summer; by appointment in winter.

A track behind the town leads towards the new crater – a cone of black, red and maroon ash that is still very warm just a couple of centimetres below the surface. There is a good view from the rim; looking down towards the harbour there are two fairly significant humps within the lavafield – these were previously joined and have moved all the way from the lower part of the rim to their

present position. This 'hill' was nicknamed 'the traveller' and at times during the eruption it moved 50 m downhill in a day. Standing at the rim it is hard to imagine that before the eruption it was nearly at the same level as the rest of the town.

Another track nearer the town runs through the lavafield, through the new 'land' that the lava has formed and towards the new seashore. There are a number of new cliffs here – made out of the molten lava that was stopped by the cold Atlantic waves. The cliffs and other rocks around them have various forms: some are vertical, others slope more gently, and have a layer of ash lying on them. A number of the rock faces are smooth while others are cracked and broken, revealing the several layers of lava that poured over the ledge before being stopped by the water. In places the sea has broken up the rocks, exposing gas holes or piles of loose clinker that were previously sheltered from the waves. Below the cliffs a beach of smooth boulders is being established as the landforms slowly begin to 'age' and take up many of the features of other sea cliffs around the country. Indeed, looking at the rocks here is a good way of beginning to understand how Iceland's coastal scenery was formed. Those visitors who have seen Dritvík cove on Snæfellsnes (see p.232) or other places with older lava flows at the coast can see what the original rocks must have looked like; soon these large blocks of lava will be eaten away by the Atlantic and will produce colourful scree slopes. Along the beach is a shipwreck (the 'Pelagus') that ran aground in 1982. The sight of this wreck is a frightening reminder of what the weather, sea conditions and an inhospitable shoreline can be like during the Icelandic winter.

The southern tip of Heimaey has a weather station and about 100 m before it there is an entrance to a lava tube or cave (on the left, towards the sea). The entrance is above the cave and is in a grassy area about 50 m away from the road. With no real landmarks it is a little difficult to find. The entrance is a hole, about 4 m deep, with convenient ledges for stepping on. The walls and floor of the cave are smooth and its end opens out to a sea cliff with a high and exposed drop.

Surtsey can be seen from the southern part of Heimaey – it is the largest island to the south-east and some 18 km from the weather station. It was formed in 1963 by an eruption in 130 m of water. Its volcanic birth must be one of the world's best-documented eruptions. Today it is still yielding a lot of information on how life-forms colonise bare ground; only scientific parties are allowed to land on it.

In the initial stages of the eruption the clouds of vapour and dust reached a height of 8,000 m as the volcano threw out vast quantities of ash and other light material. The volcano then fought a battle for survival with the sea; before the frail island could be washed away, lava poured out, flowing over the ash and consolidating it. After Heimaey, Surtsey is the largest island in the Westman Islands.

A good way to see more of the islands is to go on one of the daily cruises by motor launch: this takes approximately two hours. The islands were produced sub-glacially and are made of palagonite; this is fairly easily eroded and the constant battering of the waves has produced many huge caves as well as innumerable ledges on the steep cliffs. The ledges provide nesting spaces for enormous numbers of guillemots, gannets and fulmars, but the most common bird is the colourful and amusing puffin. Skuas are also seen chasing other birds – either to kill them or to make them disgorge their catch. Altogether there may be 5,000,000 birds during the summer, with as many as 36 species represented. For a long time the puffins were an important source of food and income for the islanders, though catching them is more of a sport than a livelihood now. Puffin eggs are collected in May and adult puffins are caught in July and August; to do this the 'catcher' is lowered down the vertical cliff and nets the birds as they fly off the ledges. During the boat trip a number of little houses can be seen perched up on top of the smaller islands. Long ropes hang down their vertical cliffs, giving the bird catchers their sole means of access to their summer homes. Above the cliffs there are often small herds of sheep, put there to take advantage of the summer grazing on the lush vegetation.

25
LÖGURINN

Distance:	86 km round trip
Route:	ring road (1) south from Egilsstaðir
	road 931 round lake
	ring road (1) back to Egilsstaðir
Map:	general map 8
Main places to visit:	Hallormsstaðarskógur (woods) ★
	Atlavík (shore of lake)
	Hengifoss (waterfall) ★
Road Conditions:	reasonable
Adjacent sections:	10 (Breiðdalsvík to Egilsstaðir)
	11 (Egilsstaðir to Mývatn)
	2 (Seyðisfjörður to Egilsstaðir)
Notes:	This is a short trip which can be made in conjunction with sections 2 or 10. It is also suitable for those with time to spare before returning by the 'Norröna'.

LÖGURINN is a 30 km-long lake on the Lagar-fljót; it is well sheltered and provides good fishing. Apart from being the country's third largest lake it is also the lowest, with its bed nearly 100 m below sea-level. Its other claim to fame is that it is reputed to be the home of a monster!

After following the ring road south for a while, the lakeside road (number 931) begins and leads through a sheltered valley. Along the shore of the green-coloured Lögurinn there are plots of hardy trees and within the even denser woods of Hallormsstaðarskógur there is an Edda hotel. These woods were first planted at the beginning of the century and are very extensive, with birch and many other trees being grown. This is an important centre for the Forestry Service and their work has been sufficiently successful for felling to start, marking the beginning of an Icelandic forestry industry. A little farther on is the Atlavík campsite, pleasantly situated in woods by the shore with plenty of secluded spots for tents. There are WCs and covered washing areas. The trees give shelter to extensive plant and bird life. From the campsite there is a view of two large clefts in the mountains on the opposite shore. In the nearer is Hengifoss, the country's third highest waterfall (118 m), while the river Bessastaðaá flows through the farther cleft.

The broad and gravelly head of the lake takes water mainly from Eyjabakkajökull and Snæfell by the glacial river of Jökulsá, hence the green colour of Lögurinn; the other main river (the first one to be crossed) is the non-glacial Kelduá. There is a final view of Snæfell just before the road turns along the western shore. There is a fine, 3 km-long, walk up to Hengifoss; it is possible to park either side of the bridge over the Hengifossá and walk up either bank. The first part of the walk up the right bank is over moorland and leads to the lower waterfall, Litlanesfoss, which has a pool below it, which is ringed with pillars of basalt. Thereafter, the climb to Hengifoss is much steeper and rockier and care has to be taken by the side of the great canyon that the waterfall has carved. The waterfall itself is hidden from the path, but this leads eventually to a rocky platform at the lip of the fall and high over the canyon, giving a spectacular view. From this high point there are views of Lögurinn, Hallormsstaðarskógur and behind them the hills crossed by the road to Seyðisfjörður. Above Hengifoss is Fljótsdalsheiði, a lake-studded moorland where there are reindeer, some of which come down to Lögurinn.

There is a pleasant journey back to Egilsstaðir through fertile farming land, with good views of the hills to the east and north-east.

26
GRÍMSSTAÐIR TO ÁSBYRGI

Distance:	60 km
Route:	road 864 to Axarfjörður
	road 85
Maps:	general map 7
	1:100 000 map of Húsavík, Mývatn, Jökulsárgljúfur
Main places to visit:	Dettifoss (waterfall, view of canyon) ★ ★ ★ ★
	Selfoss (waterfall) ★ ★
	Hafragilsfoss (waterfall, view of canyon) ★ ★ ★
	Ásbyrgi (horseshoe-shaped canyon) ★ ★ ★
Road Conditions:	the early stages may be very bad due to corrugations; the rest is reasonable.
Adjacent section:	27 (Ásbyrgi to Húsavík and Mývatn)
Notes:	Recommended: worth a detour off the ring road. The short journey allows time for exploration.

THE ROAD north of Grímsstaðir follows the boundary between the farming area of Hólsfjöll on the east and a sandy stretch of land on the west, beyond which is the river Jökulsá á Fjöllum. When Jökulsá á Fjöllum is sighted it is fairly wide, covering a flat gravel bed it has created. The river is a grey colour, being heavily laden with the material it transports from Dyngjujökull, one of the northern lobes of the massive Vatnajökull glacier. With a length of 206 km, it is the country's second longest river, reaching the sea at the northern bay of Axarfjörður. The road surface can be exceptionally bad here, with regular short-pitched corrugations that span the entire width of the road.

Fortunately the signposted track to Dettifoss is much smoother, though mud or snow may be obstacles depending on the weather and time of year. The relatively steep descent just before the car park can be tricky and may not be worth attempting in muddy conditions. Parking before this only means a short walk and may save problems for two-wheel drive vehicles. There are many viewpoints on the cliff top, both of the waterfall and of the magnificent canyon farther downstream. As the grey torrent of water pounds into the pool below Dettifoss it sends up a huge spray that drifts in the wind for a couple of hundred metres.

High above the river, the path picks its way through great basalt boulders towards the waterfall. On the massive wall on the opposite side, the regular geometric shapes of the basalt columns can be picked out, as well as caves that were burrowed out of the rock by the swirling waters many thousands of years ago. A thick band of grass grows on one of the scree slopes which is constantly wettened by the wind-blown spray.

The path to Dettifoss does not follow the edge of the canyon for a good reason: a careful inspection shows cracks in the ground a few metres from the edge, indicating where the canyon will next be widened. The roar from Dettifoss can be deafening as water plunges over the 45 m fall into the canyon below. This is the most powerful waterfall in Europe, with a flow of between 200 and 1,500 cubic metres per second, depending on the time of year. With little water the lip is quite easy to approach, but when the river is swollen the water can easily spread over a much wider approach to the falls.

To the north of Dettifoss lies Jökulsárgljúfur National Park, which was created in 1973; its main attractions, apart from Dettifoss, are

Ásbyrgi (see later in this section) and the rock formations of Hljóðaklettar which are at Vesturdalur (see section 27). Just north of Dettifoss is the Jökulsárgljúfur canyon, probably the country's finest, which is 25 km long; at this point it is 500 m wide and about 100 m deep. Along it, vertical cliffs cut by the river rest on basalt platforms at the water's edge, and rock columns and scree slopes line the canyon's twisting route.

The river can be followed upstream over a jumble of large boulders towards Selfoss, about 1 km away. In some places banks of fine black sand are being formed and at one point there is a little inlet with a beautiful black sandy 'beach'. Selfoss is rather different in character to Dettifoss with a long curving lip that crosses the river obliquely. The fall is much smaller (13 m) than Dettifoss and the lip is easily approached. The river and its banks level off above Selfoss and open out into the desert.

Less than 2 km after rejoining the road, an unsignposted track leads towards the next waterfall, Hafragilsfoss (27 m). The track is driveable for a normal vehicle but is steep at the end. From here there is a marvellous view of the canyon, arguably even better than the view from Dettifoss. Down to the left, Hafragilsfoss sends up clouds of spray that look like fountains and reach back up to the level of the fall. The best view, though, is from the red lava promontory to the right. From here the scene is breathtaking; as well as a view of the canyon to both north and south, the colours of the landscape are remarkable. There are different shades of grey in the river as the water reaches stiller pools and begins to form black sandbanks, and in some places strange patches of blue/black water can be seen where clear water from the hillsides meets the grey glacial river. Various other small canyons can be seen, each with their own river (and waterfall) feeding the main river. On the cliff top between the river and the road are the red remains of lava and ash from the Sveinar crater row which erupted some 6,000 years ago.

After the main road is regained, craters and various types of volcanic material can be seen along the route but gradually a sandy and windblown soil and its vegetation take over, with a low but quite thick plant cover towards Axarfjörður. Farther on, a track goes left to the abandoned farm of Hafursstaðir and then continues towards another part of the canyon. The main landmark by the road is Hafrafell (512 m) on the right. As the wide bay comes into view there is a view of the most northerly part of the canyon as it curves round before giving way to a wide expanse of sandur.

The bay of Axarfjörður is not really a fjord as it lacks the steep, glacially eroded mountainsides so common on the east and north-western coasts. The Jökulsá á Fjöllum is crossed by a modern suspension bridge, taking the road westwards. After passing under the bridge, the river divides into two. The major distributary, Bakkahlaup, carries sand out to the middle and western part of the bay and forms Vestursandur, while the minor distributary, the Sandá, builds up the eastern Austursandur. This is Iceland's largest sandur which is remote from a glacier and it supports a number of farms on its grasslands, some of which were destroyed by *jökulhlaups* in 1684 and 1711-1712. On the left there is the richly wooded Áshöfði and the small lake of Ástjörn, then the second road after the petrol station leads into the extraordinary canyon of Ásbyrgi.

The entrance to Ásbyrgi is spectacular: you seem to be driving through a wide and very deep canyon with sheer cliffs about 60 m high on either side when suddenly the right-hand wall stops. It is just a rock island in the middle of a much wider canyon and gives this outstanding example of erosion its 'horseshoe' shape. The canyon is about 3.5 km long and the rock island ('Eyjan', 84 m) is about half its length. An old Viking legend describes Ásbyrgi as having been made by one of the eight shoes of Sleipnir, Óðin's mount. Sleipnir (whose teeth were inscribed with ancient runes) was able to travel far and wide (over sea as well as land), and he often visited the land of the dead in order to carry warriors to Óðin's home. As further proof of Sleipnir's visit to Ásbyrgi, about midway between Eyjan and the end of the canyon is a solitary rock just where the frog (the horny part in the centre of Sleipnir's hoof) would have landed.

At the farthest end of the canyon there are a couple of small but deep ponds with a few ducks, while seabirds have made their home in the cliffs above. Paths lead to the south-west corner where there are a number of viewpoints below the cliffs that look over the big wooded area south of the island and there is a fine view of the whole canyon itself. There is also a good echo from this point.

It is difficult to imagine how this massive scar was carved by Jökulsá á Fjöllum, possibly some 3,000 years ago; the main clues to its history are a tiny waterfall above the ponds and the large piles of rubble all round the end of the canyon.

The campsite (with primitive toilets and a tap) is at the end of the canyon, with tents pitched in the woods or on a very large and flat grassy area, which is sometimes used for sports meetings. There is a warden on duty from whom a leaflet and map of the Jökulsárgljúfur National Park can be obtained. The site can be very busy at times.

27
ÁSBYRGI TO HÚSAVÍK AND MÝVATN

Distance:	120 km
Route:	road 85 to south of Húsavík
	road 87
	ring road (1)
Maps:	general maps 7 and 4
	1:100 000 map of Húsavík, Mývatn, Jökulsárgljúfur
Main places to visit:	Vesturdalur (rock formations of Hljóðaklettar and Rauðhólar) ★ ★ ★ ★
	Tjörnes (fossils) ★ ★
	Húsavík (town) ★
Road Conditions:	reasonable
Adjacent section:	12 (Mývatn)
Notes:	The visit to Vesturdalur takes a few hours but is recommended.

AFTER the main road from Ásbyrgi is regained, the next road left (number 862) climbs through the moorland of Ásheiði which is well vegetated and provides a remarkable contrast to the bare sandur at the coast. The track up to Vesturdalur is good, though it is narrow with limited passing places. Just before the main track turns left, a signpost points south where another track goes in the direction of Hólmatungur (16 km) and Dettifoss (23 km). (Two-wheel drive vehicles should not attempt the section beyond Dettifoss). The final part of the track is down a very steep hill,

with a view of the rock formation of Hljóðaklettar on the left. The Vesturdalur campsite can be busy, especially at weekends, because of its surroundings and because it is especially good for walkers. It is the most important centre in the Jökulsárgljúfur National Park and has a warden. Leaflets with a map are available, showing a number of places that can be visited on foot.

As the site is entered a good path on the left goes all the way to Hljóðaklettar (about 2 km); en route there are cliffs (on the right) with small basalt pillars fanning out – a foretaste of what is to come. Down by the river the water has exposed tall rocks whose sides are made up of these pillars, sometimes four, five, or six-sided and varying from about 2 cm to 10 cm across. These slender pillars were formed as the basaltic lava slowly cooled and contracted. It would first cool at the top and then the geometrical shape that was assumed was continued down into the mass of rock. While the faces of these columns are relatively small, it is the presence of thousand upon thousand of them in such a concentrated space that makes Hjóðaklettar such a remarkable sight. In some places the pillars' sides have been exposed and the twisted columns decorate the rock faces in intricate patterns; elsewhere the ends have been broken off, leaving behind an incredible three-dimensional mosaic. All this strange scenery was formed by volcanic eruptions some 8,000 years ago and since then the river has been slowly eroding it.

A path to the right of the main rock formation leads to the river where there is black sand, a 'beach' of smoothed boulders and a view of the cliffs above the river. The main path along the left of Hljóðaklettar goes past many places worth exploring, including caves by the main path and the maze of paths that lead off it.

The path continues to the red scoria craters at Rauðhólar – at this point, aim for the hill on the left and then cut across to the highest one on the right. These are cones of black and red ash and from the tallest (and reddest) of them there is a view down to the river where there are slender red and black lava pillars; these are the 'feeder dykes' up which the molten lava flowed that produced some of the surrounding landscape. Rauðhólar was formed at the same time as Hljóðaklettar. To the north, the tops of the canyon's cliffs are also red and on the other side of the river there are some smaller cliffs and canyons.

The main coastal road goes past the vast area of sand and gravel built up by the river, but the sandur is so flat that it is difficult to see the farms, some 10 km distant. To the left there are a few small canyons and around the higher ground before the lagoon of Lón there is a lavafield with large lava domes rising above the sand dunes. The western shore has a steep climb, leading to an excellent view of Axarfjörður from the site of the radio mast. Below, the rivers carry black sand out to the long curved sandbars that have been built up; to the south the green pasture and moorland stretches back until it meets the higher dusty desert; to the east there are red-coloured mountains, rising steeply above the farmlands.

The Tjörnes headland is the farthest north that most visitors reach (about 30 km south of the Arctic Circle). It is a good place from which to view the midnight sun. The road is usually above cliffs but once or twice it nears the sea. A few small rocks lie off the coast at Breiðavík but the only islands of note are Lágey and Háey to the north.

After the headland has been rounded there are a number of small roads going to the right. One of these (not signposted, without a gate and near the farm of Ytritunga) heads back round to reach the shore; this is the best way to reach the Tjörnes fossil beds. Park just before the new track to the shore begins (it is slippery when wet and there is hardly any turning space at the bottom). On the walk down to the small jetty there are dozens of white bands in the soft rock – these are the fossilised remains of sea shells. More are found on both sides of the stream that flows past the jetty and also on the steep slope between the old track and the sea. These are the most accessible examples of fossils in the area; elsewhere on the peninsula there is lignite (a stage between peat and coal) which was once mined near Ytritunga and shells belonging to various geological periods. The rocky shore is littered with great tree trunks carried here from overseas by the tides. A short distance offshore is the island of Lundey.

Towards the head of the broad Skjálfandi is Húsavík, a prosperous and neat-looking fishing settlement that was one of the cooperative movement's first centres. There is an information board as the town is entered. The campsite is on the left, before the football ground. The site is grassy and has a heated washroom. With a population of over 2,500 Húsavík is an important community that serves a wide area; consequently it has a good selection of shops and services with most of the facilities that visitors might require, including hotels, garages, restaurants, a museum, pool, hospital and car rental. Many of the buildings are heated by natural hot water. The harbour is worth seeing as numerous freighters, trawlers and smaller boats visit it. Behind the settlement there is a mast-topped hill (Húsavíkurfjall) from which there are good views over Húsavík and towards the impressive hills on the western side of the bay. The hill also overlooks the lake of Botnsvatn, which is easily reached from the town.

As the road heads south out of Húsavík there is moorland on the left and just before the junction with the road from Akureyri there is a view to the right of the river Laxá and the large Aðaldal-shraun lavafield in which there are many pseudocraters. Once road 87 is taken to the left, moorland stretches up on the right into Hvammsheiði, while the farms on the left shelter under the higher hillside. Around the farm of Hveravellir there is a powerful source of hot water which is used to heat homes in Húsavík; there are glasshouses here, too, and clouds of vapour coming from some of the wellheads and pipes. The moors become rather wilder as the road climbs, forming a barren windswept plateau of gravel at about 350 m in Hólasandur. There is a rescue hut here with nothing for company but the road, telephone cables and sheep fences; a few boulders litter the surface, but the landscape is mainly an undulating mass of black sand and gravel. Just before Mývatn is sighted the wasteland abruptly comes to an end, replaced by moorland leading down to the lake. The area round Mývatn is described in section 12.

28
DALSMYNNI TO BJARKALUNDUR

Distance:	123 km
Route:	road 60
Maps:	general maps 2 and 1
Road Conditions:	the mountain road at the start can be rough, otherwise reasonable.
Adjacent sections:	29 (Bjarkalundur to Ísafjörður)
Notes:	This section links the north-west fjords and Snæfellsnes to the ring road. There is no recognised campsite at Bjarkalundur.

THE MOUNTAIN road between Dalsmynni and Hvammsfjörður is steep and twisting, providing views of the fine mountains on both sides. There should be no heavy vehicles on the first section as there is a bridge with a two-tonne axle limit early on, but even so the road is badly rutted and needs great care. There are a number of waterfalls and canyons carved out by the main rivers at both ends of the pass. The pass enters a wide valley which gives a view towards the broad Hvammsfjörður and the hills beyond.

As the fjord is approached, road 57 goes left along the northern shore of the Snæfellsnes peninsula; the Guide picks up this route at Stykkishólmur in section 32. The eastern shore's settlement is Búðardalur, which boasts an hotel, swimming pool, hospital, and shops. Thereafter, the journey is through a stony moorland by the shore; before another mountain pass, road 589 turns left, north-west to Laugar which has a summer hotel, pool and campsite (Laugar is also known as Sælingsdalur).

The pass through Svínadalur has a number of fine cliffs on either side and a few waterfalls, notably Réttargil, which is on the right about halfway through. Once the valley of Hvolsdalur is reached the fine slopes of Hvolsfjall can be seen on the right, with layer upon layer of basalt atop the scree. This terraced scenery continues round the face of the mountain, while below it an extensive flat and well-irrigated area of farmland has many grassy fields. The entry into Gilsfjörður has the towering pinnacles of Hvolsfjall on one side with the other shore being ringed by smaller hills. A waterfall called Gullfoss is at the fjord's head. The headland at Króksfjarðarnes

offers very good views, looking into three fjords as well as over to the many islands in eastern Berufjörður; after that road 605 branches off to the right to the eastern side of the main peninsula. Just after the farm of Bær in Geiradalur there is a very steep hill going down to a bridge – take care as this comes with little warning.

The approach to Bjarkalundur gives the first sighting of the strange cone-shaped rock of Vaðalfjöll (509 m) which is on the moorland behind the Edda hotel. There is no proper campsite here, but tents are often erected on the flat ground on the right just beyond the hotel. Apart from walks up to Vaðalfjöll, this is a good base from which to explore the neighbouring fjords and hills. Bjarkalundur is not a settlement, only a stopping place with the hotel, its restaurant and petrol pumps.

29
BJARKALUNDUR TO ÍSAFJÖRÐUR

Distance:	231 km
Route:	road 60 to mountain road
	road 61
Map:	general map 1
Road Conditions:	the mountain road at the start may be rough in bad weather conditions.
Adjacent sections:	30 (Ísafjörður)
Notes:	This is rather a long journey, with outstanding fjord scenery providing the main attraction.

AFTER REACHING the head of Thorskafjörður, it is a hard climb up the gravelly mountain road, but the views from it are outstanding. The journey over the barren moorland of Thorskafjarðarheiði is a memorable one: it is rocky and windswept, with little or no shelter – except at the rescue hut on the plateau. The old glaciers have left behind lots of small lakes, many with snow lying over them, but there are few rivers of any magnitude. While its surface is

rather stony at times, this road is remarkably good, given its height (490 m) and isolation. As the road descends and travels above the fishing river of Langadalsá there is a waterfall on the right and a parking area at the bridge in Langidalur.

After the muddy and stony headland and a few deserted farms you come to the long Ísafjörður, surrounded by low, gently sloping hills that give only a little shelter to the more fertile land at the head. The fjord's shore can be followed (road 633) to Reykjanes (where there is a source of warm water) but the main road climbs over the moors to Mjóifjörður, of which there is a good view from an outcrop just after the bridge on the winding downhill section. Far away in the distance the beautiful Drangajökull ice cap can be seen to the north.

In the first part of Mjóifjörður, at Djúpmannabúð, there is a roadside cafe, a petrol station (the last one until Súðavík 117 km away) and a place for camping (on the right just after the bridge). Towards the end of the fjord there are good examples of rock layers split by frost-shattering. Along the shore seabirds and ducks (with their young) are plentiful.

The headland offers fine views of Drangajökull and the snow-covered mountains on the opposite side of the water. The highest point on the glacier is Jökulbunga (925 m) which is to the left of the bay of Kaldalón, where the ice-fall of the glacier over a cliff can be seen. Once the headland is turned there is an impressive view of the high and almost sheer cliffs of the northern wilderness.

There is spectacular scenery on all sides as you travel along Skötufjörður: Fossahlíð's cliffs tower above you on the left, and more giants guard the headlands of the fjords that are encountered farther on; the fjord's hills are surprisingly well vegetated, and a number of waterfalls tumble down the sides, most above the road with a few below. When the fjord's western shore is reached, the peak of Snæfjall (793 m) lies straight ahead, across Ísafjarðardjúp.

Hestfjörður is rather different with many of its slopes less steep and more vegetated. At the head there are some waterfalls. On the western side there is a sudden view of Hestur (547 m) a long, narrow and beautiful hill jutting out towards the main fjord, red bands of rock and their scree lending colour to the landscape. Hestur dominates the next small fjord of Seyðisfjörður, after which is the imposing Álftafjörður, with long bare scree slopes on either side and a grassy part at the head which gives access to the hills. Súðavík, a fishing settlement, has a number of shops and a garage as well as small industrial buildings. This is the coastal road's final sight of the hills to the north, whose awe-inspiring cliffs are 300-400 m high.

As the road turns the headland there is a narrow tunnel cut into the rock. The entry into Skutulsfjörður is dominated by three red, green and black giants of mountains in front, with the town of Ísafjörður spread out on a wide sandspit below Eyrarfjall (724 m). The description of the fjord and the main sights around Ísafjörður is contained in the next section.

30
ÍSAFJÖRÐUR

Maps:	general map 1
	1:100 000 map of Hornstrandir
Main places to visit:	Ski lodge (view) ★
	harbour ★
	trip on the mail plane ★ ★
Adjacent section:	31 (Ísafjörður to Brjánslækur and Stykkishólmur)
Notes:	An excellent centre for exploring the surrounding fjords and hills.

THE TOWN of Ísafjörður is the hub of the north-western fjords, having a population of about 3,500 and a wide selection of shops and services, including a cinema, swimming pool, library, and folk museum. It is the most convenient centre from which to explore the peninsula.

Ísafjörður has a long history; there was a farm on the fjord's sandspit during the time of the Settlement. This curious L-shaped projection into the middle of the deep fjord offers good protection to the harbour and is now the site of the main part of the town. There is newer housing below the hillside on the west.

The 'centre' of the town is by the small plot of grass with two flagpoles in front of the Hotel Ísafjörður and opposite a bank. Opposite the hotel is a street (Aðalstræti) running towards the open fjord; at the end of this is a park, with the cinema on its left and the swimming pool on the right (the library and folk museum are above the pool). The street immediately in front of the hotel is Hafnarstræti; turn right for the harbour. Fishing is of course the main industry of Ísafjörður, and so it is the home of a large fishing fleet as well as a port of call for small boats and larger freighters; the harbour and its jetties are therefore always busy and well worth a visit. The ferry boat 'Fagranes' (see p.50), which makes regular trips to Hornstrandir, is moored on the west side of the harbour, near the Hotel Ísafjörður. At the end of the harbour area there is a group of four houses, some of the town's oldest buildings, dating from 1734-1785. The town was granted municipal rights much later, in 1866.

Apart from the facilities already mentioned, the town has two hotels, a youth hostel, handcrafts centre, a tourist bureau, a state alcohol shop, a golf course, car and boat rental, hospital and a number of other shops. The factories, processing plants and warehouses can be found near the harbour.

As you approach the town there is a new housing development with, unusually, many modern wooden houses situated near the head of the fjord. North of this lies the road to the south (60) and then, immediately after a bridge, the track to the campsite turns left up the valley of the river Tunguá, just before a group of houses. The valley, which has a waterfall, is very sheltered and popular with berrypickers. The site is grassy and has WCs with sinks in washrooms. Just by the beginning of the track to the campsite another track leads up the hill to the skiing lodge where there is usually good skiing in the first few months of the year, with towbars leading to slopes of varying difficulty. Whereas the campsite track goes straight ahead, the route to the ski lodge is sharp right (thus going above and parallel to the main road) and then sharp left about 1 km later.

While Iceland has many unspoilt regions which offer good walking, one of the most interesting is Hornstrandir, the most northern area of the north-western fjords. Bad weather conditions have always made farming difficult here and during the 1950s the last of its inhabitants moved out, taking their sheep with them and thus allowing the land to revert to its former wild state. The ferry 'Fagranes' makes regular trips to the district's landing places so it is possible to spend a few days walking across the moorlands, knowing that the boat can take you back to Ísafjörður (it is of course advisable to tell someone where you are going and when you intend to return). Guided treks of 4, 5 or 10 days are available and it is also possible to go on a part-day walk from one boat-stop to another; alternatively a boat trip (5 or 11 hours) can be taken. There are no tourist huts on Hornstrandir, so camping is the only accommodation available. A 1:100 000 (1982) map of the area is published. As well as being a most attractive place to walk (when the weather is good), Hornstrandir also has bird cliffs, foxes and seals to see and an uncropped flora to admire. There is no vehicle access.

The hills around Ísafjörður are beautiful, with steep scree slopes, large cirques and plateaux that offer much to the walker. The cirques (also called corries or cwms) were produced by small glaciers nestling in sheltered hollows. A number of the hills near the settlement can be reached by sloping valleys, but many hilltops are guarded by steep slopes, too dangerous to ascend.

A spectacular way to see these mountains is to take the mail plane, which for about two hours flies the route: Ísafjörður – Suðureyri – Holt – Thingeyri – Bíldudalur – Patreksfjörður – Ísafjörður. The airstrip is on the eastern side of Skutulsfjörður.

From the air it is far easier to spot just what the ancient glaciers have produced: the U-shaped valleys, the cirques and the summit ridges, and these can be seen as parts of a whole landscape and not just individual features. While access routes to the tops may be difficult to find from ground level, they are clearly seen from above, as are difficult ridges and slopes; this may be of benefit to those planning a series of walks. The hills are about 500-700 m high, some with snow remaining on their rough plateaux or ridges. The fjords' water is quite clear, giving a view of the bed in the shallows; the water is sometimes blue, or azure, often tinted by the sandy beaches too, especially at Patreksfjörður. Towards the most southerly part of the flight there is a breathtaking view of the white-topped cone of the Snæfellsjökull glacier (see p.144).

31
ÍSAFJÖRÐUR TO BRJÁNSLÆKUR AND STYKKISHÓLMUR

Distance:	141 km then ferry crossing
Route:	road 60 to Flókalundur
	road 62 to Brjánslækur
	ferry boat 'Baldur' to Stykkishólmur
Maps:	general maps 1 and 2
Main places to visit:	Fjallfoss (waterfall)
Road Conditions:	possibly a bit rough over the mountain passes.
Adjacent section:	32 (Stykkishólmur to Búðir)
Notes:	Once again the scenery in general is the main attraction. The ferry is taken to avoid the (possibly poor) road to Bjarkalundur and the need to retrace much of section 28. The crossing also gives a chance for those with limited time to see Snæfellsnes.

THE STEEP and winding mountain road south of Ísafjörður leads past dark giants of mountains, their sides decorated with scree slopes and coloured by yellow and green mosses. The height of the road (610 m) allows fine views over many of the lower hills and of the numerous cirques, as well as allowing the walker easier access to the plateaux. Önundarfjörður is crossed by a new causeway (marked as a path on the 1:250 000 map). The fishing settlement of Flateyri is on its northern shore.

The road over the next pass runs alongside many more fine hills, some with almost vertical buttresses falling sharply into rocky cirques; others have slopes comprised solely of scree. The long Dýrafjörður has a great number of hills about 700 m high lining its sides, with many summit ridges and valleys aligned nearly at right angles to the fjord. Much of the land is bare but by the head there is a strong growth of shrubs and some good farmland. Thingeyri, a small fishing settlement, is situated halfway along the southern shore. It has a harbour, processing plant, petrol station, garage and supermarket. It sits at the foot of Sandafell (367 m), which has a commanding position over the district.

The journey south from Thingeyri starts fairly easily but the mountain pass is another of the zig-zag, ear-popping variety, with lots of steep scree slopes and perhaps some rocks lying on the road. The views on both sides are tremendous, with Arnarfjörður (which splits up into six smaller fjords) lined with one rocky crag after another. Of particular beauty are Urðarfjall (616 m) and Meðalnesfjall (409 m) which are near the fjord's head and between them is the broad – and 100m high – waterfall Fjallfoss (also called Dynjandi). At the head of the fjord there is a hydro-electric power station, taking water from the cliffs from which a few narrow waterfalls descend. As the road turns away from Dynjandi-vogur, a minor road (number 621) follows the shore and goes to a car park below Fjallfoss. The fall fans out into dozens of small streams which then rejoin to go over a few smaller falls.

The mountain road up to Dynjandiheiði is less steep and gives fine views back into Dynjandi-vogur. The landscape at the summit plateau is bleakly impressive: a jumbled mass of broken rock with hardly any big boulders as the frost has shattered anything of size into rubble; there are, however, a number of small lakes. There is a hut situated at the summit.

The long journey downhill overlooks Geir-thjófsfjörður and meets road 63 (to the right) which goes towards the settlements of Bíldudalur and Vatneyri and then on to the tall cliffs at Latrabjarg, Iceland's most westerly point. The protected area of Vatnsfjörður starts just before the coast is met; then there is a junction at which there is an Edda hotel (Flókalundur) and a number of houses. While road 60 continues round to the left, road 62 to the ferry terminal at Brjánslækur goes to the right.

The ferry boat 'Baldur' plies between Brjáns-lækur and Stykkishólmur daily (except Sunday), the journey taking 3½ hours. A car berth should be booked in advance through a tourist bureau – this is especially important at weekends or when good weather has attracted a lot of visitors to the fjords. The fares are quite reasonable; the cost of taking a vehicle depends on its weight (under/over 1200 kg). The ferry certainly saves a great deal of time when heading south towards Reykjavík and it allows a visit to Snæfellsnes to be made instead of retracing part of the Dalsmynni-Bjarkalundur route.

If you have not got a ticket you should inquire about space on the ferry on arrival – this can be done by continuing past the quay, turning sharp right after the bridge and going to the house on the left. The loading of cars (it only takes about 12) is not a sight for the nervous car owner as they are lifted on board using cradles in which the wheels sit. The axles are then securely fastened using chains. Half the vehicles are shipped under cover and the others sit on the deck; the latter group can be reached by drivers wanting to inspect the chains.

There are beautiful views of both peninsulas as the ship picks its way through the myriad of islands and reefs in Breiðafjörður. The bay is very exposed, so warm/waterproof clothing should be kept handy for going on deck. The wildlife is plentiful, with large numbers of seabirds and some seals around the islands. A few of the larger islands are inhabited and one, Flatey, provides a short stop for the ferry. The island has been inhabited since the Middle Ages but its importance has lessened considerably and it now has a permanent population of about forty.

Once disembarked at Stykkishólmur, turn left at the end of the road out of the harbour and then second right. This takes you onto the main road through the town. On its outskirts is the road to Hotel Stykkishólmur: the turning to the left immediately before the football pitch. The camping site is only a little farther (500 m, left) along the main road. Stykkishólmur is described in the next section.

Distance:	140 km
Route:	road 56
	road 57 west
	road 54 west
	road 574
Map:	general map 2
Main places to visit:	Stykkishólmur (town) ★
	Helgafell (view) ★
	Sjómannagarður (museum)
	Hólahólar (crater) ★
	Dritvík (cove) ★ ★
	Hellnar (fishing settlement, rocks) ★
	Arnarstapi (fishing settlement, rocks) ★ ★
	Búðir ★ ★
Road Conditions:	possibly poor
Adjacent section:	33 (Búðir to Borgarnes)
Notes:	The coastline, with its rock formations and sandy beaches, is well worth exploring.

STYKKISHÓLMUR is a pleasant little town with a well-sheltered harbour and a population of over 1200, and it merits some exploration. On the main road there is a chemist, bank, post office, large supermarket and a garage (opposite the camping site). On the hill to the east of the harbour are the hotel and hospital, while by the western road there is an interesting walk through an area of new buildings, a shellfish factory and a view of some of Breiðafjörður's islands and a couple of shipwrecks. From the rocky promontories round the town there are fine views of snow-covered Ljósufjöll to the south. The camping site is by the town's entrance and is grassy, though it can get muddy at times. It has a couple of WCs and a sink. There is an information board by the main road near the site's entrance.

Lining the route out of town there are often many racks of fish hanging up to dry. In a few places crushed shells from the shellfish factory have been used instead of ash or gravel to make tracks and paths. The airfield is on the right. Mountains dominate the landward view, with

Ljósufjöll (1063 m) to the south, Hólsfjall (930 m) to the south-west and, rather nearer, the coloured Drápuhlíðarfjall (527 m) also to the south. Closer to the settlement and reached by a track after a tall mast, is the grassy Helgafell (73 m). Helgafell is one of the main locations of the thirteenth-century *Eyrbyggjasaga*; the Saga (whose main character is the chieftain Snorri Goði) has been an important source of information on the life and religious ideas of the Icelanders in the tenth and eleventh centuries. The *Eyrbyggjasaga* relates how Helgafell was regarded as sacred and that no one with an unwashed face should be allowed to look at it. After Christianity was introduced, hermits took up residence there in a church, and a monastery was built in the twelfth century. There is a parking space just before the farm and a short walk gives a commanding position from the view indicator, especially over the islands near the coast. According to tradition, those who walk up the hill without talking or looking back will have three wishes granted.

Going eastwards, the green pastures of the Thórsnes peninsula give way to a more stony landscape and numerous but fairly small lavafields. The road passes a number of farms on the thin strip of land on the seaward side and there is a view of the small islands and reefs close to the shore. After the road leaves the shore, it crosses the yellow and green moss-covered Berserkjahraun lavafield which lies below Bjarnarhafnarfjall (575 m); nearby there are four hills of red and black scoria, the sources of much of the surrounding volcanic material. The name 'Berserkjahraun' comes from the story of two 'berserks' (originally battle-frenzied Norse warriors) who used their great strength to build a path through the lavafield; this mammoth task was a ploy to tire them out so that they could be killed more easily when they were exhausted. A bridge goes over the mouth of Hraunsfjörður and then the road skirts Gjafi. Hills such as this, with their smooth and coloured scree slopes, stop abruptly at Grundarfjörður, where the cliffs of the basalt hills provide a fine background to the fishing port which bears the same name. To the west is Kirkjufell (see p.150) (463 m), whose isolation from the rest of the mountain chain and its steep narrow ridge make it a very photogenic landmark. A few waterfalls line the road as Kirkjufell is passed and by Stoð (268 m) there is a long and narrow sandspit. Going round Búlandshöfði is a little daunting with the long scree slopes and bird cliffs above and a long drop below; however the end of this part of the journey provides a fine view over to the flatter farmland to the sea. There is a direction board just before Ólafsvík, a busy fishing port.

It is only on nearing the smaller fishing settlement of Rif that the peninsula's main landmark, the glacier Snæfellsjökull (1446 m), comes clearly into view. This is a composite volcano (see pp.144-145) with a beautiful conical shape (topped by three peaks); its summit is visible from Reykjavík, some 110 km away to the southeast. The volcano last erupted some 2,000 years ago. It is featured in Jules Verne's book *Journey to the Centre of the Earth:* Snæfellsjökull was the entrance to the Earth's interior used by Professor Harwick's party. Verne had the expedition eventually return to the surface at the Italian volcano of Stromboli. It is ringed by a number of hills, which are in turn surrounded by the volcano's moss-covered lavafields. Much of the seaward expanse of the lava is grassed over, while the lava by the shore has been eroded by the Atlantic, often producing grotesque shapes.

Just beyond the small settlement of Hellissandur is a small sea-faring museum ('Sjómannagarður') made up of two well-preserved buildings whose walls of turf and lava blocks are in very good condition. To gain admittance to the buildings, ask at the petrol station opposite. Behind the museum there is a view towards Snæfellsjökull and the surrounding mountains.

This district takes the full brunt of the gale-force winds coming in from the Atlantic and the coastal road may be blocked off by the snow in winter but the two roads that cross the peninsula farther east are usually clear, allowing movement of traffic. A number of small airfields in this district are used in emergencies when the roads are impassable and a navigational aid to aircraft and ships, the 400 m-high mast at Gufuskálar, lies beyond Hellissandur. As a testament to the cruel weather conditions the area has to endure at times, there are a number of disused farms near the road.

The route now passes through some lavafields, often grassed over and with views towards the glacier. The road moves away from the sea and goes past the crater of Saxhóll (125 m), then returns towards the shore and passes the (signposted) craters of Hólahólar; one of which, Berundalur (113 m), has a sloping crater rim, one part being so low down that vehicles have been driven into it, unfortunately spoiling the sparse vegetation on the crater's inner wall. The rim is easy to climb as the lava sections are grassed over but the patches of red and black ash are loose, affording less grip to feet and shelter to the plant life. The summit overlooks the sea, the glacier, and the smaller craters nearby.

An important place in Icelandic fishing history

is Dritvík cove, which used to be a fishing station from which over three hundred fishermen might set out in fifty or more open rowing boats. Now there is only a rescue hut by the pebble beach but the walk to it is pleasant and interesting as the path runs above steep cliffs and looks out over the wild Atlantic and the rock formations that the breakers are carving out of the coastline. The track to the cove is about 3 km after Hólahólar; it is not marked on the map but the rescue hut is. A car can be taken down the (signposted) track for a couple of kilometres to Djúpalón – the surface is not too bad but there are few passing places. From the parking space, a path leads down to the right to a black pebble beach ringed by tall rocks eroded by the waves.

The rocks and cliffs around the beach are worth exploring: those made of lava have been smoothed down by the Atlantic while the cliffs made of ash have been eaten away far more by its pounding seas and have produced tall, rough scree slopes, red and black in colour. This awesome backdrop to the sea continues along to the north-west as the path goes above the cliffs to Dritvík (1 km). There is another pebble beach here, littered with wood and metal; at the back there is a rescue hut. On the hill above is a cairn from which there are fine views of the coastline.

A coast as wild as that found round Snæfellsnes requires lighthouses to warn sailors of their position, and the lighthouse at Malarrif marks the most southerly point of the peninsula. Nearby are the Lóndrangar rocks, two monstrous lava blocks standing 70 m high, which are prominent landmarks. Between Lóndrangar and the fishing village of Arnarstapi are caves, pillars and other rock features hewn out of the sea cliffs by the

Atlantic. Hellnar is a small fishing settlement with a good harbour that has been important for many centuries. There is a car park above the harbour, and by the jetty there are bird cliffs, a natural arch and many rock faces made of plates of smooth rock. The area is protected and both the rocks and the bird life are of interest. More rocky inlets and bird cliffs can be reached by walking north-east along the track behind the harbour and then towards the sea once high ground is reached.

The next village, Arnarstapi (also called Stapi), is better known and a little busier. The coastline by the village is a haven for seabirds as there are many sheltered ledges on the cliffs. Near the harbour, behind its sea-wall, there are fine grey basalt pillars, their dull colour brightened by the greens and yellows of the plants. To the north there are a series of cliffs and a waterfall.

Passing through lavafields then wet meadows, the road next goes under the southern slopes of Kambsheiði and Fróðárheiði, with a long sand-bar (Hraunlandarif) skirting the coastline. Just after road 54 (which cuts across the peninsula) is encountered on the left, there is a track on the right – this leads to Búðir. The track skirts the mossy lava of Búðahraun, a protected lavafield whose southern side juts out into the sea.

Búðir has a rather rough campsite (primitive toilet, water tap) opposite the hotel. Beyond the hotel there are paths that lead through sand dunes to the shore. This is a most interesting area, with the dark lava rocks, the light brown sand and the Atlantic surf all providing spectacular scenery. There is plenty of bird life, too, with oyster catchers and terns particularly in evidence.

33
BÚÐIR TO BORGARNES

Distance:	120 km
Route:	road 54 east
Map:	general map 2
Main places to visit:	Eldborg (crater) ★ ★
	Sveðjufoss (waterfall, and
	salmon jumping) ★
Road Conditions:	reasonable
Adjacent sections:	15 (Akureyri to Borgarnes)
	16 (Borgarnes to Reykjavík)
Notes:	This is a short journey and it may be possible to continue to Reykjavík in the same day.

ONCE THE coastal road has been regained, waterfalls decorate the sides of Mælifell (566 m) and the cliffs above Búðir, with Bjarnarfoss being the most notable fall. There are no harbours between Búðir and the eastern end of the peninsula, since numerous sandbars reach out along the coast into Faxaflói, denying boats passage. Just as the road heads away from the sea, at Staðastaður, there is a fine sandy beach. At Vegamót, at the junction with road 56 (which passes north through the mountains), there is a roadside cafe, two petrol stations and a garage. To the north-east are the rhyolite hills known as Ljósufjöll, with rather less snow on this side compared with the northern view. The road continues through more wet meadows under Hafursfell, with enough good grazing land to support herds of cattle and horses.

Just after the fishing river of Haffjarðará is crossed, the road swings south round the grey and mossy Eldborgarhraun lavafield; on the right is the crater from which the lava flowed, Eldborg (100 m). The walk (about 3 km) up to Eldborg is an interesting one and is started on a path (marked on the 1:250 000 map) due east of the crater. The path, which is after the farm by the bridge, may involve wading a stream; those not wanting to risk getting wet should start on the northern side of the stream (ie before the farm). The area round the crater is a mixture of soft clay, lava, heath and dwarf shrubs; there are a few ill-defined paths, some of which are marked with occasional dots of yellow paint on wayside stones. The climb up the crater wall is to the right and is marked by yellow dots; it is rather loose and steep. At the crater rim there are dozens of exposed layers of frothy lava which the crater has poured out – grey, brown, green and a multitude of reds. The rim is narrow and the inside wall falls steeply to the same level as the surrounding land. There is a fine view from here, not only of the lavafield, the farms and the mountains but also of the sea, the small islands and the sandbars.

More farming land is now crossed, with scrub round the Barnaborg crater (112 m) and its lavafield Barnaborgarhraun; a little farther on is the fishing river Hítará, with the Brúarfoss waterfall just under the bridge. There are now great numbers of basalt outcrops along the road, mostly lying in a south-west/north-east direction, though this becomes a south/north alignment nearer Borgarfjörður. Some of these are small but others are perhaps 50 m or higher and dominate the rest of this flat region. The solid bedrock has made drainage difficult, so the area is boggy, with a great number of small lakes and only a few farms. The shore is also very rocky, with hundreds of reefs and islands, prohibiting the building of a harbour. There is a waterfall (Sveðjufoss) on the river Langá which is reached by either of two tracks to the right after the road crosses the river. This is a good salmon river and there are usually fishermen at the pools above and below the falls. The waterfall has recently been altered by building a salmon ladder and on that side there is access to the rocks above the main pool. While this is quite an attractive waterfall, its main interest is the salmon and the best place to watch them is probably below the main fall as here you can see the fish swim upstream and with a bit of skill (and luck) you can photograph them as they leap. The salmon are usually jumping in July and August. There is another waterfall (Langárfoss) just a little downstream.

The road now continues to Borgarnes which is described at the end of section 15.

34
BORGARFJÖRÐUR TO REYKHOLT AND HÚSAFELL

Distance:	40 km from ring road
Route:	road 50 east from ring road (20 km north-east of Borgarnes)
	road 518 east
Maps:	general maps 2 and 5
Main places to visit:	Reykholt ('Snorralaug') ★
	Hraunfossar (waterfall) ★ ★
	Hallmundarhraun (lava caves) ★ ★ ★
Road Conditions:	reasonable, except to Hallmundarhraun for which a four-wheel drive vehicle is needed.
Adjacent sections:	35 (Húsafell to Kaldidalur and Borgarfjörður)
Notes:	The road may have to be retraced if conditions on the route through Kaldidalur are not suitable for two-wheel drive vehicles. If the caves are omitted then sections 34 and 35 can easily be completed in a single day.

AFTER CROSSING the broad Norðurá and the salmon river of Thverá, road 50 gradually makes its way up the sloping farmlands to the hills on the east. An old and very narrow bridge carries the road over the Hvítá, whose banks are made of huge piles of gravel brought down from the Eiríksjökull glacier. Nearby, small clouds of vapour announce entry into an active geothermal area. The scenery suddenly changes into a gravelly waste and then just as abruptly turns back into farmland as the valley of Reykholtsdalur is entered by road 518. After some small farms on the right, some with glasshouses, the road enters the historically important settlement of Reykholt, by following the tree-lined road on the left.

The Edda Hotel is at the centre of Reykholt; there is a direction board by the side of the road and parking space can be found behind the church. This district was the home of Snorri Sturluson (1178-1241, see p.19), one of Iceland's most important chieftains and writers. There is a statue of him in front of the hotel and round to the right, steps lead down to 'Snorralaug', a small circular pool with clear, warm water beside which there is a small tunnel that used to come from his farm. A gravestone just to the right of the church tower, marked 'Sturlungareitur' may mark the spot where he is buried. The settlement is sheltered, with some houses and a farm; by the side of the main road it has a garage and petrol station and a shop.

The road turns left into the next valley of Hvítárdalur which is rather barer and more gravelly, its northern hills having a number of canyons. Towards the valley's end is the lavafield of Skógarhraun, where there is a very unusual type of waterfall. This is best reached by turning into the car park on the left signposted 'Hraun-fossar' after crossing the bridge and climbing the hill. This wide series of waterfalls is quite re-markable as the water is coming out of the porous lava and flowing over the lower layer of non-porous rock. This gives an idea of the immense quantity of water that may be trapped within lava and demonstrates why so few rivers are seen crossing lavafields. A little farther upstream there is a small wooden bridge and a path which leads to a more conventional type of waterfall (Barnafoss), over which tumble the green waters of the Hvítá. The Hvítá's colour comes from the fine material suspended in the swirling water; in contrast to this, the water from Hraunfossar is crystal clear, having been well filtered during its slow passage through the porous lava.

About 5 km later, and with Húsafell farm on the right, the road heads over the bridge, the tracks to the left leading to the campsite. This is a busy site as many summer homes have been built in this wooded and pleasant district and it is a good centre for walks on to the neighbouring hills. There are washrooms, WCs, a shop, petrol station and a swimming pool. Small two-berth huts can also be rented. Bus and walking tours, pony trekking and fishing are also available; you can also get plane trips and flying lessons as the site has its own airstrip!

This last part of the section deals with a journey to the lava caves at Hallmundarhraun. Although only four-wheel drive vehicles should go on the track behind Kalmanstunga, the route past this farm and round the hill of Tunga is suitable for two-wheel drive cars.

The road continues through a little wood and skirts the colourful hill of Tunga (445 m); just in front is Strútur (938 m, and a popular climb for a view); to the right is the glacier Eiríksjökull (1675 m). At the back of Tunga there is a farm (Kalmanstunga); beyond its gate there is a track up a hill towards the lava caves, a route for four-wheel drive vehicles only. The track goes above the southern end of the Hallmundarhraun, with the huge plates of lava becoming flatter as the journey goes on. After some 7 km a signpost points left to Surtshellir; this track continues for only a small distance thereafter. Take this track and park a little way up. Walking less than 1 km in a direction midway between this track and the main track leads to the caves. Do not forget to take a torch.

When the lava flows in red-hot rivers through long underground 'tubes' it sometimes leaves behind huge caves or caverns, roofed over by the massive domes of lava. In some places the roofs collapse, giving access to these great voids just beneath the surface. So it is here. The first big cave found on the left splits into two, with the left-hand part having a relatively smooth floor and wall. There are the lava equivalents of stalactites and stalagmites left by the dripping fluid. The cave's air is damp, but the porous nature of the lava allows water to pass through it easily and there are no pools on the ground or in the cave. As you head back out and over the huge jumble of rocks that once formed the roof, there is an archway (part of the original roof) and then a massive cavern. This is enormous, perhaps 80 m long, 30 m wide and 20 m high, again with smooth knobbly lava on the walls and floor. On the walls are the tell-tale signs of the old lava levels, 'tide marks' left by the molten rock. These are just two examples of the many caves to be found here.

Once road 518 is regained, the journey along the northern side of the valley goes through a well-wooded area of farmland. A bridge across the Hvítá allows the round trip from Húsafell to be completed.

Distance:	87 km
Route:	road 518 east
	track F35 ('Kaldidalur')
	road 52 north-west
Maps:	general maps 2, 5 and 3
Main place to visit:	Thórisjökull (walk towards glacier) ★ ★ ★
Road Conditions:	although the F35 is classed as a 'track', it is normally passable for two-wheel drive vehicles in summer, but check beforehand.
Adjacent sections:	15 (Akureyri to Borgarnes)
	16 (Borgarnes to Reykjavík)
Notes:	This is a short journey through a wild and beautiful pass, which can be completed in a day together with section 34 (excluding the caves). It can also be used as a route to Thingvallavatn.

BEFORE THE road out of Húsafell begins to round Tunga, track F35 branches off to the right and it soon gives a fine view of the glacier Eiríksjökull, while on the left there is a wide expanse of lava and gravel where glacial rivers come down through the area of Geitlönd. After a steep climb there is another view of this huge grey expanse with the Svartá (which comes from Langjökull) running through it. To the left of the track is the lavafield of Geitlandshraun with Hafrafell (1167 m) behind it; to the east there is a small portion of the enormous ice-cap of Langjökull. The track skirts the shield volcano of Ok (1198 m) which has a tiny glacier on its summit.

Farther along there are two prominent hills on the left (Hádegisfell and Hádegishnúkar); behind the latter is the glacier Geitlandsjökull, part of the Langjökull ice-mass. This is the beginning of the Kaldidalur pass, which runs between the two glaciers of Langjökull and Ok; however the name is often used to describe the whole route from Tunga southwards. Perhaps the finest view on the route is of Thórisjökull (1350 m), which is quite separate from Langjökull. Although not a large glacier, it has many icefalls over its cliffs and a walk towards it (a couple of kilometres after

Hádegishnúkar is passed) is well worthwhile, the more so since nature has provided a magnificent viewing platform: just a kilometre from the road is a 40 m-high fault line whose sheer cliffs look out over the lower reaches of the glacier and the glacial rivers. The walk is over a soft rock-strewn surface, light to dark-brown in colour, that supports some plant life.

Then the road climbs and, from a hill decorated with dozens of small cairns, there is another marvellous view of the glacier. From here the mountains to the south can be seen for the first time and there is also a view of Eiríksjökull's dome to the north-east. The winding, downhill journey then passes the boulder-decorated western slopes of Thórisjökull on the left; on the right there is a barren undulating wasteland of brown boulders stretching far into the distance. Ahead, the tallest hills are the group known as Botnssúlur (1095 m) and to the right is the lone bare hill of Fanntófell (901 m), sitting below Ok. The finest hill in view is the almost perfectly conical shield volcano of Skjaldbreiður (1060 m) on the left. Behind it and to its left is the steep-sided Hlöðufell (1188 m).

Soon after a small rescue hut is passed on the

left, a sheepgate across the road marks the end of the track. At this point road 52 goes south to Thingvellir (section 17); to the right it leads into the long valley of Lundarreykjadalur. Once onto this latter road, the hill just after the junction looks over to Skjaldbreiður (east) and the similarly-shaped Ok (north-east). With the lake of Reyðarvatn and then Thverfell (655 m) on the right, the scenery slowly becomes greener as the road travels down the valley. About half way through the valley, the river Grímsá appears on the right. There are quite a number of farms here, many sitting on the flat gravel moraines under the hillsides. When the first junction with road 50 is met, turning left takes you to Reykjavík, right to Borgarnes. After going right, and in less than a kilometre, road 50 is met again (from the right); after passing this junction, the cone of the volcano Snæfellsjökull can be seen, some 105 km away to the north-west.

When Borgarfjörður is reached at the junction with road 53, turning left takes you to Reykjavík (route described in section 16) while the road to the right crosses the Hvítá to meet the ring road north-east of Borgarnes (section 15).

36
GULLFOSS TO HVERAVELLIR

Distance:	95 km
Route:	track F37 ('Kjölur')
Maps:	general maps 6 and 5
Main place to visit:	Hveravellir (solfatara field) ★ ★ ★
Road Conditions:	no two-wheel drive vehicle should attempt this route up into the highlands. Conditions can get very rough when the weather is bad, especially near Bláfell. Most of the rivers are described, but descriptions refer only to conditions experienced by the author. Enquire about prevailing conditions at Geysir.
Adjacent sections:	37 (Hveravellir to Blöndudalur)
Notes:	Very fine scenery in good weather. The track to Kerlingarfjöll should not be attempted in bad weather. Fill up with petrol at Geysir; it is 183 km to the next petrol station in Blöndudalur (see section 37).

THE TRACK heads north above Gullfoss, the first section being a climb up through gravel towards the river Sandá. This glacial river is bridged; the bridge has a small hut by it. A little farther on there is a track to the left to the tourist hut at Hagavatn (15 km). Later on, three more small rivers have to be forded, providing useful practice for the Grjótá which follows and is rather bigger. Beyond it is a car park and a view towards Bláfell (1204 m), the region's highest mountain. Farther on, the Fremstavá has to be crossed.

On the western side of Bláfell, the track may sometimes split into two parts which should rejoin a little later, but if signposts or stakes are not in evidence, it may be necessary to check the alternative routes. The mountain's sides are rocky, and the fairly numerous streams or rivers coming down make the going much tougher than in the gravel areas. The height gained here – the pass of Bláfellsháls is at 610 m – gives a fine view back to the Hvítá and then forward to its source, the glacial lake of Hvítárvatn.

This is by far the largest lake below the massive ice-cap of Langjökull. Unfortunately, the track does not go very near the glacier but there are good views of it from many points on the route. There may be icebergs floating in Hvítárvatn and a good bridge crosses the river, taking the track through the moraines of Hvítársandur. At the western side of the lake, there is a remarkable view of the crag Skriðufell, with glaciers on three of its sides and Hvítárvatn on the fourth. To the rock's right is a black and deeply-crevassed ice-fall. Later on, two tracks (about 10 km apart) go left to the tourist hut at Hvítárnes (8 km and 4 km respectively).

The start of the signposted track to Kerlingarfjöll is of much the same difficulty as the main route but its second river, the Blákvísl, a tributary of the Jökulfall, is one whose level can change quickly and so may be difficult. The waterfall Gýgjarfoss on the Jökulfall is very near the Blákvísl, with both tuff and basalt rocks in evidence in the canyon it has carved out. The fall's nearness to the Blákvísl's crossing point adds spice to fording the river!

Kerlingarfjöll is a group of rhyolitic peaks standing high above the surrounding land. Some of them are over 1400 m high and have small glaciers on their summits. Not only is this a renowned climbing area, it also offers good conditions for summer skiing. In the centre of this mountain range lies the valley of Árskarðsá which has a solfatara field. En route to the Árskarðsá valley there are a tourist hut and a ski school at Árskarður.

A couple of kilometres on towards Hveravellir after the junction with the Kerlingarfjöll track there is a hut (not marked on the 1:250 000 map) and a farm building. A few kilometres later the track forks: the fork to the right should be taken. Soon the track approaches the domed glacier of Hofsjökull then heads north, with a view to the right of the rock Gœgir, three sides of which are surrounded by ice. The lake of Thórisvatn, which lies below Rjúpnafell, is to the left. After Rjúpnafell is rounded, the track to the protected area of Hveravellir is met; the huts on this track are only 2 km away. The main tourist hut (there are two) is quite large and has a kitchen. Primitive toilets are outside. Down the hill is the other tourist hut, the campsite and a toilet; there is a weather station to the right. A warden is on duty.

Hveravellir is an oasis, all the more remarkable for being found in this cold, windy and bare region, and at an altitude of around 650 m. It has a solfatara field that has built up a dome of light grey plates of silicate, upon which there are numerous pools with small jets of hot water coming up. There is one particularly strong jet of superheated steam near the top, with its own little cone. There are also some mud pools and numerous vents giving out vapour. The vegetation is lush though cropped by the sheep.

Beyond the hot area is the lavafield of Kjalhraun, which flowed from the crater Strýtur (840 m), some 6 km south of the hut. Behind Strýtur, Kjalfell (1000 m) can be seen. West of the oasis, a track goes to another tourist hut at Thjófadalir (12 km). The hut at Hveravellir sits in the 25 km-wide valley between the glaciers that is called 'Kjölur'. This name is often used (instead of the correct one, 'Kjalvegur') to describe this section and the next.

37
HVERAVELLIR TO BLÖNDUDALUR

Distance:	90 km to ring road
Route:	track F37 ('Kjölur')
	road 732 to bridge over Blanda
	road 731 on east side of Blanda
Map:	general map 5
Road Conditions:	probably easier than section 36 unless there is a lot of water in the Seyðisá
Adjacent section:	15 (Akureyri to Borgarnes)
Notes:	A short journey and not as interesting as section 36.

AFTER LEAVING the hut at Hveravellir and returning 2 km to the main track (F37), the first obstacle is quite straightforward: the gate on the sheep fence. This has been built to separate the northern flocks from the southern ones, making the sheep gathering somewhat easier in autumn. The fence runs eastwards from Langjökull to the track and then south-east to Hofsjökull.

The seemingly never-ending terrain of grey and brown gravel stretches away on either side, with the hills not very prominent because of the already great altitude of the track (about 600-700 m). There are occasional vegetated areas such as around the river Seyðisá, which has to be crossed three times, the second ford being quite wide. Farther on the narrower Kúlukvísl is encountered; it is necessary to drive upstream before crossing as the opposite bank is quite high. Another river, 20 km on, has a rescue hut and an airfield by it and the final two rivers are about 1 km and 2 km farther on. The last one has a soft bed; the area after it can be very muddy and is hard going after rain.

Thrístikla marks the beginning of a system of lakes around which the clumped vegetation thickens. On the right and hidden from view, the glacial river Blanda flows through Blöndugil, a very long canyon which it has carved out. This is the start of the northern lowlands with increasing signs of human activity including some construction work, but no farms as yet. New hydro-electric schemes are being constructed in this area so heavy vehicles may be encountered from here on. To the east, long ridges begin to appear, heralding the northern mountain chains, and then the track turns into the welcoming green scenery of Blöndudalur, above the banks of the swirling Blanda. The track here has recently been improved and after it swings round a sharp bend it becomes road 732, travelling along the western side of Blöndudalur. The first petrol station since Geysir (183 km) is situated at the junction with road 731 to Varmahlíð. The Blanda is crossed next via a narrow suspension bridge and the road continues beside the river along the widening valley.

The ring road is met after crossing the Svartá-the route to the west is described in section 15.

38
GOÐAFOSS TO NÝIDALUR

Distance:	134 km
Route:	road 842
	track F28 ('Sprengisandur')
Maps:	general maps 4 and 5
Main places to visit:	Aldeyjarfoss (waterfall) ★ ★ ★
	Ingvararfoss (waterfall)
Road Conditions:	no two-wheel drive vehicle should attempt this route. Most of it is over gravel but there are some rocky parts and a number of rivers, which are described as seen by the author. Enquire about current conditions at Goðafoss.
Adjacent section:	39 (Nýidalur to Sigalda)
Notes:	The views along this route can be breathtaking, especially in clear weather. Get petrol at Goðafoss (or at Stóruvellir 23 km later on). The next petrol is at Sigalda (234 km from Goðafoss, 211 km from Stóruvellir): for details, see section 39.

THE USUAL approach to Sprengisandur is by the western bank of Skjálfandafljót, along road 842 which goes up the long and pleasant valley of Bárðardalur. (Another road, 844, follows the valley's eastern bank south from Fosshóll and meets up with road 842 at the suspension bridge near Stóruvellir.) There are big patches of bare ground on the hills on the valley's eastern side, which contrast with the rich growth of dwarf birch on the right. At various points the river flows over lava that has come from Trölladyngja. At Stóruvellir there is a small petrol station (the last before the interior) and a suspension bridge over the green glacial river. The valley's two roads now move away from each other, and as road 842 climbs there is a good view of the river disappearing through a canyon; the waterfall Aldeyjarfoss is beyond this but hidden from view.

After the last farm, Mýri, the Mjóadalsá is bridged (there are no more bridges in this section) and a steep and fairly rough climb follows. As the lake of Íshólsvatn appears on the right, the track to Aldeyjarfoss branches off to the left. There is a car park and toilets near the falls. The

falls are very attractive, their main beauty being the rows of thick basalt columns lining the gorge and, above them, smaller twisted columns add to the decoration. Below the waterfall, the river has cut its way through the moraines and there is a good view down the valley of Bárðardalur. From the tall moraines above the falls there is a tremendous panorama over to the mountains on the east with the view stretching from the north of the country (by Tjörnes) down to the huge bulk of Dyngjufjöll. Between the viewpoint and Dyngjufjöll lies the vast lava wilderness called Ódáðahraun. These two places are described in section 40.

On regaining the main track and going downhill, another track to the left leads to the small waterfall of Ingvararfoss where a canyon is being cut by the Skjálfandafljót. Next, as the main track begins its long climb through and over the moraines there are more views into the Ódáðahraun, with the beautiful cone of the shield volcano Trölladyngja becoming visible. The track is rocky at times, alternating with some sections of smooth sand; there is wilderness all around with huge bare moraines to left and right that often obscure the view. At about 700 m, with Dyngjufjöll directly on the left, a hilltop (also to the left) offers a spectacular view from the northern mountains down to the Vatnajökull glacier. This is probably the route's finest view.

This hard, bumpy terrain continues for some distance. Shortly after the little river of Fossgíls-mosar (which has to be forded) there is a signpost to Kiðagil (3 km), which is a long narrow canyon near Skjálfandafljót. The landscape is now more open and offers good views to Vatnajökull and Tungnafellsjökull with one small river to cross before following the Kiðagilsá through a series of small moraines. Then a wide system of streams must be crossed before a track (F78) branches off to the north-west (this may be closed); a wide but shallow river bed and a number of small streams from mossy sources then follow. Since for a great deal of the journey the moraines have hidden the hills from view, it's a relief to get the view of the glaciers on both sides that now follows. On the left is Tungnafellsjökull with the smooth surface of Vatnajökull behind it; on the right is Hofs-jökull with some of its bare peaks sticking out of the ice. The sighting of these mountains may be considered to mark the start of Sprengisandur.

The whole route is often called Sprengisandur but the name should really only be applied to the (grey) sand and stone desert between the Kiðagilsá and the western edge of Hofsjökull

(where the Thjórsá begins). The track follows the curve of the green lake of Fjórðungsvatn which may have tricky patches of wet black sand; to the right is the track (F72) to the north-west. After the next track (F98 to Gæsavötn) there is a braided glacial river, neither very deep nor wide. The Tómasarhagi is an oasis, containing a wide, braided system (possibly dry) of river beds. This final part of the journey runs under the steep slopes of Tungnafellsjökull (1540 m), whose sides have many ice-falls on them. With the grey and black background of the surrounding gravel, the mountain's mossy patches and the white snow and ice give some colour to the sombre surround-ings. The final river before the campsite is braided and can be fast and deep in places, making it arguably the hardest on the route. However, it is in sight of the main tourist hut.

There are two tourist huts at Nýidalur, with a warden on duty. They offer sleeping accom-modation, kitchen, primitive toilets, running water and a campsite.

The valley of Nýidalur (sometimes called Jökuldalur) runs to the south of the glacier and was only discovered as recently as 1845. The valley is about 800 m above sea level and is an excellent place to use for exploring the highlands, so the campsite is often frequented by groups of walkers. A large scale map in the tourist hut shows a suggested walking route near the glacier.

Distance:	119 km to junction with road 26
Route:	track F28
	road 32
Maps:	general maps 5 and 6
Road Conditions:	probably easier than section 38, although crossing the river Illugaverskvísl may be tricky.
Adjacent sections:	19 (Gullfoss to Sigalda)
	20 (Sigalda to south coast)
	41 (Sigalda to Landmannalaugar)
Notes:	This route can be combined with sections 20 or 41, however the latter route should not be started late in the day.

TRACK F28 heads south, going uphill behind the huts, past the airstrip and then through moraines to a river, which is fairly wide and deep in places. The present cross-country track follows a new route, the older one being nearer the Thjórsá. Sections of this western route can still be reached and just a few kilometres after Nýidalur a track goes westwards to the hut at Hreysiskvísl; another track to this hut goes off the main route at Kistualda.

In the section between Nýidalur and Kistualda there are three rivers, with another two just after Kistualda.

The view towards Hofsjökull dominates the gravel landscape, with other hills (for instance Kerlingarfjöll, to the south-west of Hofsjökull) lining the horizon. Soon the track enters a vegetated area with the river Svartá, which is narrow, rocky and may be deep, running through it. A little after this, the great river Thjórsá can be seen, taking its load of sand and gravel from Hofsjökull down towards the sea. The scenery to the right is greener now, with the banks of the river and the streams that feed it becoming quite mossy. A number of pools and small lakes line the route, with a few of their streams to be crossed. Next, the river Illugaverskvísl is sighted on the left; this provides the most difficult crossing of the route as it is fast, wide and deep, and has

boulders in it.

A signpost beyond the river points in the direction of a new track to a construction site farther north, so watch out for fast-moving heavy lorries from now on. The track here has been widened and strengthened.

As the bridge over the Kaldakvísl is crossed there is a mass of brown lichen-covered rock on both sides of the canyon. Its walls are vertical and it has a number of horizontal rock platforms near the water, especially on the downstream side. While the route has definitely been improved and is easier to negotiate, there are still small rivers to cross and one, a couple of kilometres after the Kaldakvísl, lies in a dip and comes without warning. However, it has only a little water. The next river (the last one) is fairly deep and after the crossing the track on the right is marked by stakes as being the main route. Thórisvatn, Iceland's second largest lake, now lies on the left, but it is frequently obscured by tall moraines. The lake is a light green colour, providing a marked contrast to the surrounding hills of black sands.

From now on there are a number of tracks and other man-made landmarks that are not marked on the 1980 edition of the 1:250 000 map since new reservoirs and transmission lines have been built for the power station projects. After the second track to Veiðivötn is passed on the left, there is a track to a small, mast-topped hill that provides a tremendous view of the mountains. From here the hills of the south and the south-east can be seen, the most prominent being the fine ridge of Löðmundur (1074 m). Below are two new lakes, part of the nearby hydroelectric system.

As the main track meets the buildings beside the lower lake, it goes to the right and after rounding some hills the scenery changes dramatically, with green pastures supporting many sheep. The new power station of Sigalda is passed and after its small settlement there is a petrol station on the right, the first since Stóruvellir (211 km). Just beyond the petrol station track F22 to Landmannalaugar, described in section 41, runs off to the left.

Another big change now takes place in the landscape, this time due to the massive destructive power of Hekla, Iceland's most celebrated volcano. It dominates the scene, as it has dominated the history and landscape of this part of Iceland for centuries. Black and twisted lumps of lava litter the surrounding land, together with black and light brown volcanic ash. Such plants as are able to grow here add colour to the startling scene.

As the road approaches the Thjórsá it forks, with road 32 going west over the river (section 19) and road 26 beginning its journey to the south-west past Hekla (section 20).

40
ASKJA

Distance:	103 km from ring road (one way)
Route:	track F88
Maps:	general maps 7 and 8
Main places to visit:	Hrossaborg (crater) ★★
	Herðubreiðarlindir (oasis) ★★
	Gljúfrasmiður (waterfall)
	Drekagil (canyon) ★★
	Öskjuvatn (lake) ★★★
Road Conditions:	no two-wheel drive vehicle should attempt this route. The two sections over the lava are tricky. Enquire at Mývatn about snow and wind conditions. Also ask about sand conditions near Herðubreiðartögl (see text).
Notes:	This section takes a long time and it may not be advisable to attempt a return journey from Mývatn in a day unless weather conditions are good. However, the scenery is superb. The route has to be retraced as the track south of Askja should not be attempted. Fuel can be obtained at Grímsstaðir and Mývatn, 7 km and 34 km respectively from beginning of the track.

AFTER LEAVING the ring road, with Hrossaborg (see section 11) on the right, track F88 crosses the western section of the Grjót desert.

The narrow sandy track is fairly level as it goes through an area of black gravel dunes and then larger boulders; plant cover soon becomes scant, especially compared to the hills on the left. Then the first lavafield begins, the crevices between the blocks filled with black sand; this is fairly flat ropey lava and is low compared to the surrounding moraines. After going alongside the lavafield the track then goes through it – an extremely slow journey over plates of bare rock, that is complicated in places as the track twists and turns between the taller blocks of lava.

After this the track emerges into sandy desert with only a little vegetation in the shelter of some boulders. It passes within 100 m of the river Jökulsá á Fjöllum, which has dunes and vegetation on both its banks. A small shepherd's hut nestles under the slopes of Miðfell and a few kilometres later (at the river Grafarlandaá), the track enters the Herðubreið Nature Reserve. The river crossing is fairly straightforward being neither deep nor very wide. There is a small oasis by the river and a waterfall nearby.

To the right is the cluster of hills called Herðubreiðarfjöll (1094 m); south-west of it is Eggert (1332 m), then the beautiful cone of Kollóttadyngja (1180 m), which is some 8,000 years old. These hills rise steeply above the gently sloping lavafields. To the left the Jökulsá á Fjöllum's path slowly alters; it has recently been moving to the west, as it seeks out the easiest route through the gravel. As the river is approached again there is an airstrip and then the beginning of the second lavafield. This is another very slow and difficult stretch. Next, the river Lindaá has to be crossed. This is not deep but is fairly wide, with a smooth gravel bed. The track then goes between the river and the lava. Before the campsite and tourist hut at Herðubreiðarlindar is reached there is another river; this is the last one and it is clear, shallow and narrow.

The campsite is set in an oasis in this desert area, with a tourist hut, primitive toilets, cold water taps and an airstrip. Behind the tourist hut there is a path leading to a cave inhabited by an outlaw in the eighteenth-century which is situated just above a stream, by an extremely luxuriant patch of vegetation. Despite its isolation, this campsite is popular and offers good

walking routes. A number of tour buses stop here. A leaflet has been published in Icelandic by the Nature Conservation Council which shows two walks, including one to a hut at the south-eastern corner of Kollóttadyngja. Neither this hut nor the one at the campsite appears to be marked on the current 1:250 000 map.

The track continues through the lava and draws near to Herðubreið (1682 m), whose steep slopes seem to offer no ascent (its summit was only conquered in 1908). With a shield volcano on its plateau giving it the appearance of a circus 'big top', this is regarded as one of the country's most beautiful mountains.

Just a few kilometres after the campsite, the track nears the river, which here has formed a canyon. The waterfall Gljúfrasmiður ('canyon maker') is at the end of this. The boulders round its lip are smooth since they are under the water for prolonged periods during the year and many of the rocks have large cracks; they are being broken up as the canyon is enlarged.

From here on, light sand is the main hazard – not just as a tricky surface, but because there may be severe dust-storms which make the route impassable. The 1:250 000 map shows the track heading south-west between Miðfell and Upptyppingar but the author's route was to the west of that because of the soft sandy conditions. New routes may not be signposted, especially if the change is recent. As Herðubreiðartögl's slopes are neared there are huge sharp boulders littering the otherwise flat gravel surface, with light brown ash from the 1875 Askja eruption also in evidence. South of the mountain the layer of light-brown ash becomes thicker.

Heading west, the great mountainous mass of the Dyngjufjöll lies ahead; Vaðalda (914 m) is to the south and the vast Vatnajökull glacier can be seen beyond it. The massive Dyngjufjöll is a collection of volcanoes, many of which have erupted since the last glaciation. Its centre has collapsed, leaving the caldera Askja (about 45 sq km), with the lake Öskjuvatn in its south-eastern corner. The lake is Iceland's deepest (217 m) and on its southern shore is the Dyngjufjöll's highest peak, Thorvaldsfell (1510 m).

Before the track begins its climb up into Askja there is a tourist hut at the interesting Drekagil canyon and another track goes south-east towards Vaðalda. The track now climbs through the Öskjuop pass, going through the lava that came from the 1961 eruption. Lying underneath this lava is tephra that was produced a little earlier in the eruption; below that, the insulating qualities of the tephra have preserved the (1961) winter snow. There are steep slopes to the left and a great mass of angular and twisted blocks of lava by the track. Snow may fall here during the summer which can make conditions very difficult. There is a car park on the left: no vehicle should go beyond it.

To the north of the Dyngjufjöll lies the enormous expanse of the Ódáðahraun lavafield. This covers over 3,000 sq km and is the largest lavafield in the world, an inhospitable area to which outlaws used to be banished (its name means 'desert of misdeeds'). Its most famous inhabitant was Grettir Ásmundsson, hero of *The Saga of Grettir the Strong*, who spent some twenty years in the desert. The old volcanoes (a number of them table mountains) have covered this desert with ash, cinders and lava. The porous nature of this material allows melted snow and rainwater to percolate down through the upper layers to reach underground streams. This, as well as its position in the rain shadow of Vatna-jökull, accounts for the lack of surface water. On windless summer days, the temperature in the lavafield may go as high as 20°C. The wild and rugged landscape near Askja is so similar to the moon's surface that some of the Apollo astronauts trained there.

The walk due south from the car park to the lake Öskjuvatn may take about an hour; cold conditions may be prevalent as the altitude is about 1100 m. Three craters from the 1961 eruption are passed (one on the left, two on the right) and part of the route goes over their ash. The crater of Víti is situated just before the lake. It was formed during the catastrophic eruption of 1875, which produced more ash than any other of Iceland's eruptions and forced many people to leave the country due to the resulting famine. Today Víti ('Hell') is a deep crater with slippery clay sides which can be dangerous in wet weather. Many people have swum in its warm, green, sulphurous water, but it has a strong and unpleasant, pungent smell. The rocks that heat it are red, blue and yellow and have vapour rising from them.

Looking towards the lake, the hills opposite and to the left are very steep and high. The hills to the right have steep cliffs down to Öskjuvatn. The lake can be approached by going left of Víti and then heading farther left. The cinder island of Eyja, formed during an eruption in 1926, can be seen in the lake.

41
SIGALDA TO LANDMANNALAUGAR

Distance:	27 km
Route:	track F22 ('Fjallabak')
Map:	general map 6
Main places to visit:	(unnamed) first crater ★
	Ljótipollur (crater) ★ ★
	ridge south of Frostastaðavatn (view) ★ ★
	Landmannalaugar ★ ★ ★
Road Conditions:	no two-wheel drive vehicle should attempt this route. The section over the lava is slow and the two rivers at the end of this section may be tricky.
Adjacent section:	42 (Landmannalaugar to south coast)
Notes:	Considerable variation in scenery: sand and lava, and colourful rhyolite hills at the destination. Landmannalaugar is becoming a popular centre for walkers as there are many places to explore in the area.

FROM JUST A LITTLE south-west of the new Sigalda power station, track F22 begins to climb through and over large gravel moraines, with the ridge of Löðmundur (1074 m) to the south-west providing the most notable landmark during the first part of the journey. The gravelly surface soon gives way to an extremely slow section over bare lava. Sometimes sharp ridges of the rock have to be crossed, in other places there are gently curving domes of ropey lava. The route is marked by stakes but if the visibility is bad it can be difficult to spot these and there may seem to be a number of ways through the areas of relatively smooth rock. It is best to stop and reconnoitre on foot if no stake is seen for 100 m or more.

When the river Tungnaá is sighted at a 'cross-roads' where a minor track crosses the major one, go ahead towards the sign 'Friðland að Fjalla-baki' which indicates the start of the protected area of the Fjallabak Nature Reserve. The next section is sandy, with deep sand, dunes and block lava by the sides of the track as it skirts the mostly bare hills and passes the minor track on the left to Hófsvað. The main track now goes through a beautiful black ash desert surrounded by hills: the scenery is bare and wild. While most of the

ash is black, some is a deep red and at one point high up on the left a red 'ridge' seems to run between two mossy hills: the left one is Hnausar (759 m). This red band is part of the inside wall of an explosion crater and a track leads up to its lip. Around the lip is a layer of lava and inside the crater there is a small lake of dark green water.

When the lake of Frostastaðavatn is reached the main track goes straight on; on the right another track leads to the banks of the Thjórsá and to the left yet another goes to the great explosion crater of Ljótipollur. This is very large (about 1.5 km wide), with bands of red ash between the layers of lava on its inside walls; there is a green lake in the crater. The far side of the rim is a convenient viewpoint over to the east as it is situated just above the river Tungnaá.

Frostastaðavatn is backed by a number of hills, some of them yellow and brown in colour and at the lake's south-western corner there is a black mass of lava. Just as the track turns away from the shore there is a small place for parking on the right and a long ridge that climbs above the lavafield. This looks over the lake and the neigh-bouring hills, some of which are craters (one by the track has a smaller cone inside it).

After another lavafield there is a broad stretch of gravel by the river Jökulgilskvísl, unusual in Iceland as the gravel is brown and not the usual black colour. The sites available for camping start after the track turns right, but the tourist hut and the main area for camping can only be reached by crossing two rivers. These may be deep and fast but are in view of the tourist hut, thus lessening any danger. The tourist hut has a resident warden, a kitchen, plenty of bunks and heating. There is a toilet block with WCs outside.

At the side of the tourist hut there is a tall and steep wall of the Laugahraun lavafield; the rock surface is jagged and sharp but provides good walking through a maze of paths. From afar it looks black but on closer inspection some of it is a beautiful deep blue in colour: this is a natural glass called obsidian; it has a smooth curved surface and very sharp edges. Large fissures in the lava make it interesting to explore but rather dangerous if it is wet or when there is snow. From the lavafield there is a flow of hot water which mixes with cold stream water, providing an ideal temperature for bathing. A gangplank from the hut leads over a marshy area to the pool.

Behind the tourist hut there is a gravel embankment beyond which there is a stream (right) and a track (left), both of which provide an interesting walk. The stream runs by a remarkable collection of colourful hills, especially in the gully behind the lava wall. Dark and light greens, greys and oranges are the main colours of these slopes – often smooth but with rocks, boulders and dead ice jutting out of them. The track leads past many of these spectacular hills and then past a series of frost-shattered scree slopes, decorated with flat stones – gold, brown, red, blue and pale yellow in colour. To the left is another colourful valley, on the other side of a series of rivers. The valleys share a gently inclined bed of colourful gravel and light brown sand, crossed by many small streams that eventually make up the Jökulgilskvísl. Not surprisingly, such colourful and unusual scenery attracts many visitors during the summer and consequently the site can be very busy at times.

42
LANDMANNALAUGAR TO THE SOUTH COAST

Distance:	61 km to the ring road
Route:	track F22
	road 208
Map:	general map 6
Main places to visit:	Eldgjá (fissure) ★ ★ ★
	Ófærufoss (waterfall) ★ ★ ★
	Litla-Ófærufoss (waterfall)
Road Conditions:	part of this section runs along a river bed which may contain a lot of water. There are many other rivers en route.
Adjacent section:	6 (Vík to Skaftafell)
Notes:	Recommended. There is considerable variation in scenery.

AFTER RECROSSING the two rivers near the tourist hut and retracing the side track for about 2 km, turn right onto the main track, F22. This leads south, following the bank of the Jökulgilskvísl, with a lavafield on the left. The river has a lot of water in it but is bridged. The hills and the gravel beds are mainly black here, although there are a few red/brown rhyolite hills adding some colour to the dark surroundings. A few streams may have to be crossed as a lake is rounded and then the track divides (go right) to go over a hill to a river crossing at the Fjallabak Nature Reserve's boundary. This crossing marks the beginning of the journey along the river bed; this stage is slow but probably not too difficult unless there has been a lot of rain. Beside the track there are smooth, black, sculptured rocks with decorative erosion stripes down their sides.

At the end of this extremely wet journey, after a sharp turn left (signposted 'Eldgjá'), the track goes first up and then down a very steep hill. Care should be taken on the hill as the vehicle's brakes will now be thoroughly soaked. This is an attractive part of the journey (with a lot of streams to cross) past rounded mossy hills and gravel terraces. The most interesting aspect of the scenery in the valley of Jökuldalir is the erosion effects on the hills, with gullies, smooth rounded ridges and some hard rock left proud of the smoother surfaces; there may also be some (partially covered) dead ice lying on some of the slopes. Numerous tracks go off to construction sites on either side, however stakes mark the main route all the way.

After passing a signposted turning on the left to the lake of Langisjór, the track climbs out of the valley. There is now a breathtaking view of the Eldgjá fissure and the beautiful scenery south of it. There is a viewpoint on the left, but an even better one on the hill (Herðubreiðarháls) on the right; this should be approached from the north as the most direct route is crossed by a series of deep and slippery gullies. The main part of the fissure is the northern part (to the left of the track); the middle part, to the right of the track, can also be seen, but the southern section is much farther away.

This is the largest explosion fissure in the world, stretching for a distance of some 18 km and aligned along a south-west/north-east direction. The fissure is broken in a number of places; the various parts have produced lava and other volcanic material on different occasions. The most southerly section (about half way between the viewpoint and Mýrdalsjökull) has produced lava since the Settlement, whereas the northern and middle sections erupted around 700 AD, sending a huge quantity of lava down the Skaftá valley.

The track goes over some bare rock and once the hill is descended a track goes left into the fissure. This latter track now twists and turns as it negotiates a way between the boulders and over some lava. Two river crossings have to be made; after the second, take the track to the right to the car park where there is a toilet and limited space for camping.

A path picks its way through the rubble on the right-hand bank of the river Nyrðri-Ófæra. The fissure is very high (150 m) and wide (perhaps 500 m) and during the short walk its fine northern end is clearly visible straight ahead. With some moss on its steep scree slopes, its real charm lies in the tinge of red ash around its lip which is protected from the elements by an overlying lava flow.

The waterfall Ófærufoss is on the left: its double fall and the gracefully curved natural arch above the lower fall must be unique. The arch, one of nature's masterpieces, is a metre wide at its narrowest point so it is quite safe to cross though care must be taken when it is wet. This basalt bridge has remained after the softer, surrounding rocks have been washed away by the river falling over the fissure's lip.

The track heads south after a glimpse of the middle section of the Eldgjá fissure and travels through a fine landscape, with a covering of short grass over much of the gently rolling scenery. The broad river Skaftá flows to the left of the road; this is a very long and powerful glacial river that flows from Skaftárjökull which is on the south-western edge of Vatnajökull; the river bed is a wide and mossy lavafield. While some of the lava came from Eldgjá, the majority did not; the Skaftá's valley was virtually filled by lava from the Laki eruption of 1783 (see p.174). After the track moves away from the river there is a large hut on the right, reached by crossing a small river. Behind the hut a path runs up the hill to the waterfall Litla-Ófærufoss, which has a fine canyon below it. The fall sends up a lot of spray and can produce rainbows. Care must be taken near the falls as the vegetation is wet and there is a (hidden) vertical drop to the left of the path.

Once the lavafield has been crossed there is a fine view of the glacier Mýrdalsjökull and from here the track goes through a pleasant area of moorland with rounded hills and flat-topped gravel terraces. There are a number of streams and small rivers to cross followed by a sandy stretch. When the Skaftá is momentarily sighted there is a view southwards to the sea. New tracks have recently been built here and heavy lorries may be encountered. A couple of farms are passed on the left before track F22 ends and road 208 begins. Beyond the farms, Skálarheiði's cliffs can be seen, below which the Skaftá widens out. The first farm on the right, Hvammur, has some turfed buildings.

The road then meets the ring road at the bridge over the Kúðafljót (section 6).

43
THÓRSMÖRK

Distance:	25 km (one way) from the ring road
Route:	road 249
Map:	general map 6
Road Conditions:	probably atrocious; this is spelt out in some detail in the description of the route.
Notes:	In good conditions and with the right equipment, this could be the most exciting journey of your visit as the scenery in Thórsmörk is quite outstanding. There is no through route, so there are double the number of rivers to cross.

PROTECTED ON three sides by the glaciers Eyjafjallajökull, Mýrdalsjökull and Tindfjallajökull, Thórsmörk may enjoy blue skies while the surrounding districts get bad weather. This small area, bounded by the rivers Krossá and Markarfljót is a colourful oasis with a lush vegetation of grass and dwarf shrubs and is a popular place with walkers. Tour buses also come here and it may be best to avoid it at holiday weekends when it can get overcrowded.

However it is well protected from regular overcrowding by the fact that some of the wildest unbridged glacial rivers in Iceland flow past it – including the Krossá, which sometimes claims lives. The author counted (and crossed) some twenty open rivers between the ring road and Thórsmörk and this did not include those areas where the track and the river were the same thing! After heavy rain this number can easily double, with rivers becoming torrents impassable even to four-wheel drive tour buses. The most difficult rivers are near the end of the route; these are: Jökulsá (from Gígjökull), Steinholtsá (from Steinholtsjökull), Hvanná (just as the campsite is neared) and the infamous Krossá (which is very deep, wide, braided and extremely fast). Fortunately the Krossá crossing point is opposite the main tourist hut so if a vehicle gets stuck then rescue should not take too long. When returning, ensure that the vehicle's engine is properly warmed up before attempting the Krossá to lessen the chance of stalling.

If you are in a two-wheel drive car you should not even attempt to start the route from the ring road and those in four-wheel drive vehicles who ford any of the four rivers mentioned above should only do so if there are other vehicles around. All the points listed on pp.63-64 should be re-read and noted. Safety is paramount on this route as it is certainly the most difficult described in the Guide and these final four crossings can be frightening. It is a good idea to start the journey in the morning and wait at the big rivers for a tour bus of which there may be a couple (or more) a day. This information should be checked if possible in Reykjavík or Hvolsvöllur before you leave.

The route to Thórsmörk is quite outstanding for its beauty as it makes its way below the precipitous slopes of Eyjafjallajökull. The mountains in this district were formed by sub-glacial eruptions and are made of palagonite, a brown volcanic rock that is more easily eroded than basalt. Thus the glaciers and streams have carved fascinating shapes in the rock – producing pinnacles, caves, steep cliffs and ravines along the northern edge of Eyjafjallajökull. A carpet of grey basalt gravel that has been brought down by the big rivers lies in the main valley, the cliffs rising steeply from this gently sloping floor.

Where mosses have managed to gain a foothold, they have decorated the brown palagonite with patches of green and yellow, while the peninsula of Thórsmörk has extensive woods of dwarf birch and a good growth of grass. The district's isolation, relatively warm temperature and lack of sheep have all helped to make Thórsmörk a bright and colourful place and since 1924 it has been protected and in the care of the Forestry Department.

At the first big river (Jökulsá), the glacial tongue of Gígjökull comes down almost to the track. Its glacial lake of Lónið often has icebergs floating in it. Steinholtsá is only a couple of kilometres farther on and the glacier and glacial lake, though hidden, are only a short distance from the crossing point. In 1967 there was a huge landslide just above the lake, causing a *jökulhlaup* that flooded the area. The Hvanná may not be too difficult to cross in good weather.

Just before the Krossá is met, the Útivist tourist hut is at Básar, just up the valley. The main tourist hut is at Langidalur on the Krossá's northern bank; it has a resident warden, plenty of accommodation and a toilet block (with WCs). This is the main campsite too. Maps (on an Icelandic-language leaflet) are available and suggested walking routes are posted up in the tourist hut. A third tourist hut is in Húsadalur which can be reached by a half-hour walk from the campsite. It is on the northern side of Thórsmörk and so looks out over the other main river, the Markarfljót. This tourist hut can also be reached by a river-crossing after the Steinholtsá, but as this is below the confluence of the Krossá and the Hvanná, the crossing is very difficult.

44
GREENLAND

MANY VISITORS to Iceland also go to Greenland; this section caters for a brief visit.

The country is a new tourist destination and there are many difficulties (transport, accommodation, weather) that may pose problems for those wanting to travel around the country. Short trips can easily been arranged through tour operators and airlines, but longer (independent) trips will need a lot of research and planning. Further information is available from the Danish Tourist Board (see p.98).

Weather can play havoc with arrangements. It can be very unpredictable, even during the summer, so careful thought should be given to the type of clothes worn: heavy shoes/boots and waterproofs should certainly be taken. Flights are not infrequently cancelled and occasionally visitors are stranded for a day or more, so if you intend to go, go at the first spell of good weather. It is not advisable to go at the end of your visit as you may miss your flight or boat home.

The native language is Greenlandic though many people also speak Danish. After Danish, English is the most common language spoken by people in the tourist industry. Danish currency is the legal tender.

Greenland is the world's largest island, most of it covered by the huge ice-cap. The ice-free parts that are populated are mainly along the west coast (where most of the people live), the southern tip and stretches of the east coast. Transport between settlements is by boat, plane and helicopter; although there will be some roads and tracks leading out of individual settlements, in general the settlements cannot be connected by roads because of the fjords. The population is only just over 50,000 so the towns and villages are small and often fairly far apart. The most convenient trips from Reykjavík are to Narssarssuaq (southern tip) and Kulusuk (near the eastern village Angmagssalik). Brief descriptions of Narssarssuaq and Angmagssalik are given below, together with some of the trips available from them. A more detailed description of the day trip to the small island of Kulusuk is also provided.

Narssarssuaq

This town of 1800 people contains the ruins of farms built by Eirík the Red (see p.11) in about 986, as well as buildings dating from the seventeenth-century Eskimo settlements. There are two hotels. Sheep farming and fishing are the main occupations, with a lot of frozen food now exported. Abundant wildlife may be seen, including whales, seals and many species of birds and plants. The area is popular with walkers and anglers, and trips can be arranged to the ice-cap.

Angmagssalik

This is a much smaller settlement, which boasts the only hotel in eastern Greenland. Trips to the ice-cap by helicopter are available and there are walks to some of the valleys as well as boat trips through the fjords. During springtime, tourist 'expeditions' go on to the ice-cap using dog sledges and skis.

Kulusuk

As the aircraft approaches the small airfield the sea below is dotted with countless icebergs. The coastline is made up of a series of tall, sharp peaks, with the valleys between smoothed down by the glaciers, which have since retreated. The island also bears the marks of the old glaciers and the scores left on the rocks by the moving ice can be seen on the walk from the airfield to the village of Kap Dan. Here the scenery is very different from the post-glacial areas of Iceland, probably having more in common with the western highlands of Scotland. There is little soil on this barren land and consequently not much plant cover except in a few boggy parts that get some shelter from low-lying ridges.

The path comes out above the village, a jumbled collection of wooden buildings, some built with concrete foundations. The village was only discovered by Europeans in 1844 when a Danish naval team managed to get through the ice and visit this isolated community, then still in the Stone Age. Since then, a considerable change has taken place in the people's way of life (the population is now 450, half under 14 years old), and it is very difficult in the space of a short visit to get much more than an impression of what life was like in such a remote and unkind environment. Most of the houses are small wooden buildings, with steep roofs and small windows. As the ground is just bare and hard rock, many of the houses stand on stilts, with the gap underneath utilised as storage space. Before the village is entered there is a small 'graveyard': no graves can be dug as there is no soil, so the coffins are covered by piles of stones and these heaps are decorated with bright plastic flowers. There are some buildings that are bigger than the houses, such as the post office, supermarket, school, a few sheds and the church. The village sits on the side of a hill, overlooking a rocky bay with a few boats by a small jetty. The bay may have many icebergs floating in it; their appearance depends on the weather but they will often take on a marvellous blue colour beside the brilliant white of any snow that is lying around. The more cloudy the weather, the more pronounced is this blueness.

The people live on the very edge of existence, not only in terms of the village's geographical position but also as a result of the physical hardships that they somehow manage to endure. Before the airstrip was built they were wholly at the mercy of the sea ice and this had kept them from any real advancement during their long isolation. Now, though hustled into the twentieth century (the first tourists arrived in the 1960s), the people's livelihood still depends on fishing and on hunting seals. Additional income comes from carving bone ornaments and beadwork which the children sell to the tourists.

The trip includes visits to the post office (cards and stamps) and the church, the only building large enough to hold a plane-load of visitors. In addition, a drum dance is sometimes performed and a kayak rower may give a demonstration. It may be possible to go part of the way back to the airfield by boat (through the icebergs); this trip, the cards and stamps must be paid for in Danish currency (the rate of exchange at the post office is very poor). As the plane leaves the airstrip it flies over the village, the bay and the larger village of Angmagssalik. (The guide will undoubtedly speak English and perhaps German or a Scandinavian language.)

45
THE FAROES

THOSE TRAVELLING to Iceland on the 'Norröna' may have an enforced stay on the Faroes while the boat visits other ports; this section is intended to provide enough information to ensure that their time is well spent.

The Faroes are a group of 18 islands, the largest and most important being Streymoy. The products of long-lost volcanoes, the islands are mostly long and narrow, with a ribbon of hills running along their length. The cliffs are spectacular, sometimes rising hundreds of metres vertically out of the sea. These are the homes of countless sea-birds; kittiwakes, puffins, gulls, fulmars and guillemots. Most of the land is hilly so the settlements tend to be along the coast, connected by relatively narrow but well-surfaced tarmac roads. Due to the numerous clefts in their cliffs, none of the islands have a ring road. Travel between the islands is by a well-organised and regular boat service and the two largest islands of Streymoy and Esturoy are connected by a bridge. While sheep farming is important, the islands depend on fishing for their prosperity, the Klaksvík-based boats sailing as far as Greenland and Newfoundland for their catches. Like the Icelanders, the Faroese are trying to reduce their dependence on the sea as their chief means of earning a living.

Faroese (which is similar to Icelandic) is the native language. Danish is the main 'foreign'

GREENLAND

DISKO
Godhavn
Søndrestrømfjord
⊕Kulusuk
Angmagssalik

⊕ Airport

| 0 | km | 500 |
| 0 | miles | 300 |

Narssarssuaq

N

THE FAROES

FUGLOY
Eiði
Gjógv
VIÐOY
KALSOY
KUNOY
BORÐOY
Tjørnuvik
EYSTUROY
SVÍNOY
Klaksvik
STREYMOY
MYKINES
VÁGAR
Tórshavn
NÓLSOY
KOLTUR
HESTUR
Kirkjubøur
SANDOY
SKÚVOY
STÓRA DÍMUN
LÍTLA DÍMUN
SUÐUROY

⊕ Airport

| 0 | 10 | 20 | 30 km |
| 0 | 10 | 20 miles |

N

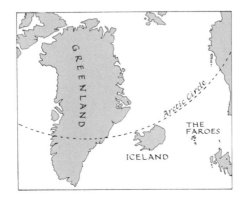

GREENLAND
Arctic Circle
THE FAROES
ICELAND

253

language taught in schools and English is the next most-used language in the tourist industry. There are Faroese banknotes but Danish currency is also used.

Tórshavn, Streymoy's largest settlement and the charming capital of the islands, is an interesting place to explore and can be used as a base from which to travel to the other islands. However, a short visit limits the number of places that can be seen, so concentrating on the two main islands may be the best plan. The following list gives suggestions for visits; three of them are on the main island and all are worth exploring:

Tórshavn: harbour, Tinganes (old buildings by harbour); Skansin (small fortress at east side of harbour); bookshops, museums, art gallery.

Kirkjubøur: village at south-west end of Streymoy: 900 year-old wooden farmhouse; partially completed cathedral; small church.

Tjørnuvík: village at north end of Streymoy: interesting houses; views of cliffs and two tall stacks on the other side of the fjord.

Gjógv: village at north end of Esturoy: natural harbour in a gorge.

Further information on the Faroes can be obtained from the Danish Tourist Board (see p.98); from your tour operator, or from the tourist bureau in Tórshavn (Ferðamannastovan, Havnargøta, PO Box 368, DK – 3800 Tórshavn, Faroes). UK visitors can obtain maps from Dick Phillips (see p.99): two maps (1:100 000 scale) cover the whole group of islands, but only the northern one is needed if no ferries are taken south of Tórshavn; a 1:200 000 map covers the whole group of islands.

Facilities Chart

This chart shows facilities available in some of the major settlements (excluding Reykjavík and Akureyri), listed according to the general map on which they appear. More everyday facilities, such as supermarkets, swimming pools and petrol stations are mentioned in the description of the settlements in the text.

Map	Settlement	Hospital	Doctor	Chemist	Dentist	Post Office	Police Station	Bank	Garage	Car Hire	Photographic shop	Information office	Tour operator
1	Bíldudalur	—	*	—	—	*	—	*	—	—	—	—	—
	Bolungarvík	*	*	—	*	*	*	*	*	*	—	—	—
	Ísafjörður	*	*	*	*	*	*	*	*	*	—	*	*
	Vatneyri	*	*	*	*	*	*	*	*	—	—	—	—
2	Borganes	*	*	*	—	*	*	*	*	*	—	—	—
	Búðardalur	*	*	—	—	*	—	*	—	—	—	—	—
	Grundarfjörður	*	*	—	*	*	*	*	—	—	—	—	—
	Ólafsvík	*	*	—	*	*	*	*	*	—	—	—	—
	Stykkishólmur	*	*	*	*	*	*	*	*	—	—	—	—
3	Selfoss	*	*	*	*	*	*	*	*	*	—	—	—
	Thorlákshöfn	*	*	*	—	*	*	*	*	—	—	—	—
4	Blönduós	*	*	*	*	*	*	*	*	*	—	—	—
	Dalvík	*	*	*	*	*	*	*	*	—	—	—	—
	Húsavík	*	*	*	*	*	*	*	*	*	*	—	—
	Ólafsfjörður	—	*	*	*	*	*	*	*	—	—	—	—
	Sauðárkrókur	*	*	—	*	*	*	*	*	*	—	—	—
	Siglufjörður	*	*	*	*	*	*	*	*	*	—	—	—
6	Heimaey	*	*	*	*	*	*	*	*	—	—	—	*
	Hella	*	*	*	*	*	*	*	—	—	—	—	—
7	Vopnafjörður	*	*	—	*	*	*	*	—	*	—	—	—
8	Búðeryri	*	*	—	*	*	*	*	*	—	—	—	—
	Búðir	*	*	—	—	*	*	*	*	—	—	—	—
	Egilsstaðir	*	*	*	*	*	*	*	*	*	—	*	*
	Eskifjörður	*	*	—	*	*	*	*	*	—	—	—	—
	Neskaupstaður	*	*	*	—	*	*	*	*	—	—	—	—
	Seyðisfjörður	*	*	*	—	*	*	*	—	—	—	—	—
9	Höfn	*	*	—	*	*	*	*	—	*	—	—	—

THIS SELECTIVE bibliography contains some 70 entries of use to visitors. Further information can be obtained from the bibliography by Horton (see **14** below). Lists of specialist research papers in a number of scientific disciplines are contained in bulletins published by the Young Explorers' Trust.

1 Guide Books

Fodor's Guide to Scandinavia (Fodor Travel Books, New York; Hodder & Stoughton, London)

The space given to Iceland is extremely limited and not particularly inspiring.

Iceland Road Guide (Iceland Travel Books, Reykjavík, 1981)

Covers all the island's roads. An English translation of a book written for Icelanders, it does not explain things that are commonplace to the Icelanders but of interest to the rest of us. The format tends to give as much space to incidental items as to the most important places to see. No pictures, but street maps of the towns.

Kidson, Peter, *Iceland in a Nutshell* (Iceland Travel Books, Reykjavík, 1974)

A good general guide to towns – especially Reykjavík and Akureyri – and a few cross-country routes, superseded by the *Iceland Road Guide.*

Nagel's Guide to Iceland (Nagel, Geneva, 1981)

This covers a number of routes from the main towns.

Reykjavík Within Your Reach (Mál og Menning, Reykjavík, 1975)

This is a guide to the city's historical buildings. Useful if you intend to spend some time exploring the capital.

Youth Hosteller's Guide to Denmark and Iceland (Youth Hostels Assoc., London, 1975)

Only a few pages devoted to Iceland.

2 Free pamphlets and brochures

Phillips, Dick, *On Foot in Iceland* (Alston, UK, see p.99)

This is Dick Phillips's programme of walks and tours in Iceland. It also contains advice useful to anyone travelling and walking independently.

Around Iceland in 1984 (Kórund hf, Reykjavík)

A free directory with numerous advertisements, written in Icelandic and English. It has recently come out annually and gives information on many towns and settlements. There are a few short articles in English on various facets of Icelandic life.

Iceland – A Touring Guide (Iceland Travel Books, 1982)

Now unavailable, largely but not entirely superseded by *Around Iceland in 1984* (see above). 272 pages, over half of them in Icelandic, the rest in English. Apart from these drawbacks, it contains information on settlements and some notes on what to see. There are a number of maps and some good colour pictures.

3 Nineteenth-century descriptions of the country

Dufferin, Lord, *Letters from High Latitudes* (John Murray, London, 1857)

Iceland was one of the main calling places during Dufferin's voyage in 1856. It deals mainly with the south-western part of the country.

Jónsonn, Jón, *Jón Jónsonn's Saga* (Ísafold, Reykjavík, 1968)

This (English) autobiography by a farmer is a marvellous account of his life at Mývatn (1829-1866).

Lock, Charles G. W., *Home of the Eddas* (Sampson Low, London, 1879)

This is a year-long diary with a summary of information for nineteenth-century 'tourists'.

Morris, William, *Journals of Travels in Iceland* from *The Collected Works of William Morris, vol 8* (Longman, London, 1911)

Descriptions of two visits made in 1871 and 1873.

4 Modern descriptions of the country

Bárðarson, Hjálmar R., *Iceland – A Portrait of Its Land and People* (H. R. Bárðarson, Reykjavík, 1982).

Briem, H., *Iceland and the Icelanders* (J. McKenna, New Jersey, 1945)

General description of the country together with some monochrome and colour photographs.

Griffiths, John, *Modern Iceland* (Pall Mall Press, London, 1969)
  Gives an outline of the country's history and discusses present-day politics and social habits.

Gunnarsson, Árni, *Volcano: Ordeal by Fire in Iceland's Westman Islands* (Iceland Review, Reykjavík, 1973)
  A record of the 1973 eruption which contains some fine photographs. It was written before the end of the eruption.

Hamar, Haraldur J., *Iceland: the Surprising Island of the Atlantic* (Iceland Review, Reykjavík, 1977)
  Photographic studies of landscapes and people.

Iceland, 874–1974 (Central Bank, Reykjavík, 1975)
  Deals mainly with economy, social habits, foreign relations, etc.

Iceland (Naval Intelligence Division, 1942)
  A good general account of the country.

Leaf, Horace, *Iceland Yesterday and Today* (George Allen & Unwin, London, 1949)
  A travel book.

Magnússon, Sigurður A., *Iceland: Country and People* (Iceland Review, Reykjavík, 1979)
  An inexpensive booklet with interesting information about the country.

Magnússon, Sigurður A., *Northern Sphinx* (C. Hurst & Co, London, 1977)
  A history of the country, from the earliest to modern times. Articles on the arts.

Scherman, Katherine, *Iceland – Daughter of Fire* (Victor Gollancz, London, 1976)
  A very readable account of life in Iceland.

Tomasson, Richard, *Iceland, The First New Society* (Icelandic Review, Reykjavík, 1980)
  A sociological review of modern Iceland.

5 Photographic studies of Iceland

Djúpalæk, Kristján frá, *Akureyri and the Picturesque North* (Iceland Review, Reykjavík, 1975)
  Of the area around Iceland's 'northern capital'.

Hannesson, Gunnar, *Reykjavík: A Panorama in Four Seasons* (Iceland Review, Reykjavík, 1974)
  Photographs of the capital.

Hannesson, Gunnar and Thórarinsson, Sigurður, *Glacier: Adventure on Vatnajökull, Europe's Largest Ice-cap* (Iceland Review, Reykjavík, 1970)
  Photographs of the country's main glacier.

Linden, F. von, and Weyer, H., *Iceland* (Robert Hale, London, 1974)
  Good photography and informative text.

McCurdy, John Chang, *Iceland* (Almenna Bókafélagið, Reykjavík, 1979)
  A fine collection of photographs, with text.

Thórarinsson, S., *Ísland – Iceland* (Hanns Reich Verlag, Munich, 1955)
  Little text but 75 photographs that capture the country well.

6 Travel, Expeditions

A Guide to Land Rover Expeditions (Land Rover)
  Free. A must for all those taking a Land Rover. (Address: Lode Lane, Solihull, West Midlands, B92 8NW).

Blashford-Snell, J., and Ballantine, A., *Expeditions* (Faber & Faber, London, 1977)
  Advice for those who are organising expeditions – equipment etc.

Cranfield, I., *The Traveller's Handbook* (Heinemann and Wexas International, London, 1982)
  Advice on vehicles, equipment etc.

Jackson, Jack and Crampton, Ellen, *The Asian Highway* (Angus & Robertson, London, 1979)
  The section on vehicles and driving is of use to anyone going through the interior.

Jackson, Jack, *The Four-Wheel Drive Book* (Gentry Books, 1982)
  This useful book lists current four-wheel drive vehicles, driving techniques, accessories available and the addresses of their suppliers etc.

Land, Tony, *The Expedition Handbook* (Butterworths, 1978)
  Advice on organising equipment etc.

Leiðabók (BSI, annually)
  Scheduled bus timetable.

7 Geology, Geography, Geomorphology

Bárðarson, Hjálmar, *Ice and Fire* (Hjálmar Bárðarson, Reykjavík, 1980)
  A good book about glaciers and volcanoes, which includes Surtsey and Grímsvötn. Fine photography.

Bemmelen, R. W. Van and Rutten, M. G., *Table*

Mountains of Northern Iceland (E. J. Brill, Leiden, 1955)
Report of a geological expedition to the mountains east of Mývatn.

Björnsson, S., *Iceland and Mid-Ocean Ridges* (Prentsmiðjan Leiftur, Reykjavík, 1967)
Highly technical.

Jökull no 29 (Iceland Glaciological Society, Reykjavík, 1979)
A review of the country's geology.

Jónasson, Pétur, *Lake Mývatn* (Iceland Literature Society, Copenhagen, 1979)
A collection of scientific studies.

MacDonald, J. G., *Volcanic Geology and Volcanicity in Iceland* (Dept. of Extra-Mural and Adult Education, Glasgow University, 1974)
A pamphlet for the interested layman.

Preusser, H., *The Landscapes of Iceland: Types and Regions* (Dr W. Junk, The Hague, 1976)
Technical (a doctoral thesis), but excellent. Expensive, however, and no index.

Rittman, A. and L., *Volcanoes* (Orbis, London, 1976)
A beautifully illustrated guide to volcanoes.

Sharp, R. P., *Glaciers* (Oregon State System of Higher Education)
A layman's guide.

Thórarinsson, Sigurður, *The Eruption of Hekla 1947-48* (several volumes) (Leiftur, Reykjavík, 1967)
Volume 1 gives an interesting account of the volcano's history with extracts from annals written at the time of each eruption.

Thórarinsson, Sigurður, *Surtsey* (Viking Press, New York, 1967)
Fine photographs show the birth of this new volcanic island.

8 Natural History

Magnússon, Sigurður A., *Stallion of the North* (Iceland Review, Reykjavík, 1978)
Icelandic horses.

Sutton, George, *Iceland Summer: Adventures of a Bird Painter* (University of Oklahoma Press, USA, 1961)
Diary of an ornithologist travelling around Iceland.

Wolseley, Pat, *A Field Key to the Flowering Plants of Iceland* (Thule Press, Shetland, 1979)
A small book with drawings of the plants.

9 History

Gilchrist, A., *Cod Wars and How to Lose Them* (Q Press, Edinburgh, 1978)

Gjerset, Knut, *History of Iceland* (George Allen & Unwin, London, 1922)
Comprehensive.

Njarðvík, Njörður, *Birth of a Nation* (Iceland Review, 1978)
The history of Iceland up until the end of the thirteenth century.

10 Language

Friðjónsson, Jón, *A Course in Modern Icelandic* (Tímaritið Skák, Reykjavík)

Glendening, P. J. T., *Teach Yourself Icelandic* (Hodder & Stoughton, London, 1981)
With dictionary section.

Pálsson, Einar, *Icelandic in Easy Stages* (2 vols) (Mímír, Reykjavík)

11 Literature, Art

Adventures, Outlaws and Past Events (Iceland Review, Reykjavík, 1977)
A collection of folk-tales.

Craigie, W. A., *The Icelandic Sagas* (Cambridge Press, 1913)

Egil's Saga (Penguin, England, 1976)
One of the greatest of the *Sagas of Icelanders*.

Einarsson, Stefán, *A History of Icelandic Literature* (John Hopkins Press, New York, 1957)
An authoritative but very technical text.

Eldjárn, K., *Ancient Icelandic Art* (Hanns Reich Verlag, Munich, 1957)
Some text and 70 photographs of woodcarvings, tapestries etc.

Elves, Trolls and Elemental Beings (Iceland Review, Reykjavík, 1977)
A collection of folk tales.

Guerber, H. A., *Myths of the Norsemen* (George Harrap, London, 1919)
Tales of the Norse Gods, from the Edda and Sagas.

Halldórsson, Haukur, *Trolls* (Örn og Örlygur, Reykjavík, 1982)
Many of the tales are from the collection of Jón Árnason.

Kristjánsson, Jónas, *Icelandic Sagas and Manuscripts* (Iceland Review, Reykjavík, 1970)

The story of the Sagas: their history and preservation.

Laxdæla Saga (Penguin, England, 1969)

Set in western Iceland, the *Laxdæla Saga* spans the period from the Settlement up to the early eleventh century.

The Vinland Sagas: The Norse Discovery of America (Penguin, England, 1965)

Contains the two major Sagas describing the discovery of America: *The Saga of the Greenlanders* and *Eirik's Saga*.

12 Economics, business

Hints to Exporters – Iceland (British Overseas Trade Board, 1983)

Useful for those going to Iceland on business.

OECD Report on Iceland (published annually)

13 Periodicals

Iceland Review (Icelandic Review, PO Box 93, 121 Reykjavík)

A glossy quarterly magazine.

News from Iceland (Icelandic Review)

A monthly newspaper.

14 Bibliography

Horton, John, *Iceland* (Clio Press, Oxford, 1983)

A major bibliography of English-language material with nearly 1,000 items (books, pamphlets, maps etc) described.

15 Maps

The maps of most immediate general interest to visitors to Iceland are listed in Part 2 on pp.85-87. The maps listed below cater to more specialized tastes.

Atlas Maps Series (1:100 000)

These cover the whole country and are based on the same projection as the General Maps Series (1:250 000). There are 87 sheets altogether, with the old 1:50 000 map series being based on a quarter of each of the Atlas Series maps.

C761 Series (1:50 000)

This is now taking over from the previous 1:50 000 maps (Quarter Maps Series), some of which are still available. The new maps were revised in 1977 and only cover the south-east corner of Iceland (S of Bogarnes and W of Selfoss). This series is based on a different projection from that of the older series.

Geological Maps Series (1:250 000)

6 of the 9 General Maps are also issued as geological maps:

Map No	Date
1	1969
2	1968
3	1980
5	1969
6	1982
7	1977

Geological Map of Reykjavík (1:40 000)

Vegetation Maps (1:40 000)

There are 64 sheets in this series, published between 1966 and 1968. They cover an area bounded roughly by the following;

a line running NE from Reykjavík.

a line running NE from Mýrdalsjökull.

only a little from map 4 of the General Map series is covered.

School Maps

There are 3 maps that cover the whole island at scales of 1:500 000, 1:2 000 000 and 1:3 000 000. There is also a set of 4 sheets (1:350 000).

Wall Maps

There is a general map (1:250 000) and 2 school maps (1:350 000 and 1:500 000).

Single Coloured Map (1:750 000)

Municipal and County Map (1:750 000)

This shows the country's administrative boundaries.

Raised Relief Map (1:1 000 000)

Geomagnetic Maps Series

These have the same boundaries as the General Maps. Numbers 2, 3, 5, 6, 8 and 9 are published as aeromagnetic profiles. Maps 2 and 3 are also published showing the total field intensity (either as single sided maps or with the respective aeromagnetic profiles on the reverse).

16 The Faroes

Williamson, Kenneth, *The Atlantic Islands* (first published, Collins, 1948; second edition, Routledge, Kegan Paul, 1970).

INDEX

Page numbers in italics refer to illustrations.

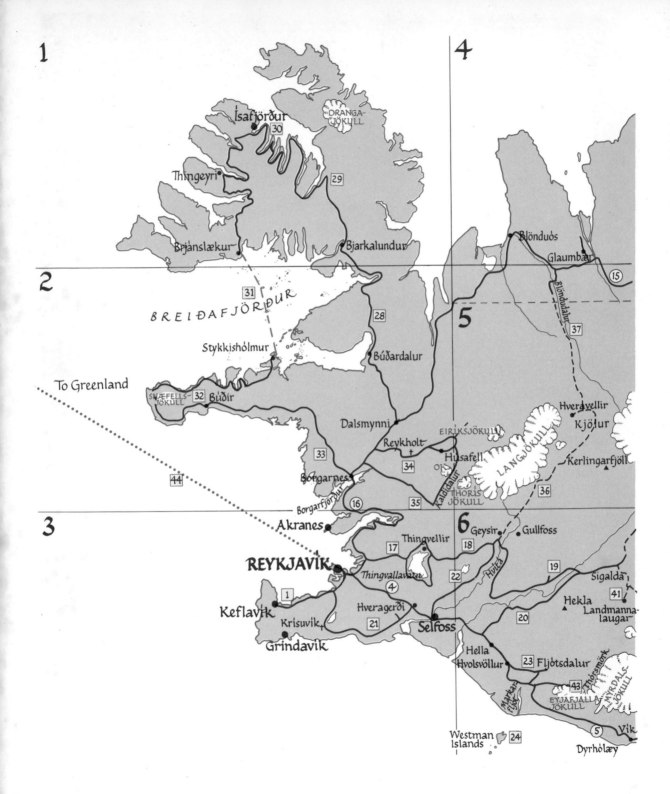